RENEWALS 458-4574

DATE DUE

GAYLORD			PRINTED IN U.S.A.

German Essays on Socialism
in the Nineteenth Century

The German Library: Volume 41
Volkmar Sander, General Editor

GERMAN ESSAYS ON SOCIALISM IN THE NINETEENTH CENTURY

Theory, History, and Political Organization, 1844–1914

Edited by Frank Mecklenburg
and Manfred Stassen

Introduction by Manfred Stassen

CONTINUUM · NEW YORK

1990

The Continuum Publishing Company
370 Lexington Avenue, New York, NY 10017

The German Library
is published in cooperation with Deutsches Haus,
New York University.

Printed in the United States of America

Library of Congress Cataloging-in-Publication Data

German essays on socialism in the nineteenth century / edited by Frank
Mecklenburg and Manfred Stassen ; introduction by Manfred Stassen.
  p.   cm. — (The German library ; v. 41)
Includes bibliographical references.
ISBN 0-8264-0323-9. — ISBN 0-8264-0324-7 (pbk.)
  1. Socialism—Germany—History—19th century—Sources.
2. Socialism—History—19th century—Sources. I. Mecklenburg,
Frank. II. Stassen, Manfred, 1939–   . III. Series.
HX273.G45   1990
335.42'0943—dc20   89-29708
                                                                 CIP

Acknowledgments will be found on page 331,
which constitutes an extension of this page.

Contents

Introduction

"A specter is haunting Europe—the specter of anti-Communism!"
(*New York Times,* Fall 1989)

At the very moment when the American bourgeois press, with unmitigated *Schadenfreude,* can easily score a point with its readers by turning the meaning of the first sentence of "The Communist Manifesto" of 1848 into its opposite, we propose that the American student of intellectual history, European affairs, and German studies have a closer look at an important chapter of the political and philosophical heritage of Western civilization—at the development of socialism in nineteenth-century Germany. We do so because we believe that, at the time of the demise of a system in Eastern Europe that traces its roots back to Marx and Engels, it is both intellectually honest and helpful to avoid misunderstandings, to go back to these roots and try to assess the original impetus of the socialist movement, its struggles, victories and defeats, its deviations from the original path, its divergent theoretical solutions, and political incarnations.

German socialism in the nineteenth century was, by no means, a unified movement: on the contrary, up until World War I, it was split into a number of internally feuding factions, even though it was perceived, from the outside, and for propagandistic purposes, as a monolithic, deadly threat to the ruling bourgeoisie.

The fight between the largest of these factions that has lasted for some seventy years, was eventually won by the so-called "revisionists." Recent developments in the socialist camp refer back to the debate on "revisionism," which is documented in this book. But up until 1917/18, Social Democracy was the organizational manifestation of the socialist movement as a whole comprising all of the factions. The ideological and organizational split between Social Democracy and Communism, as we know them today, is actually a product of the twentieth century. It is, therefore, important to note at the outset that the concept of Social Democracy denotes different things before and after World War I, that it has undergone a semantic shift: it has been narrowed down in the process. This is why the common roots of both parts of the movement need to be uncovered and put in perspective. And this is why we concentrate our selection on the years 1844–1914.

The end of communist supremacy in Eastern Europe may open a new chapter in world politics, but it hardly signals the "end of history," if by "history" we mean the manifestation of human praxis over time, the continuous struggle of mankind to improve the human condition in the context of ever-changing and new challenges.

It is worth noticing at this juncture that Stalinism was the true "grave digger" of a unified left in the thirties and forties in Europe and, eventually, also of communism itself; it represented the beginning of the end we are currently witnessing. The collapse of Stalinism (Romania) and of Neo-Stalinism in the rest of Eastern Europe—in particular in Czechoslovakia and the German Democratic Republic—reopens the forum for the debates documented in the texts of this volume, debates that had been artificially cut off by half a century of repression. There is not only no end of history in sight, but there are, inherent in this debate, quite a number of fruitful impulses for the revival of that history. This is not to deny that crucial insights have been gained in the meantime, particularly through the painful experiences of the twentieth century: it has become obvious to the left that neither is capitalism likely to disappear automatically nor would the dictatorship of the proletariat entail the end of all evil in the world.

At a moment when the largely nonviolent abdication of an ideology leaves an intellectual and political vacuum in a crucial part of the world, it is most propitious to reflect back on the origins of the socialist movement, of a time before it came to power, as a result of the Bolshevik revolution.

To many observers the essentially nonviolent character of the rapid abdication of the old regimes in Eastern Europe came as something of a surprise. This is understandable, since similar developments in capitalist dictatorships do not seem to be possible and, if they occur, the people's will is repressed with brute military force. It pays to reflect for a moment on what this may tell us about the fundamental difference of both types of regimes: it would appear that, in communist countries, the ruling elites protect only their own power—as they did in East Germany in 1953, in Hungary in 1956, and in Czechoslovakia in 1968—whereas in capitalist countries, the regimes tend to protect the power and the property of the truly powerful *behind* the scenes.

The next chapter in the history of socialism will have to be written with reference to these origins, to some of the basic tenets that inspired its founders and that are not obsolete today. Foremost among these tenets is the fundamental relationship between socialism and democracy. The fate of a united Europe and, by extension, of world peace, will ultimately depend on the peaceful resolution of this question.

The study of the socialist movement in the nineteenth century in Germany and of the development of democratic socialism or social democracy—through a close look at Germany's labor movement and the various stages in the history of the Social Democratic Party (SPD) up to World War I—is, therefore, not only an exercise in historical research into a particular, localized phenomenon: it offers an insight into the options of an international political movement that champions the idea of social justice for all, in an essentially hostile political environment. The case of Germany is exemplary in that Germany was considered crucial for the eventual victory of socialism then—according to the theory, the Revolution was supposed to occur in the most advanced industrialized country—and, because of the national and political division into two states with the same social heritage, but with as an as yet divergent notion of the road to social democracy, it will again be crucial for the further development of socialism, and of the new European order, now.

The adoption of a volume on German socialism into the canon of The German Library, intended for the American scholarly public, is a reflection at once of the essential part that German socialism played in shaping the German intellectual and national identity, and of the influence it had on the American labor movement. This contribution by German immigrants of the nineteenth century—mostly those who had to leave the country because of their involvement in the failed 1848 bourgeois revolution—to American thought and political organization, is usually neglected when, on October 6 each year, German–American Day, the German heritage in the United States is officially commemorated. It may very well be that the early American revolutionary army could make use of the military skills of a defrocked and decadent, antirepublican Prussian aristocrat, Baron von Steuben. But there can be no doubt that the more lasting German contributions to America's social conscience, its sense of equity, its trade-union movement, and its inspirations to overcome large social crises (such as, in the twentieth century, the Great Depression) have come from the likes of Carl Schurz, himself a '48er, antislavery activist under President Lincoln, and Secretary of the Interior from 1877 to 1881, and the democratically minded German socialists who organized large sections of the labor forces in New York and Chicago, and who influenced public opinion in immigrant circles through a myriad of newspapers in Milwaukee, Cincinnati, and St. Louis. It is to their credit that the German immigrants understood that their influence would ultimately be only implicit and subcutaneous and that, in a country of the geographic and social dimensions of the United States, with the pioneering spirit of an immigrant nation, ethnic diversity and racial division would prove stronger than international solidarity with the oppressed of the very countries most of the immigrants had left behind. Many of the German socialists remained locked in their German ghettos, socially and linguistically. (Some of the early and extremely awkward English translations of texts by prominent German socialists, which were done by German immigrants, and which we deliberately kept intact, show how difficult it must have been for them to communicate with their partners in a multilingual, but increasingly English-speaking society.) They never saw their efforts crowned through the formation of a strong American Socialist Party, which might have become a third political force in their new home country.

There were many more German immigrants to this country than is commonly recognized, and their contributions have by now taken root in American everyday life. Many of these stem from the early days of the labor movement, with its clubs and their rich traditions in music and sports. The memory of these contributions was all but forgotten, and the "German Huns" came under attack in the final years of the Wilhelminian Empire and World War I, and it was eventually wiped out during the Nazi terror. Today, German-American officialdom avoids the issues by linking the rehabilitation of

German contributions to American culture and society to a group of pastoral pacifists of the seventeenth century who, in 1683, founded Germantown in Pennsylvania.

The selection of texts we have assembled in this volume is also a reflection of the interdisciplinary character of German Studies in the United States to which The German Library is making a major contribution.

We are treating socialism in the nineteenth century as a philosophical doctrine, as the political movement of the class struggle, and as the unfolding of its political organization into a party. In choosing the various contributions, we tried not so much to "tell a coherent story," but to concentrate on such texts that demonstrate a particular originality of social-scientific investigation and analysis and/or political argumentation and debate at the time. The length of some of the texts does, therefore, not always reflect the importance that the particular issue treated may have had in the overall development of socialism or for the contemporary state of awareness of the contestants.

We alternate between propagandistic and soberly analytical texts, between programmatic statements and polemical refutations, popularizing manifestos and treatises pertinent to "scientific socialism"—in all, a mix of argumentation, analysis, and debate that has been lost in the process of history and is virtually unknown today. In particular, scientific socialism was the expression, in the second half of the nineteenth century, of an unerring belief in social progress and the eventual mastery of the world through scientific and rational means.

The topics we focus on as "major issues of the day" are chosen as much for their topicality then as for their current notoriety. Many milestones of socialist thought and practice that one might expect in such an anthology are either briefly included or omitted altogether since they are accessible elsewhere. In the appendix, we decided that rather than reprinting the successive party programs or the resolutions of the various Internationals, it would be more informative for the majority of our readers to witness the fight against the socialists, with the full weight of the juridical arsenal the Empire could muster, and the struggle by the socialists themselves to put one of their political weapons, the trade unions, on a legal basis (for which they had to borrow heavily from the tactical and linguistic armory of the "class enemy").

The selections that follow are not meant to be exhaustive or entirely self-explanatory. Depending on the specific needs of the reader, the texts should be read in conjunction with histories of nineteenth-century Germany, of the labor movement, and of the Social Democratic Party, as well as with literary texts of the period in question. (See the bibliography, pp. 327–30)

Theoretical Underpinnings

The essays assembled here are primarily social-scientific documents on a common theme. From the outset, though, the socialist movement in Germany has emphasized its strong ties to its theoretical heritage, the theory of dialectical materialism developed by Marx and Engels. Many of the authors cited in the anthology, in the very heat of party-political or parliamentary debates, refer back to "The Communist Manifesto" as the starting point, as the first popular theoretical articulation and, at the same time, militant pronouncement of the socialist cause as an international struggle. The terms *socialist* and *communist* were used almost interchangeably up to the 1848 revolution.

We begin the selection with the theoretical part of the "Manifesto": it is, in essence, a popularized application of Hegel's theory of dialectical progress in history to the entire field of human social development up to the present. The reader will be struck, in particular, by the author's insistence on the achievements of the bourgeoisie. This part of the canon of socialist literature contains by far the most convincing and analytically lucid eulogy of the very class whose inevitable and imminent demise at the hands of the antagonistic proletariat—a creation of its own, to promote its own glory—it predicts at the same time.

The description of the development of capitalism, of the succession of crises it inevitably generates, and of the ingenious resources it mobilizes at each juncture to gain a new lease on life, sound remarkably modern, even after almost 150 years. We know today that the theory of the gradual pauperization of the proletariat did not materialize in history, at least not when applied to the working classes of the industrialized nations in the first and second worlds. It should be noted, however, that one of the ways by which capitalism avoided the ultimate antagonism of the pauperization of the masses, which could have led to the revolution, was the *embourgeoisement* of the working classes in the West which, in turn, was only possible through the exportation of cheap, sub-subsistence-level labor conditions to the third world. And that this global third world pauperization, which is growing, bears in it the seeds of a potential global revolution, is an insight shared by many, Marxists and non-Marxists alike.

While the "Manifesto" emphasizes the dialectical aspect of the inevitable movement of history, the text from the "Critique of Political Economy" stresses the materialistic side of the theory: being determines consciousness, the economic basis of life, the praxis of men and women in the world, generates the superstructure of laws and legal institutions, constitutions, philosophies, ideologies, and religious beliefs.

Marx's brief summary of his theory shows that he has stood Hegel's idealistic philosophy upside down, from "the head unto its feet." The text also shows that once the superstructure has been generated it reflects back onto the base: the dialectic is a two-way street. And, even though the abolition of the last antagonisms, as we know them from our analysis of history to date, between the bourgeoisie and the proletariat will bring the "prehistory" of mankind to an end, it will at the same time create a new quality of social organization, with its own dynamic. The fact that, according to the theory, antagonisms based on the exploitation of man by man will disappear does not mean that the dialectic will come to an end; it will remain the motor of historical development. The events in Eastern Europe—and to a certain extent in China—demonstrate the consequences of the attempt at putting an artificial stop to the dialectical development of society and of history.

Engel's graveside speech in honor of Marx underlines in a concise form the unity of the three aspects that combine to make the work of Marx unique: He was, first of all, a great thinker and discoverer, on the order of Hegel and Darwin. Just as Darwin discovered the law of the development of organic nature, so Marx discovered the law of development of human history. He was, secondly, a foremost social scientist having laid bare, through empirical studies and the analysis of a vast body of contemporary literature, the motor behind capitalist economy: surplus value. He discovered the law of motion of capitalist production, just as Newton had discovered the law of motion of the celestial bodies. He was, thirdly, a revolutionary, a political activist for whom these discoveries were not only theoretical insights and milestones in man's struggle for knowledge, but guideposts for political action and agitation. In his so-called "Eleventh Thesis on Feuerbach," Marx himself sums up his mission: "So far philosophers have interpreted the world differently; the point, however, is to change it."

History of the Class Struggle

Short of rewriting the history of German socialism, it is inevitably somewhat arbitrary how one introduces the subject in the context of the present anthology. We have chosen to start with a text by August Bebel—the publication of this book coincides with the one-hundred-and-fiftieth anniversary of his birth—on the "Workers' Clubs" in the 1860s. It gives a rare insight into the as yet ill-developed political consciousness of the German working class at the time, and into the predominantly late-feudalistic ideology of the superiority of artisanal production, both socially and aesthetically, over industrial manufacture in German society. It also shows the working class in the city of Leipzig to be in the vanguard of the political movement of liberation from an oppressive rule then, as it is again now.

The demand in 1862, as a first step toward the liberalization of the workers, is universal suffrage. Thus, Bebel clearly establishes at the beginning of the movement the necessary linkage between socialism and democracy. The so-called "Eisenacher Programm" of August Bebel's and Wilhelm Liebknecht's "Social Democratic Workers' Party" postulates in 1869: "Political freedom is the ineluctable condition of the economic liberation of the working classes. The social question can, therefore, not be separated from the political; their solutions are mutually dependent on each other, and they are only possible in a democracy" (my translation).

Friedrich Engels's text on "Socialism in Germany" reflects a much later moment in the development of the movement. By 1890, in less than twenty years since the proclamation of the German Reich in Versailles (1871), votes for the socialists had soared, from under 100,000 to approximately 1.5 million. Engels can thus imagine the ultimate victory of the socialists to be attainable through the parliamentary process—not necessarily through a revolution—on condition that a war can be avoided in which reactionary forces in

France and Russia would bond together to crush the progressive socialists in Germany. The socialists, therefore, if for no other reason than to assure their own survival and future political success, must be in the vanguard of the pacifist movement and join any antiwar effort by other political forces. This stance is in keeping with the internationalist origins of the movement, and it did not jibe well with the nationalist and jingoistic rhetoric of the day. As a consequence, the socialists were frequently apostrophized as *vaterlandslose Gesellen,* unpatriotic scum.

Wilhelm Liebknecht's piece on "May Day" reminds us of the development of socialism as primarily the history of a struggle, one that needed its own symbols and rituals. The text is at the same time a testimony to the extreme sense of responsibility organized labor exhibited when faced with an economic recession: May Day is not to be construed as a "day off" *(freier Tag),* but as a day of celebration *(Feiertag)* of the achievements of the class struggle to date, and of demonstration for the eight-hour day. Due to the persistent opposition on the side of capital against any May Day variety, it eventually became a symbol of the internationalism and the solidarity of the socialist movement everywhere. The workers, the salt of the earth, celebrate on this day the beginning of a new era of mankind and proclaim peace and the protection of the class interests of the workers of all countries, just as, for thousands of years, Europeans have celebrated the beginning of a new life cycle in the Spring, usually on the first day of May. To this day, the first of May is the international day of labor throughout Europe and in other countries in the world, with a proud and public recognition of their socialist heritage.

Ferdinand Lassalle's essay on "Capital" is to be seen in conjunction with, and in sharp contrast to, Emil Lederer's analysis of the "salaried employee" *(Angestellte).* Whereas the former expounds the theory of bourgeois capital and its ideology, liberalism, as leading inevitably to an internecine war between large and small capitalist enterprises and, by extension, to the ultimate demise of the working class, the latter develops a critique of the bipolar antithesis of the class struggle theory, on the basis of a sociological analysis of a new class emerging in capitalist production: the salaried employee. Far from turning workers into paupers, increased automation and the relentless competition between capitalists have created the need for more sophisticated, better educated, better paid, and socially more accepted "workers" whose class consciousness, at best, puts them apart, but definitely neither in the "capital" nor in the "labor" camp. The two articles highlight the choice before the socialist movement: to stick with the orthodox Marxist bipolar theory of class struggle, or to open up gradually to accommodate new class formations or other distinct social strata hitherto unknown or irrelevant. Lederer's analysis is an early social scientific warning to the socialists that their ideology might be out of step with the development of the social makeup of the electorate, or worse even, that it might be clouding their overall perception of reality. It took the Social Democratic Party in Germany until 1959 before it shed its Marxist ideological heritage and, with its so-called "Godesberger Programm," became a catchall, magnet party *(Volkspartei)*.

The three pieces by Marx and Engels on the social classes and the labor movement in the United States are an excursion. They demonstrate to the American student of socialism that the currency of socialist ideas and their fate in the US was very much on the minds of the founders of socialism, and that there were indeed fruitful impulses from German immigrants on the American labor movement. What they also show is the early emergence of a persistent trait in American public consciousness, a certain parochialism of perception that leads the American leaders of the movement to believe that the conditions prevailing in the US are the universally normal conditions, a perception that, according to Engels, severely limits their imagination. So much so, that Engels discovers in 1885 that large segments of the American public believe that there is no separate working class in the US and that, consequently, there is no class struggle. Engels, in an effort to refute this opinion, points to a bitter and protracted coal miners' strike in Appalachia in 1889—a struggle that, by the irony of history, does not seem to be over yet, since in 1989 it is still occupying the headlines of the bourgeois press with express reference to the language of class struggle used by the miners throughout the conflict.

Engels still had some hope in the early 1890s that a significant sector of American labor could be organized into a "German–American Socialist Labor Party." This hope is fueled by an echo to Goethe's dictum, *Amerika, Du hast es besser!* ("America, you are better off!"—that is, than Europe), the belief that the organization of American workers into a party should be so much easier than a similar effort in Europe, since the various factions are free of their historical burden that had frequently limited or even paralyzed them in their respective home countries. Engels does not hide his disillusionment with American organized labor: whereas the so-called "Henry George" movement in New York was not inclined to pursue the introduction of a collective mode of production, but stuck with the program of land leasing to individual owners, and had little more than local importance, the Knights of Labor would clad their modern attempts at workers' emancipation in medieval mummery. The German immigrants themselves, who were frequently not of the best socialist stock, remained New York-centered and for the most part knew no English. But more importantly, Engels clearly diagnosed the objective reasons for the failure of socialism in the US: the constitution and the electoral system that renders every vote not given to one of the two major parties worthless; the divisiveness between the workers on the basis of ethnic origin and race; and, finally, economic protectionism which, initially and for a short time, benefits the workers to a certain extent, enough to weaken their resolve to change their condition radically.

The Social Democratic Party

The history of the Social Democratic Party of Germany is well documented, also in English. We have, therefore, concentrated on a few seminal texts referring to the very beginning of the organization of workers in Germany, to the all-out attack against an increasingly successful party by imperial Germany through the "Law against the Socialists," and to the so-called "revisionism debate," an inner-party struggle of orientation between the pursuit of a revolutionary course and one of reform.

Ferdinand Lassalle's "Open Letter" to the *Allgemeiner deutscher Arbeiterverein*—ADAV ("General German Workers' Club"), is a programmatic statement, written at the invitation of the workers of Leipzig. In it, Lassalle tries to combine the political demand of universal (equal, direct, secret) suffrage with the social claim of the appropriation of production profits by the workers (who would have to be put into a position to own the means of production by way of state-financed credits). General elections would give the workers the power to emancipate themselves by giving the state the mandate to finance their participation in the production process, on the producers', and not only on the consumers', side. If, with this political power in hand, the people—96 percent of the German population lived in misery at the beginning of the second half of the nineteenth century—were not successful in improving their condition, they would have only themselves to blame. The coalition of the ruling classes did everything imaginable to undermine the efforts of Lassalle and his followers.

Franz Mehring's account of the effects of the "Law against the Socialists" documents the Gestapo-like, or McCarthy-style, persecution of the socialists by the authorities of the German Reich, newly bolstered by its victory over France and the unification of the nation, but apparently insecure in its internal affairs. It also documents the underground strategies of a beleaguered party, including the adverse effect of a near-break that well-intentioned exile newspapers brought upon the party. What is particularly interesting about Mehring's analysis is the reference to what Hegel calls "the cunning of reason": the further the Bismarckian repression proceeded and became known, the more sympathy the socialists gained in society. The election successes of the SPD that Engels had referred to in another context are a clear demonstration of this unintended side effect.

The three articles by Eduard Bernstein, Rosa Luxemburg, and Karl Kautsky take us to the so-called "revisionism debate" of the German Social Democracy (1901 ff.). Revisionism, in the acceptation appropriate to this debate, refers to the alternative that Eduard Bernstein developed, from 1896 on, to the hitherto prevalent orthodox Marxist tenets of German Social Democracy, which had decided on the strict observance of the resolutions of the Second International. Several socialist theoreticians and some movements in other countries had come to similar conclusions, quite independently of the debate in Germany. Foremost among those were the Fabian Society in England, Benedetto Croce in Italy, and Jean Jaurès in France.

Bernstein's critique of orthodox Marxist socialist theory concentrates on three aspects: (1) Marx does not sufficiently explain the transition from a capitalist to a socialist society; (2) The few explanations in the Marxian oeuvre are contradictory in that he alternates between an evolutionary and a revolutionary scenario, and only the first of these is compatible with his scientific analysis of social forces; (3) The theory of the inevitable collapse of capitalism, because of the progressive worsening of its economic crises, was not confirmed by history. Bernstein pleads for the development and adoption of an evolutionary theory of the road to socialism, and for the transformation of the SPD from a revolutionary class party to a democratic reform party.

It cannot be overlooked today that part of the ideological baggage of Bernstein's alternative to the prevailing socialist doctrine of the party was, among other things, a dubious stance on foreign policy. He opposed colonialism only on the grounds that it would foster an already existing naval chauvinism at home, whereas he exhibited the typical cultural superiority of the European colonial powers of the day when he maintained that a "higher culture" can claim a higher right: that is, that only the appropriate cultivation of the land, which the colonial powers would presumably guarantee, gives the legal title to it, not "mere possession."

Bernstein's followers denied that there can be generally applicable principles for an internationalist socialism or an identical action program for socialist parties in different countries. Along with this softening stance on internationalism and the plea for a pluralistic socialism went the rehabilitation of patriotism and nationalism as an adequate expression of working-class sentiments. For Germany, they proposed the continued gradual promotion and adoption of socialist measures, on the basis of an improved lot of the working class through more political rights and better education.

The SPD, officially at the Dresden party convention of 1903, and through some of its more vociferous spokespersons, severely criticized Bernstein's ideas. We have selected two examples of the party's counterattack on Bernstein: Rosa Luxemburg's "Reform and Revolution" and Karl Kautsky's summary of the "Revisionist Controversy." Whereas the former charged that the revisionist theory was based on the assumption of an attenuation of the inherent contradictions of capitalism and a basically mechanistic understanding of economic processes, the latter denounces Bernstein's analysis on the grounds that his optimism reflects only a temporary economic boom in the capitalist economy, which has been dominated by the hectic formation of trusts and cartels for its survival ever since the death of Karl Marx in 1883. Rosa Luxemburg suspects in Bernstein a deep-seated aversion toward theoretical analysis and a tendency toward eclecticism and opportunism. Kautsky, on the other hand, tries to show that Bernstein has not grasped the meaning of "social revolution" in the party platform as the philosophical, scientific, and political concept that it is, but understands it, much as the hostile state authorities, in the sense of incitement to violent insurrection, thereby playing into the hands of the class enemy. Only social revolution in the sense of the Party could eventually bring about democracy, whereas no a priori link could be established between capitalism and democracy.

This section on the development of the SPD concludes with a "Report of the Executive Committee," a concrete account of the work of the parliamentary caucus of the Party in 1910. This relatively obscure document affords a unique insight into the daily political struggle, and it is a testimony to the enormous originality and vigor of a party thriving under adverse circumstances—with its emphasis on education for the masses through the popularization of theoretical knowledge, its concern for the rights of women, and the solidarity with socialist causes abroad.

Major Issues of the Day

The topics we have singled out under this rubric—women's rights, militarism, anti-Semitism, philosophy, and religion—were significant testing grounds for the application of the socialist doctrine, areas in which the socialists were either in the vanguard of the thinking of the day, or where they were on the defensive.

Women

Bebel's book "Woman and Socialism" was a best-seller of socialist literature in the nineteenth century. It contained a wealth of information on the status of women in many countries. In Germany, many basic rights that women had already won elsewhere had still to be fought for. Whereas the examples from other countries are worthy to be emulated—particularly those from the United States where, as early as 1869, a woman could be elected justice in Wyoming, and voting rights were granted nationwide by 1890—it is ultimately only through the socialization of the means of production that the fight can be won. The sole true ally of the women's movement is the proletariat, since its agenda calls for the humanization of the work place and the extension of the benefits of automation to both sexes.

Clara Zetkin formulates the socialist-feminist position of her day: whereas Marxism does not explicitly deal with feminism and women's rights, it has developed the only adequate method with which to approach them. Today, many feminists might disagree with her view that the exploitation of women will cease if and when the exploitation of man by man will have been overcome. But for Zetkin, solidarity with the socialist cause was more important, and ultimately more promising, than siding with the bourgeois suffragettes who accepted to work within the capitalist framework.

Militarism

Karl Liebknecht and Rosa Luxemburg write against militarism at a time when the Reich was bent on an imperialist foreign policy and preparing for an adventurous and rapacious war. They denounce militarism primarily as the enemy of the liberation process of the working class. It narcotizes the natural perceptions and class instincts of young workers, instills in them a jingoistic nationalism, and teaches them false virtues and values through the canonization of external appearances (parades and the tinsel of uniforms) and the bestowing of social privileges in return for military service. Since one of the rewards for military service is the taking over of past recruits into the civil service, the virus of militarism, with its emphasis on blind obedience and mindless discipline, is carried over into civilian life and weakens the immune system of the entire society against authoritarian and ultimately totalitarian rule. This is an indictment of German society that was shared by many intellectuals and writers of the turn of the century (see Heinrich Mann's "Der Untertan"). In Germany, antimilitarism has always militated against the all-pervasive preoccupation of German governments with "security" (*Sicherheit*), vis-à-vis real enemies on the outside as well as vis-à-vis imagined enemies within. Not all socialists have emphasized, as Rosa Luxemburg and Karl Liebknecht have, the inherent contradictions in militarism and its peril for the working classes in particular. At the outbreak of World War I, the representatives of the Socialist Party in Parliament voted in favor of the war credits the Kaiser had requested. The remilitarization of West Germany after

World War II, while having been initially opposed by the SPD, was later sanctioned and is no longer an issue today.

Anti-Semitism

While anti-Semitism is recognized by the German socialist elite of the nineteenth century to be a problem, this group tends to treat it as a characteristic of a backward culture, such as the one prevailing in Russia, Austria, and Prussia (Engels), or as a bourgeois, middle class problem, traceable to Jewish competition to small merchants, farmers, businesses, the professions, and students, particularly in times of economic depression (Bebel). Both recognize anti-Semitism as a European phenomenon, and both categorically declare that it is incompatible with socialism and will disappear with the disappearance of the class that harbors it. Subsequent history has shown that there was no reason for such optimism: anti-Semitism has persisted and continues to exist, even under so-called socialist regimes. While anti-Semitic sentiment had not entirely disappeared in the countries of the "really existing socialism" and may even over time have dictated much of public policy toward Jews in general or, at least, Jews in dissident circles, it is apparent that the Communist Parties in the East did not allow any anti-Semitic excesses, pogroms, or propaganda. This certainty has vanished with their demise, as some of the occurrences in the East since the fall of 1989 have indicated.

Philosophy and Religion

The contributions by Joseph Dietzgen and Franz Mehring on philosophy are examples of the popularization of theoretical issues of socialism for the masses, and a tribute to the socialist initiatives of educating the workers and immunizing them against the potentially nefarious influences of philosophies such as Nietzsche's, which was considered to be apologetic of a ruthlessly egoistical capitalism and of decadent amorality.

The two texts on socialism and religion are examples of a persistently ambiguous relationship. The orthodox Marxist atheist heritage often stands in the way of treating the phenomenon of religion analytically or, at least, pragmatically. The present texts are no exception. Whereas Dietzgen sees in religious education of the working classes in public schools not much more than a form of spiritual force-feeding, Mehring merely paraphrases Marx when he attributes the existence of religion to the existence of a deficiency. Dietzgen can only conclude that religion is a private matter and that the party must take this into account in its propaganda efforts against it, since members of the working class do take this private matter very seriously. Mehring cannot do much more than reiterate the orthodox opinion of the irreconcilable contradiction between the proletariat and religion. Redemption for the working class, in the socialist, secular sense, can only come through the overthrow of capitalism. The state should not nourish the private matter of religion, but the state should also not curtail the private practice of it. In these pragmatic views on the subject there is no hint anymore of Marx's tremendous appreciation of religion as an indicator of social deficiencies on earth and a thorn in the side of oppressive societies, and hence for its revolutionary potential. But the tone of Dietzgen and Mehring is one of tolerance. Today, socialism and religion in Germany are reconciled, at least insofar as the official party line is concerned.

It may very well be true that in the industrialized world, which we have come to consider the first world, the "laborers and wages (no longer) dance upon the outer circle of the conditions constituting a bare existence." In the third world, this precarious dance is the everyday tune, and it is far from over. But even if one does not agree with this assessment, which lends continued credence to much of what the socialist theoreticians have written and stood for, and concentrates on the errors, unfulfilled prophecies, and obsolescences of the texts presented here, who would deny respect to the authors of these documents, which are the milestones of the labor movement of a major industrialized country and that have caught the imagination of whole continents, a movement whose successes over the years have benefited people in many parts of the world, whether they are conscious of it or not?

M. S.

February 22, 1990

Chronology

[Adapted from Suzanne Miller and Heinrich Potthoff, *Kleine Geschichte der SPD*, Fifth edition, Bonn, 1983.]

1848

February	"The Communist Manifesto," by Karl Marx and Friedrich Engels, is published in London.
March	Revolutions in France, Germany, Austria, Hungary.
April	Workers' Associations are founded in numerous cities.
August 23– September 3	A labor congress meets in Berlin; The "Workers' Fraternity" is founded under the direction of Stephan Born.

1854

July	All Workers' Associations are dissolved based on the law banning associations (*Vereinsgesetz*) promulgated by Parliament (*Bundestag*).

1861

The ban on coalitions is lifted in Saxony.

1863

March 1

Ferdinand Lassalle answers the Leipzig Committee in an "Open Letter"; he advocates the creation of an independent political party for workers.

May 23

Founding of the "General Association of German Workers" (ADAV) in Leipzig. Lassalle is elected its president for five years. The ADAV proclaims as its most important goal the introduction of the universal, equal, and direct right to vote.

1864

August 31

Lassalle dies after a duel.

September 28

Creation of the International Workers' Association (First International) in London.

1865

December

Creation of the "United German Cigar Workers Association" in Leipzig.

1866

May

Creation of the German Book Printers' Association.

August 19

Bebel and W. Liebknecht form the "Saxonian People's Party" together with other bourgeois democrats.

1867

February 12

Karl Marx publishes the first volume of his major work, *Capital*.

Bebel, W. Liebknecht and Schraps are elected to the North German Reichstag.

September 5	At the Congress of the German Workers' Association a majority of the congress resolves to uphold the Program of the First International; the creation of trade unions is supported.

1869

August 7–8	Creation of the Social Democratic Workers' Party in Eisenach; the SDAP expressly proclaims itself to be the German branch of the International Workmen's Association.

1871

The revolt of the Paris Commune.

1875

Fusion of the Lassallean and the Eisenach group at the Party Congress in Gotha becomes the Socialist Workers' Party of Germany. Promulgation of the Gotha Program, which is harshly criticized by Marx in his "Marginal Notes" *(Randglossen)*.

1876

October 1	The first issue of *Vorwärts (Forward)*, the primary press organ of the Socialist Workers' Party, is published in Leipzig.

1878

July 30	Despite the government's efforts to prevent a significant electoral turnout, the Socialist Workers' Party obtains 437,158

	votes and with that nine mandates in the elections to the Reichstag.
October 19	Legislation introduced by Bismarck in May ("the law against the dangerous activities of social democracy")—antisocialist law—passes in the Reichstag by a vote of 221 to 149.

1880

August 20–23	Congress of the Socialist Workers' Party in Wyden, Switzerland.

1883

March 14	Karl Marx dies in London.

1889

July	An International Congress of Laborers selects the First of May as Day of Struggle for the eight-hour work day.

1890

January 25	The Reichstag rejects an extension of the antisocialist law.
February 20	The SPD receives 1,427,000 votes in the Reichstag elections and becomes the party with the strongest numerical representation.
November–December	Creation of the General Commission of the Trade Unions of Germany.

1891

August 16–23	Congress of the Second International.

October 14–20	Party Congress in Erfurt. Promulgation of the Erfurt Program.

1895

August 5	Friedrich Engels dies in London.

1899

January	Eduard Bernstein publishes *Evolutionary Socialism: A Criticism and Affirmation*.
October 9–14	Confrontations regarding revisionism at the Party Congress in Hanover.

1903

September 13–20	Revisionism is rejected and denounced at the Party Congress in Dresden.

1905

May 22–27	Debate regarding a general strike at the Fifth Trade Union Congress in Cologne. The Congress rejects agitation for a political mass strike.
September 17–23	At its Party Congress in June, the SPD declares its support for mass strikes only as a defensive instrument of the class struggle.

1906

September 23–29	Continuation of the discussion over mass strikes at the Mannheim Party Congress. Trade unions are granted far-reaching independence according to the Mannheim Agreement.

1912

January 12	The SPD acquires 34.8 percent of the votes (4.25 million) in the Reichstag elections.

1913

August 13	August Bebel dies in Switzerland.

1914

August 3	The SPD's parliamentary caucus resolves to support the government's demands for war credits by a vote of 78 to 14.
August 4	The SPD faction in the Reichstag votes unanimously for the war credits proposal. The party chairman, Haase, declares: "We will not abandon the fatherland in its hour of greatest need."
December 2	Karl Liebknecht is the only one to vote against the second proposal for war credits.

German Essays on Socialism
in the Nineteenth Century

THEORETICAL
UNDERPINNINGS

Karl Marx and Friedrich Engels

From The Communist Manifesto

A specter is haunting Europe—the specter of communism. . . .

The history of all hitherto existing society is the history of class struggles.

Freeman and slave, patrician and plebeian, lord and serf, guild-master and journeyman, in a word, oppressor and oppressed, stood in constant opposition to one another, carried on an uninterrupted, now hidden, now open fight, a fight that each time ended, either in a revolutionary reconstitution of society at large, or in the commmon ruin of the contending classes.

In the earlier epochs of history, we find almost everywhere a complicated arrangement of society into various orders, a manifold gradation of social rank. In ancient Rome we have patricians, knights, plebeians, slaves; in the Middle Ages, feudal lords, vassals, guild-masters, journeymen apprentices, serfs; in almost all of these classes, again, subordinate gradations.

The modern bourgeois society that has sprouted from the ruins of feudal society has not done away with class antagonisms. It has but established new classes, new conditions of oppression, new forms of struggle in place of the old ones.

Our epoch, the epoch of the bourgeoisie, possesses, however, this distinctive feature: It has simplified the class antagonisms. Society as a whole is more and more splitting up into two great hostile camps, into two great classes directly facing each other—bourgeoisie and proletariat.

From the serfs of the Middle Ages sprang the chartered burghers of the earliest towns. From the burgesses the first elements of the bourgeoisie were developed.

The discovery of America, the rounding of the Cape, opened up fresh ground for the rising bourgeoisie. The East-Indian and Chinese markets, the colonization of America, trade with the colonies, the increase in the means of exchange and in commodities generally, gave to commerce, to navigation, to industry, an impulse never before known, and thereby, to the revolutionary element in the tottering feudal society, a rapid development.

The feudal system of industry, in which industrial production was by closed guilds, now no longer sufficed for the growing wants of the new markets. The manufacturing system took its place. The guild-masters were pushed aside by the manufacturing middle class; division of labor between the different corporate guilds vanished in the face of division of labor in each single workshop.

Meantime the markets kept ever growing, the demand ever rising. Even manufacture no longer sufficed. Thereupon, steam and machinery revolutionized industrial production. The place of manufacture was taken by the giant, modern industry, the place of the industrial middle class by industrial millionaires, the leaders of whole industrial armies, the modern bourgeois.

Modern industry has established the world market, for which the discovery of America paved the way. This market has given an immense development to commerce, to navigation, to communication by land. This development has, in its turn, reacted on the extension of industry; and in proportion as industry, commerce, navigation, railways extended, in the same proportion the bourgeoisie developed, increased its capital, and pushed into the background every class handed down from the Middle Ages.

We see, therefore, how the modern bourgeoisie is itself the product of a long course of development, of a series of revolutions in the modes of production and of exchange.

Each step in the development of the bourgeoisie was accompanied by a corresponding political advance of that class. An oppressed class under the sway of the feudal nobility, an armed and self-governing association in the medieval commune; here independent urban republic (as in Italy and Germany), there taxable "third estate" of the monarchy (as in France); afterwards, in the period of manufacture proper, serving either the semi-feudal or the absolute monarchy as a counterpoise against the nobility, and, in fact, cornerstone of the great monarchies in general—the bourgeoisie has at last, since the establishment of modern industry and of the world market, conquered for itself, in the modern representative state, exclusive political sway. The executive of the modern state is but a committee for managing the common affairs of the whole bourgeoisie.

The bourgeoisie, historically, has played a most revolutionary part.

The bourgeoisie, wherever it has got the upper hand, has put an end to all feudal, patriarchal, idyllic relations. It has pitilessly torn asunder the motley feudal ties that bound man to his "natural superiors," and has left no other nexus between man and man than naked self-interest, than callous "cash payment." It has drowned the most heavenly ecstasies of religious fervor, of chivalrous enthusiasm, of philistine sentimentalism, in the icy water of egotistical calculation. It has resolved personal worth into exchange value, and in place of the numberless indefeasible chartered freedoms, has set up that single, unconscionable freedom—Free Trade. In one word, for exploitation, veiled by religious and political illusions, it has substituted naked, shameless, direct, brutal exploitation.

The bourgeoisie has stripped of its halo every occupation hitherto honored and looked up to with reverent awe. It has converted the physician, the lawyer, the priest, the poet, the man of science, into its paid wage laborers.

The bourgeoisie has torn away from the family its sentimental veil, and has reduced the family relation to a mere money relation.

The bourgeoisie has disclosed how it came to pass that the brutal display of vigor in the Middle Ages, which reactionaries so much admire, found its fitting complement in the most slothful indolence. It has been the first to show what man's activity can bring about. It has accomplished wonders far surpassing Egyptian pyramids, Roman acqueducts, and Gothic cathedrals, it has conducted expeditions that put in the shade all former exoduses of nations and crusades.

The bourgeoisie cannot exist without constantly revolutionizing the instruments of production, and thereby the relations of production, and with them the whole relations of society. Conservation of the old modes of production in unaltered form was, on the contrary, the first condition of existence for all earlier industrial classes. Constant revolutionizing of production, uninterrupted disturbance of all social conditions, everlasting uncertainty and agitation distinguish the bourgeois epoch from all earlier ones. All fixed, fast frozen relations, with their train of ancient and venerable prejudices and opinions, are swept away, all new-formed ones become antiquated before they can ossify. All that is solid melts into air, all that is holy is profaned, and man is at last compelled to face with sober senses his real conditions of life and his relations with his kind.

The need of a constantly expanding market for its products chases the bourgeoisie over the whole surface of the globe. It must nestle everywhere, settle everywhere, establish connections everywhere.

The bourgeoisie has through its exploitation of the world market given a cosmopolitan character to production and consumption in every country. To the great chagrin of reactionaries, it had drawn from under the feet of industry the national ground on which it stood. All old-established national industries have been destroyed or are daily being destroyed. They are dislodged by new industries, whose introduction becomes a life and death question for all civilized nations, by industries that no longer work up indigenous raw material, but raw material drawn from the remotest zones; industries whose products are consumed, not only at home, but in every quarter of the globe. In place of the old wants, satisfied by the production of the country, we find new wants, requiring for their satisfaction the products of distant lands and climes. In place of the old local and national seclusion and self-sufficiency, we have intercourse in every direction, universal interdependence of nations. And as in material, so also in intellectual production. The intellectual creations of individual nations become common property. National one-sidedness and narrow-mindedness become more and more impossible, and from the numerous national and local literatures there arises a world literature.

The bourgeoisie, by the rapid improvement of all instruments of production, by the immensely facilitated means of communication, draws all, even the most barbarian, nations into civilization. The cheap prices of its commodities are the heavy artillery with which it batters down all Chinese walls, with which it forced the barbarians' intensely obstinate hatred of foreigners to capitulate. It compels all nations, on pain of extinction, to adopt the bourgeois mode of production; it compels them to introduce what it calls civilization into their midst, i.e., to become bourgeois themselves. In one word, it creates a world after its own image.

The bourgeoisie has subjected the country to the rule of the towns. It has created enormous cities, has greatly increased the urban population as compared with the rural, and has thus rescued a considerable part of the population from the idiocy of rural life. Just as it has made the country dependent on the towns, so it has made barbarian and semibarbarian countries dependent on the civilized ones, nations of peasants on nations of bourgeois, the East on the West.

The bourgeoisie keeps more and more doing away with the scattered state of the population, of the means of production, and of property. It has agglomerated population, centralized means of production, and has concentrated property in a few hands. The necessary consequence of this was political centralization. Independent, or but loosely connected provinces, with separate interests, laws, governments, and systems of taxation, became lumped together into one nation, with one government, one code of laws, one national class interest, one frontier and one customs tariff.

The bourgeoisie, during its rule of scarce one hundred years, has created more massive and more colossal productive forces than have all preceding generations together. Subjection of nature's forces to man, machinery, application of chemistry to industry and agriculture, steam navigation, railways, electric telegraphs, clearing of whole continents for cultivation, canalization of rivers, whole populations conjured out of the ground—what earlier century had even a presentiment that such productive forces slumbered in the lap of social labor?

We see then: the means of production and of exchange, on whose foundation the bourgeoisie built itself up, were generated in feudal society. At a certain stage in the development of these means of production and of exchange, the conditions under which feudal society produced and exchanged, the feudal organization of agriculture and manufacturing industry, in one word, the feudal relations of property became no longer compatible with the already developed productive forces; they became so many fetters. They had to be burst asunder; they were burst asunder.

Into their place stepped free competition, accompanied by a social and political constitution adapted to it, and by the economic and political sway of the bourgeois class.

A similar movement is going on before our own eyes. Modern bourgeois society with its relations of production, of exchange and of property, a society that has conjured up such gigantic means of production and of exchange, is like the sorcerer who is no longer able to control the powers of the nether world whom he has called up by his spells. For many a decade past the history of industry and commerce is but the history of the revolt of modern productive forces against modern conditions of production, against the property relations that are the conditions for the existence of the bourgeoisie and of its rule. It is enough to mention the commercial crises that by their periodical return put the existence of the entire bourgeois society on its trial, each time more threateningly. In these crises a great part not only of the existing products, but also of the previously created productive forces, are periodically destroyed. In these crises there breaks out an epidemic that, in all earlier epochs, would have seemed an absurdity—the epidemic of overproduction. Society suddenly finds itself put back into a state of momentary barbarism; it appears as if a famine, a universal war of devastation had cut off the supply of every means of subsistence; industry and commerce seem to be destroyed. And why? Because there is too much civilization, too much means of subsistence, too much industry, too much commerce. The productive forces at the disposal of society no longer tend to further the development of the conditions of bourgeois property; on the contrary, they have become too powerful for these conditions, by which they are fettered, and so soon as they overcome these fetters, they bring disorder into the whole of bourgeois society, endanger the existence of bourgois property. The conditions of bourgeois society are too narrow to comprise the wealth created by them. And how does the bourgoisie get over these crises? On the one hand, by enforced destruction of a mass of productive forces; on the other, by the conquest of new markets, and by the more thorough exploitation of the old ones. That is to say, by paving the way for more extensive and more destructive crises, and by diminishing the means whereby crises are prevented.

The weapons with which the bourgeoisie felled feudalism to the ground are now turned against the bourgeoisie itself.

But not only has the bourgeoisie forged the weapons that bring death to itself; it has also called into existence the men who are to wield those weapons—the modern working class—the proletarians.

In proportion as the bourgeoisie, i.e., capital, is developed, in the same proportion is the proletariat, the modern working class, developed—a class of laborers, who live only so long as they find work, and who find work only so long as their labor increases capital. These laborers, who must sell themselves piecemeal, are a commodity, like every other article of commerce, and are consequently exposed to all the vicissitudes of competition, to all the fluctuations of the market.

Owing to the extensive use of machinery and to division of labor, the work of the proletarians has lost all individual character, and, consequently, all charm for the workman. He becomes an appendage of the machine, and it is only the most simple, most monotonous, and most easily acquired knack, that is required of him. Hence, the cost of production of a workman is restricted, almost entirely, to the means of subsistence that he requires for his maintenance, and for the propagation of his race. But the price of a commodity, and therefore also of labor, is equal to its cost of production. In proportion, therefore, as the repulsiveness of the work increases, the wage decreases. Nay more, in proportion as the use of machinery and division of labor increases, in the same proportion the burden of toil also increases, whether by prolongation of the working hours, by increase of the work exacted in a given time, or by increased speed of the machinery, etc.

Modern industry has converted the little workshop of the patriarchal master into the great factory of the industrial capitalist. Masses of laborers, crowded into the factory, are organized like soldiers. As privates of the industrial army they are placed under the command of a perfect hierarchy of officers and sergeants. Not only are they slaves of the bourgeois class, and of the bourgeois state; they are daily and hourly enslaved by the machine, by the overseer, and, above all, by the individual bourgeois manufacturer himself. The more openly this despotism proclaims gain to be its end and aim, the more petty, the more hateful, and the more embittering it is.

The less the skill and exertion of strength implied in manual labor, in other words, the more modern industry becomes developed, the more is the labor of men superseded by that of women. Differences of age and sex have no longer any distinctive social validity for the working class. All are instruments of labor, more or less expensive to use, according to their age and sex.

No sooner is the exploitation of the laborer by the manufacturer, so far at an end, that he receives his wages in cash, than he is set upon by the other portions of the bourgeoisie, the landlord, the shopkeeper, the pawnbroker, etc.

The lower strata of the middle class—the small tradespeople, shopkeepers, and retired tradesmen generally, the handicraftsmen and peasants—all these sink gradually into the proletariat, partly because their diminutive capital does not suffice for the scale on which modern industry is carried on, and is swamped in the competition with the large capitalists, partly because their specialized skill is rendered worthless by new methods of production. Thus the proletariat is recruited from all classes of the population.

The proletariat goes through various stages of development. With its birth begins its struggle with the bourgeoisie. At first the contest is carried on by individual laborers, then by the work people of a factory, then by the operatives of one trade, in one locality, against the individual bourgeois who directly exploits them. They direct their attacks not against the bourgeois conditions of production, but against the instruments of production themselves; they destroy imported wares that compete with their labor, they smash to pieces machinery, they set factories ablaze, they seek to restore by force the vanished status of the workman of the Middle Ages.

At this stage the laborers still form an incoherent mass scattered over the whole country, and broken up by their mutual competition. If anywhere they unite to form more compact bodies, this is not yet the consequence of their own active union, but of the union of the bourgeoisie, which class, in order to attain its own political ends, is compelled to set the whole proletariat in motion, and is moreover yet, for a time, able to do so. At this stage, therefore, the proletarians do not fight their enemies, but the enemies of their enemies, the remnants of absolute monarchy, the landowners, the nonindustrial bourgeois, the petty bourgeoisie. Thus the whole historical movement is concentrated in the hands of the bourgeoisie; every victory so obtained is a victory for the bourgeoisie.

But with the development of industry the proletariat not only increases in number; it becomes concentrated in greater masses, its strength grows, and it feels that strength more. The various interests and conditions of life within the ranks of the proletariat are more and more equalized, in proportion as machinery obliterates all distinctions of labor, and nearly everywhere reduces wages to the same low level. The growing competition among the bourgeois, and the resulting commercial crises, make the wages of the workers ever more fluctuating. The unceasing improvement of machinery, ever more rapidly developing, makes their livelihood more and more precarious; the collisions between individual workmen and individual bourgeois take more and more the character of collisions between two classes. Thereupon the workers begin to form combinations (trade unions) against the bourgeois; they club together in order to keep up the rate of wages; they found permanent associations in order to make provision beforehand for these occasional revolts. Here and there the contest breaks out into riots.

Now and then the workers are victorious, but only for a time. The real fruit of their battle lies, not in the immediate result, but in the ever expanding union of the workers. This union is helped on by the improved means of communication that are created by modern industry, and that place the workers of different localities in contact with one another. It was just this contact that was needed to centralize the numerous local struggles, all of the same character, into one national struggle between classes. But every class struggle is a political struggle. And that union, to attain which the burghers of the Middle Ages, with their miserable highways, required centuries, the modern proletarians, thanks to railways, achieve in a few years.

This organization of the proletarians into a class, and consequently into a political party, is continually being upset again by the competition between the workers themselves. But it ever rises up again, stronger, firmer, mightier. It compels legislative recognition of particular interests of the workers, by taking advantage of the divisions among the bourgeoisie itself. Thus the Ten-Hours Bill in England was carried.

Altogether, collisions between the classes of the old society further in many ways the course of development of the proletariat. The bourgeoisie finds itself involved in a constant battle. At first with the aristocracy; later on, with those portions of the bourgeoisie itself, whose interests have become antagonistic to the progress of industry; at all times with the bourgeoisie of foreign countries. In all these battles it sees itself compelled to appeal to the proletariat, to ask for its help, and thus, to drag it into the political arena. The bourgeoisie itself, therefore, supplies the proletariat with its own elements of political and general education, in other words, it furnishes the proletariat with weapons for fighting the bourgeoisie.

Further, as we have already seen, entire sections of the ruling classes are, by the advance of industry, precipitated into the proletariat, or are at least threatened in their conditions of existence. These also supply the proletariat with fresh elements of enlightenment and progress.

Finally, in times when the class struggle nears the decisive hour, the process of dissolution going on within the ruling class, in fact within the whole range of old society, assumes such a violent, glaring character, that a small section of the ruling class cuts itself adrift, and joins the revolutionary class, the class that holds the future in its hands. Just as, therefore, at an earlier period, a section of the nobility went over to the bourgeoisie, so now a portion of the bourgeoisie goes over to the proletariat, and in particular, a portion of the bourgeois ideologists, who have raised themselves to the level of comprehending theoreticially the historical movement as a whole.

Of all the classes that stand face to face with the bourgeoisie today, the proletariat alone is a really revolutionary class. The other classes decay and finally disappear in the face of modern industry; the proletariat is its special and essential product.

The lower middle class, the small manufacturer, the shopkeeper, the artisan, the peasant, all these fight against the bourgeoisie, to save from extinction their existence as fractions of the middle class. They are therefore not revolutionary, but conservative. Nay, more, they are reactionary, for they try to roll back the wheel of history. If by chance they are revolutionary, they are so only in view of their impending transfer into the proletariat; they thus defend not their present, but their future interests; they desert their own standpoint to place themselves at that of the proletariat.

The "dangerous class," the social scum (lumpen proletariat), that passively rotting mass thrown off by the lowest layers of old society, may, here and there, be swept into the movement by a proletarian revolution; its conditions of life, however, prepare it far more for the part of a bribed tool of reactionary intrigue.

In the conditions of the proletariat, those of old society at large are already virtually swamped. The proletarian is without property; his relation to his wife and children has no longer anything in common with the bourgeois family relations; modern industrial labor, modern subjection to capital, the same in England as in France, in America as in Germany, has stripped him of every trace of national character. Law, morality, religion, are to him so many bourgeois prejudices, behind which lurk in ambush just as many bourgeois interests.

All the preceding classes that got the upper hand, sought to fortify their already acquired status by subjecting society at large to their conditions of appropriation. The proletarians cannot become masters of the productive forces of society, except by abolishing their own previous mode of appropriation, and thereby also every other previous mode of appropriation. They have nothing of their own to secure and to fortify; their mission is to destroy all previous securities for, and insurances of, individual property.

All previous historical movements were movements of minorities, or in the interest of minorities. The proletarian movement is the self-conscious, independent movement of the immense majority, in the interest of the immense majority. The proletariat, the lowest stratum of our present society, cannot stir, cannot raise itself up, without the whole superincumbent strata of official society being blown to pieces.

Though not in substance, yet in form, the struggle of the proletariat with the bourgeoisie is at first a national struggle. The proletariat of each country must, of course, first of all settle matters with its own bourgeoisie.

In depicting the most general phrases of the development of the proletariat, we traced the more or less veiled civil war, raging within existing society, up to the point where that war breaks out into open revolution, and where the violent overthrow of the bourgeoisie lays the foundation for the sway of the proletariat.

Hitherto, every form of society has been based, as we have already seen, on the antagonism of oppressing and oppressed classes. But in order to oppress a class, certain conditions must be assured to it under which it can, at least, continue its slavish existence. The serf, in the period of serfdom, raised himself to membership in the commune, just as the petty bourgeois, under the yoke of feudal absolutism, managed to develop into a bourgeois. The modern laborer, on the contrary, instead of rising with the progress of industry, sinks deeper and deeper below the conditions of existence of his own class. He becomes a pauper, and pauperism develops more rapidly than population and wealth. And here it becomes evident that the bourgeoisie is unfit any longer to be the ruling class in society, and to impose its conditions of existence upon society as an overriding law. It is unfit to rule because it is incompetent to assure an existence to its slave within his slavery, because it cannot help letting him sink into such a state, that it has to feed him instead of being fed by him. Society can no longer live under this bourgeoisie, in other words, its existence is no longer compatible with society.

The essential condition for the existence and for the sway of the bourgeois class, is the formation and augmentation of capital; the condition for capital is wage labor. Wage labor rests exclusively on competition between the laborers. The advance of industry, whose involuntary promoter is the bourgeoisie, replaces the isolation of the laborers, due to competition, by their revolutionary combination, due to association. The development of modern industry, therefore, cuts from under its feet the very foundation on which the bourgeoisie produces and appropriates products. What the bourgeoisie therefore produces, above all, are its own grave diggers. Its fall and the victory of the proletariat are equally inevitable.

Translated by S. Moore

Karl Marx

From A Contribution to the Critique of Political Economy

. . . Some remarks as to the course of my own politico-economic studies may be in place here.

The subject of my professional studies was jurisprudence, which I pursued, however, in connection with and as secondary to the studies of philosophy and history. In 1842–43, as editor of the *Rheinische Zeitung,* I found myself embarrassed at first when I had to take part in discussions concerning so-called material interests. The proceedings of the Rhine diet in connection with forest thefts and the extreme subdivision of landed property; the official controversy about the condition of the Mosel peasants, into which Herr von Schaper, at that time President of the Rhine Province, entered with the *Rheinische Zeitung;* finally, the debates on free trade and protection gave me the first impulse to take up the study of economic questions. At the same time a weak, quasi-philosophic echo of French socialism and communism made itself heard in the *Rheinische Zeitung* in those days when the good intentions "to go ahead" greatly outweighed knowledge of facts. I declared myself against such botching, but had to admit at once in a controversy with the *Allgemeine Augsburger Zeitung* that my previous studies did not allow me to hazard an independent judgment as to the merits of the French schools. When, therefore, the publishers of the *Rheinische Zeitung* conceived the illusion that by a less aggressive policy the paper could be saved from the death sentence pronounced upon it, I was glad to grasp that opportunity to retire to my study room from public life.

The first work undertaken for the solution of the question that troubled me was a critical revision of Hegel's *Philosophy of Law;* the Introduction to that work appeared in the *Deutsch-Fran-zösische Jahrbücher,* published in Paris in 1844. I was led by my studies to the conclusion that legal relations as well as forms of state could be neither understood by themselves nor explained by the so-called general progress of the human mind, but that they are rooted in the material conditions of life, which are summed up by Hegel after the fashion of the English and French of the eighteenth century under the name "civil society"; the anatomy of that civil society is to be sought in political economy. The study of the latter, which I had taken up in Paris, I continued at Brussels, whither I immigrated on account of an order of expulsion issued by Mr. Guizot. The general conclusion at which I arrived and which, once reached, continued to serve as the leading thread in my studies may be briefly summed up as follows: In the social production which men carry on they enter into definite relations that are indispensable and independent of their will; these relations of production correspond to a definite stage of development of their material powers of production. The sum total of these relations of production constitutes the economic structure of society—the real foundation, on which rise legal and political superstructures and to which correspond definite forms of social consciousness. The mode of production in material life determines the general character of the social, political, and spiritual processes of life. It is not the consciousness of men that determines their existence, but, on the contrary, their social existence determines their consciousness. At a certain stage of their development the material forces of production in society come into conflict with the existing relations of production, or—what is but a legal expression for the same thing—with the property relations within which they had been at work before. From forms of development of the forces of production these relations turn into their fetters. Then comes the period of social revolution. With the change of the economic foundation the entire immense superstructure is more or less rapidly transformed. In considering such transformations the distinction should always be made between the material transformation of the economic conditions of production, which can be determined with the precision of natural science, and the legal, political, religious, aesthetic, or philosophic—in short, ideological—forms in which men become conscious of this conflict and fight it out. Just as our opinion of an individual is not based on what he thinks of himself, so can we not judge such a period of transformation by its own consciousness; on the contrary, this consciousness must rather be explained from the contradictions of material life, from the existing conflict between the social forces of production and the relations of production. No social order ever disappears before all the productive forces for which there is room in it have been developed, and new, higher relations of production never appear before the material conditions of their existence have matured in the womb of the old society. Therefore mankind always takes up only such problems as it can solve, since, looking at the matter more closely, we will always find that the problem itself arises only when the material conditions necessary for its solution already exist or are at least in the process of formation. In broad outlines we can designate the Asiatic, the ancient, the feudal, and the modern bourgeois methods of production as so many epochs in the progress of the economic formation of society. The bourgeois relations of production are the last antagonistic form of the social process of production—antagonistic not in the sense of individual antagonism, but of one arising from conditions surrounding the life of individuals in society; at the same time the productive forces developing in the womb of bourgeois society create the material conditions for the solution of that antagonism. This social formation constitutes, therefore, the closing chapter of the prehistoric stage of human society.

Friedrich Engels, with whom I was continually corresponding and exchanging ideas since the appearance of his ingenious critical essay on economic categories (in the *Deutsch-Französische Jahrbücher*), came by a different road to the same conclusions as myself (see his *Condition of the Working Class in England*). When he, too, settled in Brussels in the spring of 1845, we decided to work out together the contrast between our view and the idealism of the German philosophy; in fact, to settle our accounts with our former philosophic conscience. The plan was carried out in the form of a criticism of the post-Hegelian philosophy. The manuscript in two solid octavo volumes had long reached the publisher in Westphalia when we received information that conditions had so changed as not to allow of its publication. We abandoned the manuscript to the stinging criticism of the mice the more readily since we had accomplished our main purpose—the clearing up of the question to ourselves. Of the scattered writings on various subjects in which we presented our views to the public at that time, I recall only the *Manifesto of the Communist Party,* written by Engels and myself, and the *Discourse on Free Trade,* written by myself. The leading points of our theory were first presented scientifically, though in a polemic form, in my *Misère de la Philosophie,* etc. directed against Proudhon and published in 1847. An essay on *Wage Labor,* written by me in German, and in which I put together my lectures on the subject delivered before the German Workmen's Club at Brussels, was prevented from leaving the hands of the printer by the February revolution and my expulsion from Belgium, which followed it as a consequence.

Translated by N. I. Stone

Friedrich Engels

Speech at the Graveside of Karl Marx

On the 14th of March, at a quarter to three in the afternoon, the greatest living thinker ceased to think. He had been left alone for scarcely two minutes, and when we came back we found him in his armchair, peacefully gone to sleep—but forever.

An immeasurable loss has been sustained both by the militant proletariat of Europe and America, and by historical science, in the death of this man. The gap that has been left by the departure of this mighty spirit will soon enough make itself felt.

Just as Darwin discovered the law of development of organic nature, so Marx discovered the law of development of human history: the simple fact, hitherto concealed by an overgrowth of ideology, that mankind must first of all eat, drink, have shelter and clothing, before it can pursue politics, science, art, religion, etc.; that therefore the production of the immediate material means of subsistence and consequently the degree of economic development attained by a given people or during a given epoch form the foundation upon which the state institutions, the legal conceptions, art, and even the ideas on religion, of the people concerned have been evolved, and in the light of which they must, therefore, be explained, instead of *vice versa,* as had hitherto been the case.

But that is not all. Marx also discovered the special law of motion governing the present-day capitalist mode of production and the bourgeois society that this mode of production has created. The discovery of surplus value suddenly threw light on the problem, in trying to solve which all previous investigations, of both bourgeois economists and socialist critics, had been groping in the dark.

Two such discoveries would be enough for one lifetime. Happy the man to whom it is granted to make even one such discovery. But in every single field which Marx investigated—and he investigated very many fields, none of them superficially—in every field, even in that of mathematics, he made independent discoveries.

Such was the man of science. But this was not even half the man. Science was for Marx a historically dynamic, revolutionary force. However great the joy with which he welcomed a new discovery in some theoretical science whose practical application perhaps it was as yet quite impossible to envisage, he experienced quite another kind of joy when the discovery involved immediate revolutionary changes in industry, and in historical development in general. For example, he followed closely the development of the discoveries made in the field of electricity and recently those of Marcel Deprez.

For Marx was before all else a revolutionist. His real mission in life was to contribute, in one way or another, to the overthrow of capitalist society and of the state institutions which it had brought into being, to contribute to the liberation of the modern proletariat, which *he* was the first to make conscious of its own position and its needs, conscious of the conditions of its emancipation. Fighting was his element. And he fought with a passion, a tenacity and a success such as few could rival. His work on the first *Rheinische Zeitung* (1842), the Paris *Vorwärts** (1844), the *Deutsche Brüsseler Zeitung* (1847), the *Neue Rheinische Zeitung* (1848–49), the *New York Tribune* (1852–61), and in addition to these a host of militant pamphlets, work in organizations in Paris, Brussels, and London, and finally, crowning all, the formation of the great International Working Men's Association—this was indeed an achievement of which its founder might well have been proud even if he had done nothing else.

And, consequently, Marx was the best hated and most calumniated man of his time. Governments, both absolutist and republican, deported him from their territories. Bourgeois, whether conservative or ultra-democratic, vied with one another in heaping slanders upon him. All this he brushed aside as though it were cobweb, ignoring it, answering only when extreme necessity compelled him. And he died beloved, revered, and mourned by millions of revolu-

---

* *Vorwärts (Forward):* A radical newspaper of the German socialists in emigration, one of whose contributors was Karl Marx. It appeared in German in Paris in 1844. Not to be confused with the official press organ of the Social Democratic Party from 1876 to 1989.

tionary fellow workers—from the mines of Siberia to California, in all parts of Europe and America—and I make bold to say that though he may have had many opponents he had hardly one personal enemy.

His name will endure through the ages, and so also will his work!

HISTORY OF
SOCIALISM:
LABOR MOVEMENT
AND CLASS STRUGGLE

August Bebel

On Workers' Clubs and Labor Associations in the 1860s

While the industrial development of Germany had made considerable headway at that time, nevertheless this country was still overwhelmingly a land of small businessmen and small farmers. Three-fourths of the industrial laborers were artisans. With the exception of work in the heavy industries, such as mining, iron construction, and machine building, factory labor was despised by the artisan journeymen. The products of factories were considered cheap as well as nasty, a stigma which the representative of Germany at the world's exposition at Philadelphia, Privy Counselor Reuleaux, still impressed upon Germany factory labor sixteen years later. In the eyes of the artisan, the factory laborer was an inferior, and to be called a laborer instead of a journeyman or an apprentice, was considered an insult by many. Moreover, the vast majority of the journeymen and apprentices still harbored the delusion that they would be masters some day, particularly when professional liberty was proclaimed in Saxony and other states in the beginning of the sixties. The political intelligence of these workers was low. In the fifties, during the period of blackest reaction, in which all political life was dead, they had been raised and had not been given any opportunity to educate themselves politically. Workingmen's clubs or artisan's clubs were exceptions and served every other purpose but political enlightenment. Workingmen's clubs of a political nature were not even tolerated in most German states, or were even prohibited by a decision of the federal parliament in 1856, for in the opinion of this parliament in Frankfort-on-Main, a workingmen's club was identical with the spreading of socialism and communism. And to us of the younger generation, socialism and communism were at that time utterly strange conceptions. It is true that here and there, for instance in Leipsic, a few individuals, like Fritzsche, Vahlteich, the tailor Schilling, existed, who had heard of Weitling's communism, and had read his writings, but these men were exceptions. Never did I hear at that time of any laborer who knew anything of the *Communist Manifesto,* or of the activity of Marx and Engels during the years of the revolution in the Rhineland.

All this shows that the working class at that time occupied a position in which it had neither a class interest of its own, nor knew anything of the existence of a social question. For this reason the laborers flocked in droves to the clubs formed by the assistance of the liberal spokesmen, who appeared to the workingmen as the heralds of genuine friends of "Labor."

These workingmen's clubs sprouted in the early sixties like mushrooms after a warm summer rain. This was true, particularly of Saxony, but it took place also in other parts of Germany. Such clubs arose in localities, and it required many years before the socialist movement found a favorable soil there, although by that time the old workingmen's clubs had disappeared.

In Leipsic, political life was wide-awake, for the city was regarded as one of the principal seats of liberalism and democracy. One day I read an invitation to attend a popular meeting for the purpose of founding an educational club. The notice appeared in the democratic *Middle German People's Paper,* of which I was a subscriber, and which was edited by Dr. Peters, a participant in the revolution of 1848, the husband of the late well-known champion of women's rights, Louise Otto-Peters. This meeting took place on February 19, 1861, in Vienna Hall, a resort located near Rose Valley, in a garden. When I entered the hall, it was already overcrowded. With much difficulty I found a place in the gallery. It was the first public meeting which I attended. The president of the Polytechnic Society, Professor Dr. Hirzel, was the speaker. He made the announcement that a club for technical education was to be founded as a second department of the Polytechnic Society, because workingmen's clubs were forbidden in Saxony by the federal decision of 1856. This started the opposition. Together with Professor Rossmaessler, who had been a member of the parliament in Frankfort-on-Main and had been ousted from his position at the Academy of Forestry in Tharand by Mr. von Buest, other speakers took the floor, especially Vahlteich and Fritzsche, and demanded full independence for this club, which should be a political one. The cultivation of lines of instruction, they said, was the business of the school, not of a club for grown people. I was not in agreement with these speakers, but I admired the keen way in which these laborers took issue with the learned gentlemen, and I secretly wished that I might also be able to speak like that.

The club was founded, and the opposition joined it, although they had not accomplished their purpose. I likewise became a member that evening. This club became, in its way, a sort of model institution. Lecturers for scientific subjects were available in plenty. Among them were the Professors Rossmaessler, Bock—the editor of *Gartenlaube* and author of the *Book of Man in Health and Disease*—Wuttke, Wenck, Marbach, Dr. Lindner, Dr. Reyher, Dr. Burckhardt, and others. These were followed later by Professor Biedermann, Dr. Hans Blum, of whom it was said that in his student's years he carried a visiting card with the inscription, "Student of the Rights of Man," Dr. Eras, Liebknecht, who came to Leipsic in the summer of 1865, and Robert Schweichel. One of the most diligent lecturers during the first year was Dr. Dammer, who later on became the first vice-president of the General Association of Workingmen appointed by Lassalle. Lessons were given in English, French, in stenography, in commercial bookkeeping, in the German language, and in arithmetic. A turning and singing section were also founded. Vahlteich, who was a great turner, joined the former, and Fritzsche and myself joined the singing section. Fritzsche sang an excellent second bass, as every one does who has no singing voice.

At the head of the club stood a committee of twenty-four, and in this committee the fight over the presidency became fierce. Rossmaessler was beaten in the race by the architect, Mothes, but the opposition continued its work systematically. At the first anniversary of the club in February, 1862, Vahlteich made the address, which was decidedly political. He demanded universal suffrage. At the new election of the committee, I was likewise elected a member of it. My longing for public speaking was soon gratified in the frequent debates of the club. A friend of mine told me later that when I, for the first time, spoke a few minutes in justifying a motion, the members sitting at his table had looked at each other, and some one had asked: "Who is that man that bears himself like that?" Since various departments had been formed for the different lines of administration, I was chosen for the library and the entertainment department. I became the chairman of both of them. The election of the president of the club, which the committee had to undertake, called forth a violent struggle at this time. Four times the ballots were cast, without resulting in a plurality for any candidate. The votes were always equally distributed. At last Professor Rossmaessler was beat once more by one vote in favor of the architect, Mothes, who had voted for himself. Now the opposition carried the struggle to the general assembly, which met on Good Friday, 1862. The club then had more than 500 members. The opposition once more advanced its old demand that the club should be made a purely political one, and that school instruction should be excluded. After a violent debate of many hours, in which I took part also, the opposition was defeated by a majority of three-fourths of the votes. If the opposition had operated more adroitly, if they had demanded that political lectures on events of the day should be delivered from time to time and discussed, they would have won out easily. But that instruction should be banished from the club, which was of the greatest interest to the younger members of the club, called out their resistance. I, for instance, took a course in bookkeeping and stenography. A few days before that decisive meeting, Fritzsche and Vahlteich had been trying hard to bring me over to their side. I could not follow them.

The opposition now withdrew from the club, and founded the "Vorwaerts" club, which opened its headquarters in the Hotel de Saxe. The hotelkeeper was the former pastor, Wuerkert, who had been dismissed during the years of reaction. He had a peculiar method of spreading enlightenment and doing business at the same time. Every week he gave lectures, delivered by himself, on a wide variety of subjects, such as the birthdays and deathdays of famous men, political events, etc. On such days his establishment was crowded. It made a queer impression when Wuerkert, after moving among his guests and bringing beer to this one or that one, took his place on the landing of the stairs leading from the lower to the upper room, and gave his lecture from there, visible to every one. Not in opposition, but rather as a supplement to these meetings in the Hotel de Saxe, acted the restaurant of the "Good Spring" on the Bruehl. It was a large cellar, recently built, and its owner was Grun, one of the men of '48. In one of the corners of the cellar stood a large table, called the criminals' table. This signified that only the venerable heads of democracy were permitted to take a seat there, men who had been sentenced to the penitentiary or to prison, or who had been removed from their positions. Sometimes both things had gone together. There sat Rossmaessler, Dolge, who had been sentenced to death for taking part in the May revolt, then pardoned to penitentiary for life, and then had spent eight years in Waldheim. Among the "criminals" were also Dr. Albrecht, who taught stenography in our club; Dr. Burckhardt, Dr. Peters, Frederick Celkers, Dr. Fritz Hofmann, called Gartenlaube-Hofmann, etc. We young men considered it as a special honor to be permitted to drink a glass of beer at this table in the company of the old men.

The leaders of the Club "Vorwaerts" did not confine themselves to the mere club meetings, but carried the agitation into the meetings of the laborers and of the people in general. They called such public meetings from time to time and discussed labor and political questions in them. These discussions were very confused. Among the subjects discussed were the insurance of invalids, the opening of a world's exposition in Germany, the question of joining the National Club, and demanding that this club should levy its dues of three marks per year also in monthly instalments, in order that the working people might be able to join. Furthermore, a demand was discussed for universal suffrage in state elections, and for a German parliament that should take care of the laborers. The calling of a general congress of German workingmen was also discussed, for the purpose of debating the rising demands. This question of calling a general congress of German laborers appeared simultaneously also in the labor circles of Berlin and Nuremberg.

Translated by E. Untermann

Friedrich Engels

Socialism in Germany

1

German socialism goes back well before 1848. Initially, it consisted of two independent currents. On the one hand, there was a true labor movement, an offshoot of French workers' communism and among its further stages of development, it gave rise to Weitling's utopian communism. On the other hand, there was a theoretical movement, emerging from the decay of Hegelian philosophy that was to be dominated by the name of Marx from the very start. The "Communist Manifesto" of January 1848 marks the fusing of these two currents. In fact, it turned into a fusing process, completed and hardened in the furnace of the revolution, in which all of them—workers as well as ex-philosophers—proved themselves worthy to a man.

After the defeat of the European revolution in 1848, socialism in Germany had to limit itself to a secret existence. It was only in 1862 that Lassalle—a student of Marx's—raised the socialist flag again. But this was no longer the intrepid socialism of the Manifesto; what Lassalle was demanding in the interest of the working class was the setting up of cooperatives by means of state credits. In fact, it was a new version of the program of the Paris workers' group that before 1848 had followed Marrast's real republican nationalist group, a program set up by authentic republicans in opposition to Louis Blanc's "Organization of Labor." As can be seen, Lassallian socialism was very modest. Even so, it represented the starting point for the second stage of the development of German socialism. Through this talent, enthusiasm, and boundless energy, Lassalle created a workers' movement that became the point of convergence for all the positive and negative, friendly and hostile activities by means of which the German proletariat kept its independence alive for ten years.

In fact, would Lassallianism as it originally came into being be able to satisfy the socialist demands of the nation that had been aroused by the Manifesto? This was impossible, and therefore, mainly due to the efforts of Liebknecht and Bebel, a workers' party soon arose to proclaim openly the principles of the 1848 Manifesto. Then in 1867 three years after Lassalle's death, *Das Kapital* by Marx was published, and from then on the specific Lassallianism began its decline. The tenets of *Das Kapital* became more and more the shared possession of the German socialists, to the Lassallians just as much as to the others. More than once and with great enthusiasm, entire groups of Lassallians went over to the new "Eisenach" party. The latter grew in strength continuously so that it soon came to open hostilities between them and the Lassalians; the fights—even with clubs—were getting worse just at a time when there was no longer any real cause for friction between the contenders and when the principles, points at issue, and even methods of combat were essentially much the same.

This was the very moment when delegates of both persuasions sat next to each other in the "Reichstag," and when the need for joint action became all the more pressing. As seen by the law and order parties, the attacks of the socialists against each other were simply ridiculous. The situation was really becoming intolerable. Finally in 1875, they merged. And since then, the formerly antagonistic brothers have persisted in becoming a single tightly knit family. And had there been the slightest possibility of renewed division, this was prevented thanks to Bismarck, who declared German socialism illegal in 1878 by his infamous emergency law. The impartial pressure of persecution once and for all forged the Eisenach faction and the Lassallians into one homogeneous block. Today, on the one hand the social democratic party is publishing the official edition of Lassalle's works while on the other hand, and with the assistance of the old Lassallians, it is erasing the last traces of the original Lassallianism from its program.

Do I really need to give a detailed account of the vicissitudes, fights, defeats, and triumphs that our party has experienced in its lifetime? When universal suffrage opened the doors to the Reichtstag, the party was represented by two delegates and one hundred thousand voters; today it has thirty-five delegates and half a million voters, more voters than can be claimed by any other party in the elections of the nineties. Eleven years of exclusion and siege by the Empire have quadrupled its strength and have turned it into the most powerful party in Germany. In 1867 the law and order party delegates could still regard their socialist colleagues as strange beings, fallen down from another planet; today, whether they like it or not, they must see them as representatives of the power to which the future belongs. The social democratic party that brought Bismarck down, which, after a struggle of eleven years, overturned the law against the socialists; the party, which like the rising tide sweeps across all obstacles, which floods town and country down to the reactionary farming districts, this party has today reached the point where it can determine with almost mathematical exactitude the time when it will come to power.

The number of socialist votes was:

1871	101,927	1884	549,990
1874	351,670	1887	763,128
1877	493,447	1890	1,427,298.

In fact, ever since the last elections, the government has been doing everything possible to drive the masses towards socialism; it has tracked down trade associations and forbidden strikes; and despite the current rise in the cost of living, it has maintained the duties that raise the price of bread and meat for the poor to the benefit of the big landowners. Therefore, in the election of 1895 we can expect to receive at least 2.5 million votes; by 1900, these should go up to between 3.5 and 4 million. A pleasant "end of the century" for our bourgeoisie!

Facing this compact and ever-swelling block of social democrats, we find only the fractured bourgeois parties. In 1890, the Conservatives (two factions combined) had 1,377,417 votes; the National-Liberals 1,177,807 votes; the free Thinking Germans won 1,159,915 votes; the Center Party 1,342,113 votes. What this really means is that a strong party, with over 2.5 million votes at its disposal, might topple any government.

In no way does the major strength of German social democracy lie in its number of voters. In our country, we only become voters at the age of twenty-five but we enlist as soldiers at the age of twenty. Since the younger generation provides our greatest followership, it is easy to conclude that the German Army will be more and more contaminated by socialism. Today, one soldier in five is ours and in a few years, we will have one in three; by about 1900, the army—formerly the most Prussian element in the country—will have a socialist majority. All of this is coming inexorably closer like an act of fate. The government in Berlin sees it coming just as we do—but it is powerless. The army is slipping away from it.

How often has the bourgeoisie expected us to stop using revolutionary means under all circumstances and to remain within the law now that the emergency law has fallen and common law has been reestablished for everybody—even for the socialists? Unfortunately, we are not in a position to do these gentlemen that favor. But for the moment it is not we who are "breaking the law." On the contrary, it is working so well in our favor that we would be fools to go against it as long as things stay like this. The question is rather whether it is the bourgeoisie and its government who are breaking the law in order to crush us? We will wait and see. In the meantime, "Gentlemen of the bourgeoisie, it is up to you to fire the first shot."

No doubt about it, they will shoot first. One beautiful morning the German bourgeoisie and its government will find that they have grown tired of looking on with folded arms as the spring tide of socialism washes over everything; they will have to turn to lawlessness and violence. But what good will it do them? Force can at best suppress a small group in a corner of the country, but that power has yet to be invented that is able to wipe out a party with more than two or three million members, spread over an entire empire. Counterrevolutionary superiority may perhaps delay the triumph of socialism by a few years, but only in such a way that it will then be all the more complete and final.

2

The above predictions could only be considered valid if Germany is permitted to pursue its economic and political development in peace. A war would change all that. And a war can start at any moment.

Everybody knows what is meant by "war" nowadays. It means: France and Russia on the one side, against Germany, Austria, perhaps Italy on the other side. The socialists in all these countries, called up against their will, would have to fight each other; what would the German Social Democratic Party do in such a case, what would become of it?

The German empire is a monarchy with a semifeudalistic structure, but actually guided by the economic interests of the bourgeoisie. Thanks to Bismarck, this monarchy has made monstrous mistakes. Its domestic policy—police ridden, narrow-minded, oppressive, and unworthy of a major nation—has earned it the contempt of all bourgeois liberal countries, and its foreign policy the distrust, even the hate, of its neighbors. Through the forcible annexation of Alsace-Lorraine, the German government has made reconciliation with France impossible for years to come and, without achieving any real advantage for itself, has turned Russia into the arbiter of Europe. This is so obvious that on the very day after Sedan the General Council of the International was able to predict the present situation in Europe. In its address of September 9, 1870, it said, "Do the Teutonic patriots really believe they would be able to secure peace and freedom by forcing France into the arms of Russia?" If Germany, carried away by its feat of arms and by the thrill of victory, robs France of territory through dynastic intrigue, then one of two things will happen: either it will become the notorious tool of Russian expansionist policy, or it will have to fight another "defensive war"—not a war like the newfangled "localized" wars, but a race war, a war against the united front of Slavs and Romanics.

No doubt about it: against a Germany such as this even the present French Republic represents the revolution—albeit a bourgeois revolution, but still a revolution. But the situation will change as soon as the republic falls under the authority of the Russian czars. Russian czarism is the enemy of all Western nations—even of their bourgeoisie. If the czarist hordes were to come to Germany, they would not bring freedom but servitude, not development but devastation, not progress but brutalization. Arm in arm with the czar, France could no longer pass ideas of freedom to the Germans; were a French general then to speak of a German republic, he would become the laughingstock of Europe and America. France would be betraying its revolutionary role in history and would permit the Bismarckian Empire to pose as the representative of Western progress in contrast to oriental barbarism.

But now socialist Germany stands behind the official Germany; it is to this party that the future—the near future—of the country belongs. Once in office, this party will not be able to exercise or maintain its power unless it undoes the injustices committed against other nations by its predecessors. It will work for the restoration of Poland, which has now been so disdainfully betrayed by the French bourgeoisie; it will make it possible for North Schleswig and Alace-Lorraine to decide their political future. All these questions will therefore be resolved easily and in the near future provided that Germany is left alone. A socialist Germany and a socialist France would never permit the problem of Alsace-Lorraine to come between them; the problem would be solved on the spot. It is just a question of waiting another ten years or so. The entire proletariat of France, England, and Germany is still waiting for its liberation. Couldn't the patriots in Alsace-Lorraine also wait a little while? Should an entire continent be devastated because of their impatience, and then be delivered over to the czarist knout? Is the game worth such high stakes?

Should it come to a war, first Germany then also France would become the main battlefield; before all others, these two countries would have to carry the cost of war and devastation. And right from the start, this war will be characterized by a series of betrayals between allies of such nature as to make those of the arch-traitor—i.e., diplomacy—pale in comparison, and again the main victims of these betrayals will be France or Germany—or both of them. Having these kinds of perspectives in mind, neither of the two countries will provoke direct confrontation. Russia on the other hand, protected against a disastrous series of defeats by its geographic and economic position, and particularly official Russia, is the only one that can attain its aims in such a war and can be striving in this direction. In any case, whatever may be the political situation today, one can bet ten to one that when the first shot is fired on the Vistula, the French armies will march to the Rhine.

And then Germany will be fighting simply for her existence. If she wins, she will not find any territory for annexation; to the West and to the East, she will only find provinces speaking foreign languages, and of those she already has more than enough. If she is defeated, crushed between the French hammer and the Russian anvil, she will lose East Prussia and the Polish provinces to Russia, all of Schleswig to Denmark, and the left bank of the Rhine to France. Even if France turns down this acquisition, Russia would force it on her. Above all, Russia needs a bone of contention, a means for continual strife between France and Germany. Reconciliation between these two great countries would mean the end of Russian hegemony in Europe. Broken up into pieces this way, Germany however would be incapable of fulfilling the role incumbent upon her in the historical development of Europe. Pushed down again into the condition forced upon her by Napoleon at Tilsit, she would only be able to survive by preparing for a new war so as to reestablish her national way of life. In the meantime, she would be the docile tool of the czar, who would not hesitate to use her against France.

Under these conditions, what would happen to the Social Democratic Party? This much is certain: neither the czar, nor the French bourgeois republicans, nor the German government itself would pass by such a good opportunity to repress the one party, which is the "enemy" for all three of them. We saw how Thiers and Bismarck joined hands over the ruins of the Paris Commune; we then would live to see how the czar, Constans and Caprivi—or their respective successors—would fall into each other's arms over the dead body of German socialism. But now after the unceasing struggles and sacrifices of thirty years, the German Social Democratic Party has attained a position like no other socialist party in the world—a position that will assure it the devolution of political power within a short time. Socialist Germany assumes the first, most honored and most responsible position in the international workers' movement; she has the duty to defend this position to the last man against any and all attackers.

But what if a Russian victory against Germany were to mean the repression of German socialism, where would the duty of German socialists then lie? Should they let go by passively the events that threaten to destroy them; should they give up positions—without fighting back—for which they have accepted responsibility before the proletariat of the whole world?

Not at all. In the interest of the European revolution, they are obliged to defend all conquered positions and not to capitulate before the internal or external enemy. And they can only do this by fighting Russia and all her allies, whoever they may be, to the utmost. Should the French Republic put herself at the service of His Majesty the Czar and Autocratic Ruler of all the Russians, the German socialists would have to fight them with regrets—but fight them they would. In the eyes of the German monarchy, the French Republic can possibly represent the bourgeois revolution. But in contrast to the Republic of Constans, Rouvier, and even Clemenceau, and particularly compared to the Republic in the service of the Russian czar, German socialism most definitely represents the proletarian revolution.

A war, in which Russians and Frenchmen were to invade Germany, would mean for her a life and death struggle, in which she could only preserve her national existence through revolutionary measures. Unless it is forced to do so, the present government will certainly not unleash the revolution. But we have a strong party—the Social Democratic Party—which can force it to act or, if necessary, could replace it.

And we have not forgotten the magnificent example, that France gave us in 1793. The centenary of 1793 is approaching. Were the czar's desire for conquest and the chauvinistic impatience of the French bourgeoisie to put a halt to the victorious but peaceful advance of the German socialists, then—you may depend on it— they are ready to prove to the world that the German proletariat of today is not unworthy of the French sansculottes of a hundred years ago and that 1893 will be as important a year as 1793. And then, when the soldiers of Mr. Constans set foot on German soil, they will be greeted with the words of the Marseillaise:

> Quoi, ces cohortes étrangères
> Feraient la loie dans nos foyers!

> (What! Shall these foreign bands of soldiers
> Lay down the law for us at home!)

In short, times of peace will ensure the victory of the Social Democratic Party within approximately ten years. War will either bring the party victory in two or three years, or complete and utter ruin for at least some fifteen to twenty years. In view of all this, German socialists would have to be simply crazy to wish for a war in which they have everything at stake instead of waiting for the triumph of peace. And that is not all. No socialist, whatever his nationality may be, could wish the military victory either of the present German government or the French bourgeois republic and least of all the czar, which would be synonymous with putting Europe under the yoke. Therefore despite all of this, socialists everywhere are for peace. If there will be a war, then only one thing is certain: this war, in which an armed force of fifteen to twenty million will be slaughtering each other and in which the whole of

Europe will be devastated as never before—this war must either bring about the immediate victory of socialism, or it must topple the old order of things in such a way and leave so much wreckage behind that the old capitalist society would become less possible than ever and that the social revolution—after a delay of ten or fifteen years—would find an ever more speedy and straight path to victory.

[The above text was originally published in the "French Workers' Almanac" and later republished in the German socialist journal *Die Neue Zeit* together with the text that follows.—*eds.*]

This is where the article for the French workers' almanac ends. It was written during the late summer when the French bourgeoisie was still intoxicated by the champagne of Kronstadt and when the memory of the great maneuvers on the battlefields between the Seine and the Marne had brought patriotic fervor to a high pitch. At that time, France—the France that finds its expression in the big press and in the Chamber majority—was in fact ready to commit immeasurable follies in the interest of Russia, and the possibility of war was moving ever closer. And if indeed this were to be, and in order to avoid any last minute misunderstanding between the French and German socialists, I thought it necessary to make clear to the former what position I felt convinced the latter would necessarily take in regard to such a war.

But then a sudden check was put to Russian warmongering. The bad harvest at home with the resulting expectation of starvation was the first misfortune to become known. Then came the failure of the Paris loan, which meant the final breakdown of Russian state credit. It was said that the four hundred million marks had been over-subscribed many times. When, however, the Paris bankers wanted to pass on the bonds the public, all their efforts were in vain. The subscribers were forced to let go of their good securities in order to be able to pay up on these bad ones, and to such an extent that this massive sale brought about a downturn in the other major stock markets of Europe; the new "Russians" sank several percentage points below their issue price—in short, there was such a crisis that the Russian government had to recall 160 million bonds, and only received payment for 240 million instead of 400 million of them. Hence, the renewed attempt by Russia—well-publicized throughout the world—to get another loan this time for a full eight hundred million marks fell through. And thus it was shown that French capital knows no "patriotism" but does have, notwithstanding the tales it has the press tell, a holy terror of war.

Since then the bad harvest has really led to famine on a scale not known in Western Europe for a long time and as does not even often occur in India, the land typical for such calamities. Even the holy Russia of earlier times, when there were no railroads, seldom suffered starvation to such an extent. How did this happen? How can it be explained?

Very simply. The Russian famine is not only the result of a single bad harvest; it is part and parcel of the social revolution that Russia has been going through since the Crimean War; what the bad harvest really did was to make the chronic suffering connected with this revolution more acute.

The old Russia went irrevocably to the grave when Czar Nicholas—despairing of himself and Holy Russia—poisoned himself. The Russia of the bourgeoisie is now being built on its ruins.

The beginnings of a bourgeoisie already existed at that time. It was partly composed of bankers and partly of importers—mainly Germans and German Russians or their descendants—partly Russians who had worked their way up in domestic trade, specifically distillers and army suppliers grown rich at the expense of the state and the people, and it already included a few manufacturers. Hereupon, the growth of the bourgeoisie, specifically its industrial segment, was practically encouraged through massive state aid, subsidies, awards, and gradually also through ever-increasing protective duties. The vast Russian Empire was to become a self-sufficient unit of production, which could completely or almost completely do without foreign imports. The wish to promote not only the development of the domestic market but also to provide the interior of the country with products grown in warmer climates, led to a continuous striving for conquest on the Balkan Peninsula and in Asia, with Constantinople here and British India over there as the final goal. This is the secret, the economic basis for the expansionist drive so rampant among the Russian bourgeoisie, which when moving southwestwards is known as Pan-Slavism.

The system of serfdom came to be absolutely irreconcilable with these industrial plans. It fell in 1861. But how! The gradual emancipation of the serfs in Prussia from 1810 to 1851 was taken as the model; but it was all to be completed within a few years. In order to break the resistance of the land and "soul" owners all the more quickly, they were given many more concessions than those given to the landed gentry by the Prussian state and its corrupt officials. And as to bribery, the Prussian bureaucrat seems an innocent child when compared to the Russian *tschinovnik*. In the resulting land reform, the nobility ended up with the lion's share—namely, the land made fertile by the labor of generations of peasants—whereas the peasants received a bare minimum of what was often barren land. The land-owners obtained the common land and woods; unable to survive without them, the peasant had to pay the gentry for using them.

In order to ruin both landed nobility and peasants as quickly as possible, the nobility received the capitalized repayment in the form of state bonds from the government in one lump sum, whereas the peasant was to pay them off in installments stretching over years. As was to be expected, the nobility squandered most of this money immediately; in contrast the peasant was suddenly cast out of a barter economy and into a money economy as a result of having to make excessive payments.

The Russian peasant, who previously had made hardly any payments in money except for minimal taxes, from hereupon was not only expected to live on his impoverished and shrunken plot after the enclosure of the common land with its free firewood and pastures, but also to bring his domestic animals through the winter, improve his land, pay the rising taxes, and now make his yearly installment payment in cash. He was thus placed in a position in which he could neither live nor die. Another problem was the competition of newly developed industry, which deprived him of a market for the cottage industry that was the mainstay for innumerable Russian peasants; or if this was not yet to occur, then his cottage industry became dependent on the good will of the merchant, i.e., the intermediary, the Saxon distributor or English sweater manufacturers, thereby turning him into a direct slave of capitalism. In short, whoever is interested in learning how badly the Russian peasant has been treated during the last thirty years, only needs to refer to the first volume of Marx's *Capital* on the "Impact of the Agricultural Revolution on Industry" (chapter 24, section 5).

The devastation caused among the peasants by the transition from a barter economy to a money economy as the main means of creating a domestic market for industrial capital are shown in the classical analysis made by Boisguilbert and Vauban of the France of Louis XIV. But what happened at that time is peanuts compared to what is happening in Russia. First of all, everything is on a scale three to four times greater and, secondly, the change of the conditions of production, in the service of which this transition is being forced on the peasants, is far more decisive. Whereas the French peasant was slowly drawn into manufacturing, the Russian peasant is being sucked into the whirlwind of industry overnight. If manufacturing knocked peasants down with a light flintlock musket, then big industry is now doing so with a magazine rifle.

Such was the situation when the bad harvest of 1891 at one stroke exposed the whole process of upheaval, which had been going on silently for years, but which had remained invisible to European Philistines. The situation was simply such that the first bad harvest had to bring about a national crisis. It turned into a crisis of such proportions that it will take years to recover. Any government would become powerless in the face of such a famine, particularly the Russian government that trains its officials in thievery. Since 1861, the old communist ways and customs of the Russian peasants have in part undermined by economic development and in part systematically destroyed by the government. The old communist community has crumbled or is in the process of crumbling; yet at the very moment when the individual peasant is being put on his own feet, the floor is pulled away from underneath him. Is it surprising that only a few districts had managed to plant the seed for the winter in the previous autumn and, if so, that it was ruined by the weather? Is it surprising that the peasant's main asset, his domestic animals, first had to go without food and were then inevitably eaten up by the peasants themselves? Is it surprising that the peasants then had to abandon house and farm and to flee to the cities, vainly to search for work but all the more surely to bring typhus along with them?

In brief, this was no ordinary famine but a momentous crisis resulting from years of silent economic revolution, and merely made acute by the bad harvest. For its part, this acute crisis is again becoming chronic and threatens to go on for years. Economically, it is accelerating the dissolution of the old communist peasant community, the enrichment and conversion of the village usurer (kulak) into landowner, and altogether the passing of land ownership from the nobility and peasants into the hands of the new bourgeoisie.

For now, this means peace for Europe. The Russian agitation for war has been slowed down for a number of years. Instead of millions of soldiers dying on the battlefield, millions of Russian peasants are dying of starvation. We will have to wait and see what all of this will mean for the future of Russian despotism.

Translated by Irene Schmied

Wilhelm Liebknecht

On May Day

The resolution to establish a May Day celebration was made on the first international congress in Paris, in 1889. It simply made the point of saying that in all countries where there are organized workers, May 1 should be celebrated simultaneously as a day of international solidarity by demonstrating for the eight-hour day and for other demands made by the working class, in ways most compatible with the manners and customs of the individual countries. Requesting a day of rest has never been an issue. The idea of a day off was introduced at a later point! I presided over the Paris congress myself, and if there had been the slightest hint of an intention to propose a general work stoppage I would have protested and the majority of the German workers would have supported me as much as the representatives of other countries, who have organized masses of workers themselves. The reason why in Germany a dispute flared up over this question lies in the fact that reference has been made to a "holiday" and to a "celebration" of May 1, and, due to the double meaning of the German words "celebration" [*Feier*] and "celebrate" [*feiern*] a misunderstanding arose, leading many to believe that the resolution passed in Paris was not referring to just merely a celebration in the sense of commemorating the day, but in terms of celebrating work, that is a day of rest. This misunderstanding already sprang up in Germany immediately after the Paris congress, but since the upcoming elections at the end of 1889 and the beginning of 1890 preoccupied us completely, we only noticed this misunderstanding—I can certainly say that for myself—only after resolutions in favor of a day off had been passed in many places, which were binding on the party comrades.

At that time no doubts were raised anywhere against the date of May 1. With the elections over, one of the first actions to be undertaken by the newly elected Reich's parliamentary group was to make an appeal from Halle, pointing out that stopping work was not in compliance with the Paris resolution and enforcing a day off could not even be seriously considered, due to the unfavorable economic situation. Such a step taken generally at a convenient time for the adversaries would merely be used by the opponents to incite an enormous class battle, in which our defeat would be next to certain, thus transforming our tremendous electoral victory into a triumph of the bourgeoisie. In our appeal we, therefore, advised against a rest day in those places, where it might provoke serious conflicts with the entrepreneurs, without, however, abandoning the idea of a rest day entirely. In this regard the appeal stated:

"German social democracy does not have a need to organize a military review after the great demonstration and the victory of February 20.* What is important and what was intended by the Paris congress is a general, awe-inspiring workers' demonstration in favor of the eight-hour day and national and international workers' protection legislation. The German labor force as a whole should celebrate May 1, if possible, and this would be achieved entirely by holding workers' meetings, workers' festivals, and similar rallies, where mass resolutions will be passed in the spirit of the Paris congress."

Wherever it is possible to get a day of rest on May 1 without conflicts, it should come about.

Even then we took this position, which is still shared by the majority of the comrades today, which then found its expression during the following international congresses as well as in the resolution suggested to you.

An additional question was then thrown in, namely, whether a celebration should take place on May 1 in the first place, or on the first Sunday in May. In England, where the workers have a powerful organization in the form of trade unions, they immediately recognized—with the instinct bestowed by power—that a rest day on May 1 was not feasible right now under the prevailing economic situation and that, due to the circumstances at the moment, not a workday, but a Sunday was appropriate for real mass demonstrations, which

*February 20, 1890, was a big success for the SPD in the elections, winning 1.5 million votes, and thirty-five members in parliament.

is the day when the English proletariat has been holding its impressive mass meetings for generations with hundreds of thousands of people. They chose the first Sunday in May. The German parliamentary group dealt with the question and, with the exception of one, consented to the English view and in early 1891 suggested to the Brussels congress that the May Day celebration be generally rescheduled to the first Sunday in May. There must have been serious reasons leading the parliamentary group to vote almost unanimously for this resolution. I do not criticize it; I have to mention it, however, because in Brussels and also elsewhere it gave rise to an accusation of the Germans for a certain halfheartedness concerning the international May Day celebration. I do not want to attack any group here. Luckily, things turned out in such a way that the thought of holding the celebration on the first Sunday in May has now, after the decisions of two international congresses, also been given up in Germany. Among the suggestions submitted to us here, only one still returns to a celebration on the first Sunday in May. And this was the only remaining issue under dispute between the various nations; now it was ruled out. Then, however, the French, Austrians, and Americans accused the Germans of wanting to evade a conflict with the entrepreneurs by our suggestion, saying we were political pussyfooters, opportunists, etc. Doing so, they did not consider, however, that the nation with the strongest trade unions, the English, shared the same view and actually already celebrated the first Sunday in May. Be that as it may, at the second international congress in Brussels the German suggestion was confirmed and voting by call during our party convention in Berlin last year proved that the overall majority of the German comrades is in favor of a celebration on May 1.

Now, concerning the May 1 celebration it was regretted that nobody had already pointed out in Paris which difficulties might arise for many comrades by choosing May 1, instead of the first Sunday in May. I believe that we still would have preferred May 1, namely for the same reason, valid in the entire civilized world, why those who made the suggestion to the congress did so: because for thousands of years May 1 has been a holiday not only in all Germanic, but also in all Romanic countries—a celebration of the spring of the newly born earth. Hence May 1 is the most appropriate conceivable choice for a universal workers' celebration, sanctified by the traditions of thousands of years. These traditions are more alive with our neighbors in the South and in the North, even today, than in North and East Germany. And we would not have a concerted celebration if we had insisted on choosing the first Sunday in May in Germany and England. But concerted it must be, if the celebration is not to defeat its purpose. For one day the entirety of the proletariat is conscious of its perfect solidarity, sharing the same thoughts, the same demands; there lies something edifying and strengthening in this; the proletariat raises its eyes across the borders of the individual nations, across the entire world. A division would weaken, even eliminate this great idea. Therefore, nothing has been attempted since the Brussels resolution by the Germans anymore in advocacy of the first Sunday. In Zurich it was no longer taken into consideration. Now we are entirely in accordance with the resolution accepted in Brussels and reissued in Zurich. The Brussels resolution reads:

> In order to keep the special economic character of May 1, that is, the demand for the eight-hour day with the demonstration of class struggle, the congress resolves:
> May 1 is a mutual holiday of the workers of all countries, in the course of which the workers are to express the common ground of their demands and their solidarity. This holiday shall be a rest day, as far as this is not rendered impossible by the conditions in the individual countries.

The Zurich resolution went somewhat beyond that, according to the German version, the following was added:

> The congress resolves: each country's social democracy has the duty to strive for a rest day on May 1 and to support all attempts made in this direction in individual places or by individual organizations.

We Germans unanimously declared that we are unable to vote in favor of the addendum in this form, because we would thereby bind ourselves to support every attempt made in the direction of a rest day in solidarity and with all of the party's power: every bold attempt made by a more enthusiastic than wise comrade would then involve the party in a general fight, and this responsibility we could not take. To say it with one word: the resolution was unacceptable to us, it would actually have proclaimed the general strike for May 1, and this was not compatible with our principles and our duties, considering the actual situation. Already the very first May Day celebration gave us the opportunity to test the issue of a rest day. The Hamburg chapter had actually committed itself before May 1, due to the misleading interpretation of the word *celebration* that I just discussed. When it became clear that the employers wanted to lure them into a trap, the prudent comrades found it impossible to stop the embittered masses. The organized workers in Hamburg went on strike—and they are the best-organized ones in all of Germany; the entire party backed it. Did we have a chance to win? No! With the economic situation it was simply impossible. We were defeated and how many sacrifices were made in vain! And now just think, we had initiated the fight all over Germany! One may commit a foolish act once—this can happen to everybody—but it may not be repeated, this is unforgivable! The leadership—to use the term for once— would act unscrupulously, as generals act unscrupulously, driving their troops into their enemies' bayonets. German social democracy was ridiculed by its opponents for its thoughtful attitude, but knowing our strength, we can easily bear this derision. In Zurich we soon found out that we Germans were not alone in our views. The English, who had decided for the first time to accept May 1 as the day of celebration in the interest of international solidarity, stated to the commission that supporting any attempt to enforce a rest day did not serve the organized proletariat's interest, and this view was taken into account in the English version of the resolution.

As a matter of fact, there were two versions of the resolution. I, who was not in the commission in question, found out about it only very late, and none of us knew about it, otherwise it would have been prevented. Incidentally, one can see from this how enormous the difficulties of linguistic communication are at an international congress, which we can overcome only by a staff of reliable interpreters, and how justified our demand in the *Vorwärts* [Forward] referring to this was. These differences could not at all have arisen with better linguistic communication. The German version you know. Now listen to the English one:

"It is the duty of every country's social democracy to strive for the celebration of May 1 as a day of rest from work and to support the endeavors of the local organizations in this direction."

In the German text "attempt" [*Versuch*], in the English one "endeavor" [*Bemühung*]. Now there is—and I certainly won't have to elaborate on that—an immense difference between "endeavor"

[*Bemühung*] and "attempt" [*Versuch*]. An endeavor is not concrete action identical with agitation; an attempt, however, is a concrete fact—as much as a decision made somewhere it is some kind of proceeding. In short, the German party would be forced to jump after each individual who jumps into water and rescue him. We were willing to accept the resolution according to the English version. Then we were reminded, however, that the German translation was the literal translation of the authoritative French original text, and this is correct. The latter says "tentative," i.e., attempt—while another version had been chosen for the English, namely, "endeavor," which satisfied the English, who would not have accepted otherwise and would also have satisfied us, as I mentioned already.

The resolution we suggest to you for the party convention is in exact compliance with the Zurich resolution. It completely ignores the question of May 1 or the first Sunday in May. We consider this question over and done with—we do not even state that in those places, where a celebration of May 1 does not seem feasible, it should be made up for on the following Sunday. Such a regulation would leave a back door open and leave an imprint of feeble compromising on it. Furthermore—and this is how the resolution is different from the resolution made last year—we based our decision on all the resolutions of the earlier international congresses and we extended the purpose of the celebration. We do not merely talk in terms of the eight-hour day and the workers' protection, but in general of the demands of the workers as a class, and in addition we expressed the idea of international fraternization and universal peace, in accordance with the resolution of the congress in Zurich. Consequently, we do not just say platonically that we consider a rest day as the most dignified form of celebration on principle, but we went further and interpreted the resolution according to its substance. We strive for a day of rest and incorporated the meanings of the English expressions "endeavor" and "to strive for" into our resolution.

And now some words concerning the addendum of the proposed resolution. We cannot recommend a general day of rest, even less propagate it. While already two and a half years ago we had to advise the workers against attempting to enforce a rest day and to start fighting against the entrepreneurs because of the serious economic situation, today this is twice as necessary and our duty to do so. Since then the economic situation has deteriorated even more and that is true in all countries, without exception. This is an international and persistent crisis, the industrial reserve labor force has increased enormously as a result of unemployment, so that any gap generated by the organized labor force staying away could immediately be filled in abundance. How hopeless a general strike, a general test of strength would be right now, will become clear to every thinking person, recounting the fact that during the past two years all major strikes in Europe were instigated and provoked by employers, realizing the fact that circumstances were favorable to them and unfavorable for the workers and expecting for sure to weaken or to destroy the workers' organizations. And, indeed, in the interest of their own class, the entrepreneurs could do nothing smarter than enticing the workers into a struggle that wastes their energies. In short, at present the employers hold the reins in the class struggle and they are in total control of the situation. And they know it. They have the instinct of power, springing from the possession of power, and not so much the function, but power gives comprehension—the insight into what is useful—and this insight is more sharply developed and much greater with the ruling classes than with the working classes, which have just begun striving upwards. Who in Germany agitated for a strike on May 1 more than anybody else? Did not our industrialists' papers ridicule the workers after the Paris congress, calling them wretched cowards not daring to come out? And since then this has been repeated before every May 1. This proves that the action they have been wanting to provoke us into was in the interest of our enemies. There one may well clench one's teeth—but surely, when we're reproached with cowardice by the world's most cowardly bourgeoisie, it only makes us laugh. One cannot always prevent young troops, who are provoked in such a way, from plunging themselves into battle and storming off in the direction where the enemy wants them to be; experienced veteran troops, like ours, do not step into such a trap. If we are to accept or offer to do battle, it will be only at the moment when we may not have the victory safely in our pocket, as the cynical saying goes, but when we know that it is not our enemies who have it in their pocket. This is the view we have been taking then and are still taking today.

Under the prevailing circumstances the question of a rest day on May 1 actually coincides with the question of a general strike. Our opponents would turn the fight, flaring up over one issue, immediately into a general one; however, a general strike in one country or a worldwide strike, even, is nonsense, this the Paris congress and also the one in Zurich unanimously stated. There it was said: once we have the power to bring the entire machinery to a standstill, we will also have the power to smash the present society to pieces, or rather, to change it into a socialist society: and once we can do that, we will not bring the machinery to a "standstill," but, to the contrary, we will even work much harder, but not in the interest of some few, but the interest of the entirety. The idea of a general strike has to be rejected because it is nonsense. "All machinery comes to a standstill, if only your strong arm wants it to be" is the slogan of those who do not have an overall view. Well, but there are millions of German workers. If a general strike were called today, we would drive exactly the best, the most competent, the organized ones into a hopeless fight. Does the proletariat have one arm after all? It has millions of arms in Germany, ten million double arms. One arm does it and so do hundreds of thousands of others, but what about the other millions? Does it mean they are led by one will, by one insight? No, they are not! The majority still stand outside of the organization; the entire class-conscious labor force would suffer a devastating defeat in such an insane fight and be thrown back for decades.

Translated by Renate Steinchen

Ferdinand Lassalle

What Is Capital?

When the way to India round the Cape of Good Hope was discovered by the Portuguese, the rich family of the Fuggers, of Augsburg, sent an expedition thither on which they made a profit of 175 percent. The profits of the world commerce were enormous, and to them must be added the gains of the usurers, who, in the Middle Ages, carried on their business through mortgages and advances on agricultural products.

Thus what was in embryo in ancient times developed in the Middle Ages and became full-grown capital. The tendencies of the time, the rise of the Middle Class, were all in the direction of invention and discovery, of division of labor, of economy in production, increase of sale, that is, in the direction of developing and perfecting those instruments and aids of production which were powerless in the olden times.

Thus, gradually, capital threw off the fetters that had hitherto confined it, and at the end of the last century all limitations and regulations of the period of rights and services had disappeared, free competition was assured, and capital appeared in its gigantic strength. "Liberty," as the middle class understood it, was established; each and everyone was free to become a millionaire—if he could!

A single glance at the distinctive features of this period will show that they are all summed up in "free competition." The bourgeois producer, in industrial as well as in agricultural production, knows nothing of particular rights. All the distinctions and conditions which arose out of the recognition of "rights" have disappeared: in their place we find the one essential condition: that of having capital in hand to make the necessary advances without which there is no production. All the old limitations having been removed the principle of division of labor comes to the front and production is divided up into a never ending series of partial operations and of production for the world commerce. All is now exchange value; everyone produces that which he does not want and cannot use; and, as opposed to the services and the production of value in use of the Middle Ages, we have now the products of industry exchanging with each other in the money form.

This is as much the case with agricultural as with industrial production; for the latter form stamps the character of the age. Anyone who now, for example, produces corn does so not for his own consumption but for the world market; and he can no longer discharge his liabilities with the product of his work, whether he uses large capital and incurs great expenses, or is only a small producer with liabilities that press even more severely upon him; he depends upon the prices quoted in the great markets of London, Paris, Berlin, and Amsterdam; so that even in the supply of food he produces only exchange value and the production of use value sinks into a shadow.

The law of Ricardo that the prices of products are regulated by the cost of production is now in full force. In the Middle Ages prices were fixed by the producer, who could always insist upon a regular profit. But under the influence of capital all this is altered. Each one underbids the other to obtain fresh custom or to retain that which he already has. For the consumer this is a benefit in the shape of cheapness. But this lowering of prices is only obtained by an increase of sale; the small profit obtained on each article is only compensated by the sale of a larger number of articles. The natural result is that production is carried on upon a larger scale, with greater concentration of work, larger supply of raw material, and an augmented output. In other words: under free competition the greater the capitalist the more he overpowers and swallows up smaller capitalists.

Here we have the productive power of capital; the pound of today produces another pound. Here also we find the origin of our complicated system of credit; the capital which is in excess of the requirements of a business, whether temporarily or permanently, is employed by way of loan, partnerships, shares, etc., in other forms of production.

Up to the present we have regarded the producer simply as a producer. Let us now look at him in his two capacities: employer or contractor, and worker; and distinguish the particular features which free competition imposes. The fate of both is determined by the price of the product in its sale, and by the proportion of it which free competition gives to each. The value of the product is at first to be found in the market price; that is, it depends at each and every moment upon the relation between the supply of the article and the demand for it. But this in its turn is subject to the fundamental law that, in the long run, the price of a product is the same as its cost of production. Say, for example, that the supply of an article is so great that the price falls below the cost of production, then the production of that article will either cease or be moderated; on the other hand, if the price of an article be so high as to yield more than the usual profit, then by virtue of free competition capital will be attracted to that particular industry, and the supply will be increased until the price is brought down to the cost of production.

The market price of a product oscillates like a pendulum, but with great irregularities, and its many changes very often have unpleasant and ruinous consequences for the individual capitalist; for he may be forced to sell his wares when prices are low and may not be able to place his wares on the market when prices are high. But this only concerns the individual; the capitalist class, as a class, is not affected by it; for it is at such times that the smaller capitalists are crushed, and the supremacy of large capitals over small capitals is established.

As regards capital these oscillations in prices compensate one another on the average, and not a single hour of labor, not one drop of the sweat of the worker is lost to capital; they are all paid back to capital by the consumer. If this be the position of the capitalist as regards the consumer, what is it that determines the proportion of the proceeds of the product which shall come to the worker? What is it that determines and settles the wages of the worker?

Under the present system of production the average wages are limited by an iron law to the necessary means of subsistence, to the minimum of food, etc. This has been disputed by certain political economists. In opposition they assert that the price of labor is regulated by the demand for it as compared with the supply of it. The people who assert this look upon labor as they do upon any other kind of merchandise, and they do this quite rightly, for it is with labor as with merchandise or wares, its price is determined by demand and supply. But what is it that regulates, that determines the market price between demand and supply? As we have already seen, this is determined by the cost of production. There is only one measure for everything that comes on the market, whether it be Chinese porcelain, American cotton, assafœtida, Circassian slave girls, or European workers; that measure is to be found in the demand for and the supply of the article, and the average relation of demand and supply is ultimately determined by the cost of production.

How much, then, does it cost to produce a worker? Evidently only just so much as is required to enable another worker to obtain the absolutely necessary means of subsistence for himself and his family. Give him this and he will provide the youngster fast enough, though not solely, perhaps, for the capitalist's sake, and will not even require to be tempted by a profit as do the producers of other wares. In short, wages under free competition, or the cost or production of labor, consist solely of the cost of producing workers.

Where it is customary to employ children in the factories then a fresh calculation is made. It is very soon found that the father does not require the means of subsistence, say, for a family of average number, but can do with less, as the children themselves contribute towards their own support.

It requires no explanation to show that of all producers the seller of labor is most unfavorably situated under the system of competition. Where would the sellers of other wares be if they could not keep their produce back when the demand was slack? The seller of labor cannot do this. He *must* sell. Hunger compels him. Further, when the price of labor rises, it only makes the lot of the workers ultimately worse, for it brings about an increase in the number of the workers. Neither need we explain how it is that no charitable employer can alter this. Whoever attempts to do so is struck down by the dagger of competition.

Under free competition the relation of an employer to the employed is the same as to any other merchandise. The worker is work, and work is the cost of its production. This is the leading feature of the present age. In former times the relations were those of man to man: after all, the relations of the slaveowner to the slave, and of the feudal lord to the serf were human. The relations in former times were human, for they were those of rulers to the ruled; they were relations between one man and another man. Even the ill-treatment of the slaves and serfs proves this; for anger and love are human passions; and those ill-treated in anger were still treated as men. The cold, impersonal relation of the employer to the employed, as to a thing which is produced like any other ware on the market, is the specific and thoroughly inhuman feature of the Middle Class Age.

The middle class hate the idea of a state; they would replace the state by a middle class society permeated with free competition; for in a state workers are still treated as man, whilst under the middle class regime the workers are like any other merchandise, and are only taken into consideration according to the cost of production.

Ancient civilization is shown by what Plutarch wrote of Marcus Crassus and his slaves. "He (Crassus) used to attend to their education and often gave them lessons himself; esteeming it the principal part of the business of a master to inspect and take care of his servants, whom he considered as the living instruments of the economy. In this he was certainly right if he thought, as he frequently said, that other matters should be managed by servants, but the servants by the master." Contrast this with the words of a liberal professor: "Swiss manufacturers boast that they can manufacture at less cost than the Germans because the Swiss have no compulsory education."

We have seen that wages, on the average, are reduced to the necessary means of subsistence. But if this be the reward of labor what becomes of the excess of the prices paid for the articles produced over the cost of subsistence of the workers whilst the articles are being made? This excess is divided between the employer and other capitalists, pure and simple, such as the holders of land, bankers, etc.

We said that there is not a single drop of the sweat of the workers that is not paid back to capital in the price of product, and that every pound in the hands of the employers produces another pound. With this increase the power of capital increases, so that every effort of the workers enables the capitalist to compel the workers to further toil. And when it is possible to reduce the prices of the products and thus cheapen the means of subsistence, then the increase of the workers does not increase with the increased produce of labor, but the power of capital does.

Take all those who have worked together in the production of some article—those who have worked with their brains as well as those who have worked with their hands; add together what they have received for their work and they will not be able to recover the product of their labor! And when machinery is employed, thus causing a greater production with the same amount of labor, then it becomes more and more impossible for the workers to buy back with their wages the product of their work, and they become poorer and poorer.

But the capitalists say that the profit of capital is really the recompense of the brain work of the capitalist, the reward for his management. In reality, however, only a very small portion of the income of the capitalist can come under this head; and the English economists have always treated the profits of the employers as the premium of capital, and have left unnoticed the reward for brain work on account of its smallness. If you want to know how small it is, look at the salaries paid to stewards of estates, to managers of factories, etc., etc., who do the brain work, while the principals travel for pleasure or attend to other matters! Only the amount so paid for management can be regarded as the recompense for such work when the employer or capitalist does this work himself. This feature is still more strongly marked in the case of railways, joint stock banks, and industrial companies. Here, those who possess the capital are many and they live on their dividends, whilst the "brain work" of the business is being done by salaried officials. Of course, some of these salaries are absurdly high; but taken them all together and compare the total with the amount paid away in dividends and then you will have some idea of the smallness of the amount paid for brain work and management.

Say that the total amount of the produce of labor during one year is £100,000, and that the cost of the subsistence of the workers—in other words, their wages—is £20,000. Now whether the employers are sharp or stupid, idle or industrious, the remaining £80,000 will fall to the share of the employers, as a class, and how much each individual employer will receive will depend upon his personal qualities.

Economics can only deal with the question of how much of the produce of labor the employers as a class can obtain for themselves, how much the workers as a class can obtain for themselves, and what quantity of the products of labor the individual worker can obtain. The question as to how one individual employer can get more for himself than other individual employers is really a part of practical business and in no way comes under economics. All this shows that capital is not ever-present, that it is not a law of nature, but is the effect of certain historical conditions; and that its productivity in altered surroundings must and will disappear.

Let us contrast the commencement of this historical analysis with the end. In the primitive state of individual, isolated labor with which we commenced, the instrument or tool—the bow and arrow of the Indian—was in the hands of the worker, and thus work alone was productive. Under the system of division of labor, work and production became social, although the distribution of the result of the work remained individualistic; and through division of labor, the system of exchange values and free competition, this result is rapidly brought about, viz.: the separation of the instruments or tools from the worker becomes complete, the productivity of labor is appropriated by the holders of the tools, and the reward of the worker is reduced to that which will keep him alive whilst he works.

Translated by F. Keddell

Emil Lederer

The Problem of the Modern Salaried Employee

Society is composed of organizations representing group interests, namely, voluntary and compulsory associations, which aim to bring together and orient their individual members by virtue of common interests, regardless of their political and cultural beliefs, their intellectualized attitudes towards life, nationality, etc. Transformation presupposes a broadening of the bases of these organizations as time proceeds. As an interest group comes into being either as an addition to, or in opposition to, political parties, it is effective only—and this is a correlative condition—when it has reached maximum size and matches the voters of the political parties in membership. Such an evolution, however, implies that the association conforms to class viewpoints to which group interests are subordinate. In fact, it is characteristic of the latest developments that class consciousness has been growing and that economic class interests, overcoming many conflicts between the group interests, govern the minds of men and contend for achievement. This has been facilitated and effected on a larger scale by the sharper separation of society into classes. Of course, definite class lines can be drawn only when an individual remains attached to one class and, as a rule, cannot shift from one class to another.

The materialistic interpretations of history, as explained by Marx, sets out its theory of future economic development in the following way: Above all, the class distinction between employer and employee or employer and worker dominates the situation at the present time. This social class conflict will be intensified to the point of unbearable social disharmony and will finally act with increasing severity as a handicap to the productive forces; thus the road to acute conflicts will be open. The simple antithesis, employer-worker, becomes a social equivalent of the partly broader, partly narrower formulation, capitalist-proletarian, in the correct economic terminology. This antithesis, as expressed by both formulas, refers to the root principle of sharp contrast inherent in the methods of production. The tendency to concentration of industrial enterprises (according to some, agricultural enterprises are also involved), due to techno-economic conditions, accentuates the class struggle—a conception of Marx—and allows contrasts to take on such gigantic proportions that they overshadow the entire economic development. The social aspects of inequality, also inseparable from the formula "capitalist-proletarian" are glossed over. The materialistic interpretation of history treats the strength of class interests of the various strata of society alike and, similarly, it oversimplifies the stratification of the classes itself. The formula "capitalist-proletarian" blurs all contrasts within the economic order and thus obscures all distinctions outside of and within the process of production. Socialists have constructed the term "composite reactionary mass" in which they include landowners, industrialists, merchants, all independent businessmen, and groups that identify themselves with these, e.g., officers, civil service employees, etc. This "mass" they contrast with the "proletarian mass." On the one hand, socialists lump all the propertied together; on the other, they put into a single class all those who have no, or relatively small, means of production, irrespective of their position outside of the industrial system. Although this division overlooks the continuous absolute and relative growth of the gainfully employed who are neither employers nor workers and consequently cannot definitely be classified as capitalists or proletarians, it could perhaps be defended on the ground that the fundamental contrast within the economic system attracts all strata outside the processes of industrial capitalism and assigns them to either the capitalist or the proletarian class. A more important incongruity, however, may be detected when one penetrates to the core of the problem in production itself.

Socialist doctrine stresses concentration of enterprises, brought about by modern technical methods, and the ever-growing mass of workers opposed to an ever-dwindling number of employers. It reduces development of the industrial economy to quantities and attempts to prove that the latent forces of the socially and economically oppressed classes will irresistibly break their bonds and create techno-economic methods of production appropriate to the control by the working class. But the concentration of undertakings, apart from the decrease in employers and the increase in workers, produces other phenomena as well. Above all, there emerges a class of technicians who, from a social point of view, cannot categorically be classified as either employers or workers. The importance of this class is heightened by the creation of socially analogous strata in commerce and public service, which make up an ever-increasing portion of the population. It is characteristic of the general acceptance of the classification "employer-worker" by social thinkers that (according to the class concept of the observer) this stratum of specific origin, composition, income as well as economic and social functions, is labeled either a new middle class—in order to increase the number of independents at least socially—or simply proletariat (white-collar proletarians), in order to signify an acceleration in the evolution of the economy.

The following investigation has set as its task the analysis of the economic and social functions of the dependent gainfully employed, the description of their efforts at organization—a symptom of their group consciousness—and the discussion of the laws pertinent to this stratum of society as well as the social policies pursued. In this manner we may be able to supplement the incomplete information relative to the social correlates of economic evolution.

At the outset it may be noted that all these groups, which are better classified under the generic heading "salaried employees" *(Angestellte)* than that of "private officials" *(Privatbeamte)*, are vertically and horizontally infinitely differentiated. The absence of a uniform law for all "employees" in itself proves the different economic origins of these groups; in fact, the character of their technical functions forbids treating them alike.

Vertically, salaried employees are still more differentiated than wage earners. Although the economic, social and cultural distances between the unskilled, irregularly employed hour laborer at the bottom of the proletarian pyramid and the skilled, highly qualified, organized, steadily employed worker are enormous, they cannot be compared with the gulf separating a clerk in a country store from an officer in a banking institution. Still, in the eyes of the law, the two latter types bear the same classification, "commercial help" *(Handlungsgehilfen)*. The technical functions of the chief groups also vary greatly. The functions of commercial employees are determined by the very nature of business. Wholesale and retail trading concerns are preeminently establishments of salaried employees because their functions carry and characterize the undertaking (in contradistinction to handicraft and factory). The position and activity of the laborer in wholesale and retail businesses are merely accessory. Consequently, the date of origin of the commercial employee antedates that of the laborer. Indeed, the modern commercial employee resembles the commercial employee of the past more than the labor employed by large-scale industry resembles the journeyman of the Middle Ages. Methods of doing business have hardly changed in the majority of cases. Even large-scale enterprises are only expanded small-scale businesses. Since no new technique has come to the fore, they exhibit no essentially new methods.

On the other hand, the technical employees are the product of industrial concentration. Neither trade nor industry knew the modern technician and specialist. Certainly, any sizable undertaking requires an organizing staff. In the simplest form of undertakings the foreman is the manager. The modern giant enterprises, however, have created an entire superstructure of technicians, an apparatus without which they would be unable to operate. The modern giant enterprise is neither an aggregation of small variegated units (as, for instance, the department store) nor an expanded retail establishment (such as a large specialty store may be judged to be) but something totally different, resting on a totally different basis. The functions of the technical employees are twofold: either they are analogous to those of the workingman, only on a higher level (such as draftsmen and engineers) who prepare the production process, or they are managers, foremen, etc., plus the commercial employees of industry, who organize the production process.*

The above-mentioned social and technical differentiations also defy a precise definition of the term "salaried employee." One can make only the general statement that the term embraces all those workers in private business who are not employed as wage earners, i.e., exclusively as manual laborers. The concept cannot be expressed concisely and definitely by a positive criterion because the

---

*These technical functions of the various groups of salaried employees will have to be discussed later. Here we make only a few introductory remarks in order to point out the variety of these groups and to show how the setup within the factory, in other words, the purely technical aspects of the industrial system, tends to form classes among principal employees also.

strata involved perform a great variety of functions in the undertaking; and yet, "employees" can be characterized as "salaried" in opposition to manual workers only on account of their technical functions. Furthermore, the social position of these strata has to be taken into consideration. In order best to understand the essential characteristics of the salaried employee who is here contrasted with the manual laborer, we proceed from the two main groups, the commercial and technical salaried employees. We designate an employee as a "salaried employee," apart from the fact that he performs directed functions, if his work is exclusively manual, similar to that of the laborer, but concurrently assumes a special character on account of his intellectual contribution, or if his work is neither intellectual nor exclusively manual (i.e., only concerned with production).

These two criteria form the boundaries between the activities of the salaried employee and the manual laborer. The purely intellectual activities of the principal employees are within these boundaries; the exclusively manual activities of the laborer are beyond. Concretely expressed, the performance of the technical employee is predominately manual and, concomitantly, intellectual (e.g., the activities of a draftsman, a construction or chemical engineer); moreover, it is as a rule preparatory. The function of the commercial employee is frequently not intellectual (e.g., those of the store salesman or, even more, those of the stockroom clerk); yet it is not merely manual like the work of the laborer engaged in production; within the stated boundaries are the absolutely intellectual functions, such as those of the accountant or factory manager, as we have said above.

The distinction between commercial and industrial (technical) employees, as just defined, is based upon the character of the enterprise. Commercial establishments are concerns that employ salaried workers exclusively and, consequently many very simple and nonintellectual duties are performed in these businesses by salaried employees. Industrial establishments add to manual labor a technical superstructure with technical employees who therefore perform in part just such manual work as the laborer does but who, nevertheless, distinguish themselves from him by the character of their work, namely their trained and intellectual performance. The grouping of the two principal categories, technical and commercial employees, under the heading "salaried employees," is traceable to the analogous social positions that at least the great majority of each group occupies. In neither of these groups is social esteem, which determines their peculiar position, based upon the nature of their technical or economic work; on the contrary, their social valuation is chiefly decided by their relationship to the important classes—the employers and laborers. This middle position between the two classes—a negative characteristic—rather than definite technical functions, is the social mark of the salaried employees and establishes their social character in their own consciousness and in the estimation of the community. Hence, apart from their technical function, the social position of the salaried employees is of great significance.*

Furthermore, the rating of the white-collar workers by the sharply demarcated classes of the employers and manual laborers is important for the improvement of their position.†

We may summarize the foregoing statements as follows: A uniform technical function does not definitely characterize all salaried employees, rather, the two chief groups of the white-collar workers are to be treated separately. Their social position, the cementing factor of these main groups, has not as yet been clarified and therefore is not easy to determine uniformly. The manifold aspects of their social position impede the application of a satisfactory unifying principle of social estimation. Social appraisal of this stratum is still in flux and its final valuation depends upon both the development of improved techniques and the relations of the salaried employees to the already established social classes.

*It must be understood that one may speak of the "same social position" only with many reservations: The lower strata of the salaried employees merge with the proletariat and the highest stratum of the salaried employees overlaps with the class of employers and managers, immediately above them. Still, uniformity may be established in a higher degree than at first seems possible by taking the relation of each group of employees to the employers and manual workers, between whom the employee group stands, as a criterion. Thus the foreman in a medium-sized enterprise stands between the employer and his help, i.e., in a position similar to that of a factory manager who stands between the large-scale employer and the industrial working class.

†In my opinion this social function has been insufficiently stressed. The attempt to define the salaried employees as a technical group must therefore fail because they form not a technical but—with some reservations—a social unit. The Austrian law, regulating the salaried employees' retirement system, has also attempted to define the persons to be insured from the viewpoint of their technical function and, consequently, the definition is absolutely unsatisfactory: "Salaried employees are employees with the character of officials, as well as, in general, employees who render intellectual services exclusively or at least predominantly."

The above-mentioned classes of employers and manual laborers have up to now tended to absorb considerable portions of the salaried employees, but this tendency does not preclude the possibility that these employees will more and more become an independent group, not only on account of their increase in number, but also in consequence of a growing consciousness of their special interests. Consequently, the theory, first propounded by Marx, of a decreasing number of capitalists controlling ever-increasing capitalist concentration as opposed to an ever-growing homogeneous proletarian mass, receiving, at least relatively, a diminishing share in the products of industry, does not conform altogether to reality. This view no longer holds true because industrial enterprises, the basis of economic development according to socialist theory, are not built as conceived by Marx and because employees are distributed among socially different strata whose relations to the employers are not necessarily analogous. The consequences to be drawn from these facts, in the formation of an opinion on the evolution of the industrial system and, incidentally, on the march of history, can be discussed only after the shift in the stratification of society has been thoroughly examined.* So far we have merely hinted at this shift.

Translated by E. E. Warburg

---

*The aforementioned social homogeneity of the salaried employees, so far as it exists, is strengthened by the custom of placing the private employees together with the civil service employees who are recognized by law as a special group. Both groups perform technical functions; in fact, the services of the major part of the civil service employees do not differ fundamentally from those of the private employees. There are enterprises, such as the Post Office Department and Railways, in which not intellectual activity, but a nonmanual and not directly productive occupation characterizes the employee. On the other hand, there are governmental departments in which the civil service employees have technical functions. The formerly stressed state functions par excellence of administration of justice and government, recede into the background when considered from the standpoint of the number of civil servants employed who put their stamp on the entire class. The social homogeneity of the predominant number of civil service employees and their equality in the eyes of the law of necessity influence the stratum employed by private business. The more the concentration of enterprises tends to set up a consummate hierarchy, the less the activities of private employees are distinguishable from those of the civil service employees.

Karl Marx

Social Classes in America

Marx to Joseph Weydemeyer

London, March 5, 1852

. . . How far bourgeois society in the United States still is from being mature enough to make the class struggle obvious and comprehensible is most strikingly proved by C. H. Carey (of Philadelphia), the only American economist of importance. He attacks Ricardo, the most classic representative (interpreter) of the bourgeoisie and the most stoical adversary of the proletariat, as a man whose works are an arsenal for anarchists, socialists, and all the enemies of the bourgeois order of society. He reproaches not only him, but Malthus, Mill, Say, Torrens, Wakefield, MacCulloch, Senior, Whately, R. Jones, and others, the masterminds among the economists of Europe, with rending society asunder and preparing civil war because they show that the economic bases of the different classes are bound to give rise to a necessary and ever growing antagonism among them. He tried to refute them, not indeed like the fatuous Heinzen by connecting the existence of classes with the existence of *political* privileges and *monopolies,* but by attempting to make out that *economic* conditions—rent (landed property), profit (capital), and wages (wage labor), instead of being conditions of struggle and antagonism, are rather conditions of association and harmony. All he proves, of course, is that he is taking the "undeveloped" conditions of the United States for "normal conditions."

And now as to myself, no credit is due to me for discovering the existence of classes in modern society or the struggle between them. Long before me bourgeois historians had described the historical development of this class struggle and bourgeois economists the economic anatomy of the classes. What I did that was new was to prove: (1) that the *existence of classes* is only bound up with *particular historical phases in the development of production*, (2) that the class struggle necessarily leads to the *dictatorship of the proletariat*, (3) that this dictatorship itself constitutes only the transition to the *abolition of all classes* and to a *classless society*. Ignorant louts like Heinzen, who deny not merely the class struggle but even the existence of classes, only prove that, despite all their bloodcurdling yelps and the humanitarian airs they give themselves, they regard the social conditions under which the bourgeoisie rules as the final product, the *non plus ultra* of history, and that they are only the servitors of the bourgeoisie. And the less these louts realize the greatness and transient necessity of the bourgeois regime itself, the more disgusting is their servitude. . . .

Translation by the Foreign Languages
Publishing House Moscow

Friedrich Engels

The Labor Movement in the United States

Ten months have elapsed since, at the translator's wish, I wrote the Appendix to this book; and during these ten months a revolution has been accomplished in American society such as in any other country would have taken at least ten years. In February 1885, American public opinion was almost unanimous on this one point: that there was no working class, in the European sense of the word, in America; that consequently no class struggle between workmen and capitalists, such as tore European society to pieces, was possible in the American republic; and that, therefore, socialism was a thing of foreign importation, which could never take root on American soil. And yet, at that moment, the coming class struggle was casting its gigantic shadow before it in the strikes of the Pennsylvania coal miners, and of many other trades, and especially in the preparations, all over the country, for the great eight-hour movement, which was to come off and did come off in the May following. That I then duly appreciated these symptoms, that I anticipated a working-class movement on a national scale, my Appendix shows; but no one could then foresee that in such a short time the movement would burst out with such irresistible force, would spread with the rapidity of a prairie fire, would shake American society to its very foundations.

The fact is there, stubborn and indisputable. To what an extent it had struck with terror the American ruling classes was revealed to me, in an amusing way, by American journalists who did me the honor of calling on me last summer; the "new departure" had put them into a state of helpless fright and perplexity. But at that time the movement was only just on the start; there was but a series of confused and apparently disconnected upheavals of that class which, by the suppression of Negro slavery and the rapid development of manufactures, had become the lowest stratum of American society. Before the year closed, these bewildering social convulsions began to take a definite direction. The spontaneous, instinctive movements of these vast masses of working people, over a vast extent of country, the simultaneous outburst of their common discontent with a miserable social condition, the same everywhere and due to the same causes, made them conscious of the fact that they formed a new and distinct class of American society: a class of—practically speaking—more or less hereditary wage workers, proletarians. And with true American instinct this consciousness led them at once to take the next step towards their deliverance: the formation of a political workingmen's party, with a platform of its own, and with the conquest of the Capitol and the White House for its goal. In May the struggle for the eight-hour working day, the troubles in Chicago, Milwaukee, etc., the attempts of the ruling class to crush the nascent uprising of labor by brute force and brutal class justice; in November the new Labor party organized in all great centers, and the New York, Chicago, and Milwaukee elections. May and November have hitherto reminded the American bourgeoisie only of the payment of coupons of U.S. bonds; henceforth May and November will remind them, too, of the dates on which the American working class presented *their* coupons for payment.

In European countries it took the working class years and years before they fully realized the fact that they formed a distinct and, under the existing social conditions, a permanent class of modern society; and it took years again until this class consciousness led them to form themselves into a distinct political party, independent of, and opposed to, all the old political parties formed by the various sections of the ruling classes. On the more favored soil of America, where no medieval ruins bar the way, where history begins with the elements of the modern bourgeois society as evolved in the seventeenth century, the working class passed through these two stages of its development within ten months.

Still, all this is but a beginning. That the laboring masses should feel their community of grievances and of interests, their solidarity as a class in opposition to all other classes; that in order to give expression and effect to this feeling they should set in motion the political machinery provided for that purpose in every free country—

that is the first step only. The next step is to find the common remedy for these common grievances, and to embody it in the platform of the new Labor party. And this—the most important and the most difficult step in the movement—has yet to be taken in America.

A new party must have a distinct positive platform, a platform which may vary in details as circumstances vary and as the party itself develops, but still one upon which the party, for the time being, is agreed. So long as such a platform has not been worked out, or exists but in a rudimentary form, so long the new party, too, will have but a rudimentary existence; it may exist locally, but not yet nationally; it will be a party potentially, but not actually.

That platform, whatever may be its first initial shape, must develop in a direction which may be determined beforehand. The causes that brought into existence the abyss between the working class and the capitalist class are the same in America as in Europe; the means of filling up that abyss are equally the same everywhere. Consequently the platform of the American proletariat will, in the long run, coincide as to the ultimate end to be attained with the one which, after sixty years of dissensions and discussions, has become the adopted platform of the great mass of the European militant proletariat. It will proclaim as the ultimate end the conquest of political supremacy by the working class, in order to effect the direct appropriation of all means of production—land, railways, mines, machinery, etc.—by society at large, to be worked in common by all for the account and benefit of all.

But if the new American party, like all political parties everywhere, by the very fact of its formation aspires to the conquest of political power, it is as yet far from agreed upon what to do with that power when once attained. In New York and the other great cities of the East the organization of the working class has proceeded upon the lines of trade societies, forming in each city a powerful central labor union. In New York the central labor union, last November, chose for its standard-bearer Henry George, and consequently its temporary electoral platform has been largely inbued with his principles. In the great cities of the Northwest the electoral battle was fought upon a rather indefinite labor platform, and the influence of Henry George's theories was scarcely, if at all, visible. And while in these great centers of population and of industry the new class movement came to a political head, we find all over the country two widespread labor organizations: the Knights of Labor and the Socialist Labor party, of which only the latter has a platform in harmony with the modern European standpoint, as summarized above.

Of the three more or less definite forms under which the American labor movement thus presents itself, the first, the Henry George movement in New York, is for the moment of a chiefly local significance. No doubt New York is by far the most important city of the States, but New York is not Paris and the United States are not France. And it seems to me that the Henry George platform, in its present shape, is too narrow to form the basis for anything but a local movement, or at least for a short-lived phase of the general movement. To Henry George the expropriation of the mass of the people from the land is the great and universal cause of the splitting up of the people into rich and poor. Now this is not quite correct historically. In Asiatic and classical antiquity the predominant form of class oppression was slavery, that is to say, not so much the expropriation of the masses from the land as the appropriation of their persons. When, in the decline of the Roman Republic, the free Italian peasants were expropriated from their farms they formed a class of "poor whites" similar to that of the Southern slave states before 1861; and between slaves and poor whites, two classes equally unfit for self-emancipation, the old world went to pieces.

In the Middle Ages it was not the expropriation of the people *from*, but, on the contrary, their appropriation to the land which became the source of feudal oppression. The peasant retained his land, but was attached to it as a serf or villein, and made liable to tribute to the lord in labor and in produce. It was only at the dawn of modern times, towards the end of the fifteenth century, that the expropriation of the peasantry on a large scale laid the foundation for the modern class of wage workers who possess nothing but their labor power and can live only by the selling of that labor power to others. But if the expropriation from the land brought this class into existence, it was the development of capitalist production, of modern industry and agriculture on a large scale which perpetuated it, increased it, and shaped it into a distinct class with distinct interests and a distinct historical mission. All this has been fully expounded by Marx (*Capital*, Part VIII: "The So-called Primitive Accumulation"). According to Marx, the cause of the present antagonism of the classes and of the social degradation of the working class is their expropriation from *all* means of production, in which the land is of course included.

If Henry George declares land monopolization to be the sole cause of poverty and misery he naturally finds the remedy in the resumption of the land by society at large. Now the socialists of the school of Marx, too, demand the resumption, by society, of the land, and not only of the land but of all other means of production likewise. But even if we leave these out of the question, there is another difference. What is to be done with the land? Modern socialists, as represented by Marx, demand that it should be held and worked in common and for common account, and the same with all other means of social production, mines, railways, factories, etc.; Henry George would confine himself to letting it out to individuals as at present, merely regulating its distribution and applying the rents for public instead of, as at present, for private purposes. What the socialists demand implies a total revolution of the whole system of social production; what Henry George demands leaves the present mode of social production untouched, and has, in fact, been anticipated by the extreme section of Ricardian bourgeois economists, who, too, demanded the confiscation of the rent of land by the state.

It would of course be unfair to suppose that Henry George has said his last word once for all. But I am bound to take his theory as I find it.

The second great section of the American movement is formed by the Knights of Labor. And that seems to be the section most typical of the present state of the movement, as it is undoubtedly by far the strongest. An immense association spread over an immense extent of country in innumerable "assemblies," representing all shades of individual and local opinion within the working class; the whole of them sheltered under a platform of corresponding indistinctness and held together much less by their impracticable constitution than by the instinctive feeling that the very fact of their clubbing together for their common aspiration makes them a great power in the country; a truly American paradox, clothing the most modern tendencies in the most medieval mummeries, and hiding the most democratic and even rebellious spirit behind an apparent, but really powerless, despotism—such is the picture the Knights of Labor offer to a European observer. But if we are not arrested by mere outside whimsicalities, we cannot help seeing in this vast agglomeration an immense amount of potential energy evolving slowly but surely into actual force. The Knights of Labor are the first national organization created by the American working class as a whole; whatever be their origin and history, whatever their shortcomings and little absurdities, whatever their platform and their constitution, here they are, the work of practically the whole class of American wage workers, the only national bond that holds them together, that makes their strength felt to themselves not less than to their enemies, and that fills them with the proud hope of future victories. For it would not be exact to say that the Knights of Labor are liable to development. They are constantly in full process of development and revolution, a heaving, fermenting mass of plastic material seeking the shape and form appropriate to its inherent nature. That form will be attained as surely as historical evolution has, like natural evolution, its own immanent laws. Whether the Knights of Labor will then retain their present name or not makes no difference, but to an outsider it appears evident that here is the raw material out of which the future of the American working-class movement, and along with it, the future of American society at large, has to be shaped.

The third section consists of the Socialist Labor party. This section is a party but in name, for nowhere in America has it, up to now, been able actually to take its stand as a political party. It is, moveover, to a certain extent foreign to America, having until lately been made up almost exclusively of German immigrants, using their own language and, for the most part, little conversant with the common language of the country. But if it came from a foreign stock, it came, at the same time, armed with the experience earned during long years of class struggle in Europe, and with an insight into the general conditions of working-class emancipation far superior to that hitherto gained by American workingmen. This is a fortunate circumstance for the American proletarians, who thus are enabled to appropriate and to take advantage of the intellectual and moral fruits of the forty-year struggle of their European classmates, and thus to hasten on the time of their own victory. For, as I said before, there cannot be any doubt that the ultimate platform of the American working class must and will be essentially the same as that now adopted by the whole militant working class of Europe, the same as that of the German-American Socialist Labor party. In so far this party is called upon to play a very important part in the movement. But in order to do so they will have to doff every remnant of their foreign garb. They will have to become out and out American. They cannot expect the Americans to come to them; they, the minority and the immigrants, must go to the Americans, who are the vast majority and the natives. And to do that they must, above all things, learn English.

The process of fusing together these various elements of the vast moving mass—elements not really discordant, but indeed mutually isolated by their various starting points—will take some time, and will not come off without a deal of friction, such as is visible at different points even now. The Knights of Labor, for instance, are here and there, in the Eastern cities, locally at war with the organized trade unions. But then this same friction exists within the Knights of Labor themselves, where there is anything but peace and harmony. These are not symptoms of decay, for capitalists to crow over. They are merely signs that the innumerable hosts of workers, for the first time set in motion in a common direction, have as yet found out neither the adequate expression for their common interest nor the form of organization best adapted to the struggle, nor the discipline required to ensure victory. They are as yet the first *levées en masse* of the great revolutionary war, raised and equipped locally and independently, all converging to form one common army, but as yet without regular organization and common plan of campaign. The converging columns cross each other here and there; confusion, angry disputes, even threats of conflict arise. But the community of ultimate purpose in the end overcomes all minor troubles; ere long the struggling and squabbling battalions will be formed in a long line of battle array, presenting to the enemy a well-ordered front, ominously silent under their glittering arms, supported by bold skirmishers in front and by unshakable reserves in the rear.

To bring about this result the unification of the various independent bodies into one national labor army, with no matter how inadequate a provisional platform, provided it be a truly working-class platform—that is the next great step to be accomplished in America. To effect this, and to make that platform worthy of the cause, the Socialist Labor party can contribute a great deal, if they will only act in the same way as the European socialists acted at the time when they were but a small minority of the working class. That line of action was first laid down in the *Communist Manifesto* of 1848 in the following words:

"The communists [that was the name we took at the time and that even now we are far from repudiating] do not form a separate party opposed to other working-class parties.

"They have no interests separate and apart from those of the proletariat as a whole.

"They do not set up any sectarian principles of their own, by which to shape and mold the proletarian movement.

"The communists are distinguished from the other working-class parties by this only: (1) In the national struggles of the proletarians of the different countries they point out and bring to the front the common interests of the entire proletariat, independent of all nationality; (2) In the various stages of development which the struggle of the working class against the bourgeoisie has to pass through, they always and everywhere represent the interests of the movement as a whole.

"The communists, therefore, are on the one hand, practically, the most advanced and resolute section of the working-class parties of every country, that section which pushes forward all others; on the other hand, theoretically, they have over the great mass of the proletariat the advantage of clearly understanding the line of march, the conditions, and the ultimate general results of the proletarian movement. . . .

"The communists fight for the attainment of the immediate aims, for the enforcement of the momentary interests of the working class, but in the movement of the present they also represent and take care of the future of that movement."

That is the line of action which the great founder of modern socialism, Karl Marx, and with him I and the socialists of all nations who worked along with us have followed for more than forty years, with the result that it has led to victory everywhere, and that at this moment the mass of European socialists, in Germany and in France, in Belgium, Holland, and Switzerland, in Denmark and Sweden, as well as in Spain and Portugal, are fighting as one common army under one and the same flag.

London, January 26, 1887

Translated by Florence Kelley Wischnewetzsky

Friedrich Engels

Why There Is No Large Socialist Party in America

Engels to Friedrich A. Sorge

London, December 2, 1893

Dear Sorge:

. . . The repeal of the silver-purchase law has saved America from a severe money crisis and will promote industrial prosperity. But I don't know whether it wouldn't have been better for this crash to have actually occurred. The phrase "cheap money" seems to be bred deep in the bone of your Western farmers. . . .

The German socialists in America are an annoying business. The people you get over there from Germany are usually not the best— they stay here—and in any event, they are not at all a fair sample of the German party. And as is the case everywhere, each new arrival feels himself called upon to turn everything he finds upside down, turning it into something *new*, so that a new epoch may date from himself. Moreover, most of these greenhorns remain stuck in New York for a long time or for life, continually reinforced by new additions and relieved of the necessity of learning the language of the country or of getting to know American conditions properly. All of that certainly causes much harm, but, on the other hand, it is not to be denied that American conditions involve very great and particular difficulties for a steady development of a workers' party.

First, the Constitution, based as in England upon party government, which causes every vote for any candidate not put up by one of the two governing parties to appear to be *lost*. And the American, like the Englishman, wants to influence his state; he does not throw his vote away.

Then, and more especially, immigration, which divides the workers into two groups: the native-born and the foreigners, and the latter in turn into (1) the Irish, (2) the Germans, (3) the many small groups, each of which understands only itself: Czechs, Poles, Italians, Scandinavians, etc. And then the Negroes. To form a single party out of these requires quite unusually powerful incentives. Often there is a sudden violent *élan*, but the bourgeois need only wait passively and the dissimilar elements of the working class fall apart again.

Third, through the protective tariff system and the steadily growing domestic market the workers must have been exposed to a prosperity no trace of which has been seen here in Europe for years now (except in Russia, where, however, the bourgeois profit by it and not the workers).

A country like America, when it is really ripe for a socialist workers' party, certainly cannot be hindered from having one by the couple of German socialist doctrinaires. . . .

Your

F. Engels

Translated by Leonard E. Mins

THE
SOCIAL DEMOCRATIC
PARTY

Ferdinand Lassalle

Open Letter to the
National Labor Association of Germany

The working-class must constitute itself an independent political party, based on universal equal suffrage; a sentiment to be inscribed on its banners, and forming the central principle of its action. The representation of the working class must be a fact in the legislative bodies of the nation. Nothing less will satisfy the awakened demands of the working classes.

We must open, for this end, a peaceful, lawful agitation. Let this be the program of the party of labor, without reference to the Progressive Party. The workers must regard their organization as that of an independent party, utterly and completely separate and distinct from all political affiliation with the Progressivists; recognizing it only when their common interests bring them into copartnership at the polls.

This must be the policy of the Workingmen's Party. Whatever of leaning toward the Progressive Party will be made apparent, must be by the Progressivists coming up to their standard; giving them a chance either to develop, or to sink deeper in the mire of impotence—where it is already knee-deep. Such must be the tactics pursued by the Workingmen's Party toward the Progressive Party. So much for politics.

Now to the social question you have broached, and which interests you in a much greater degree.

I confess that it was with a grim smile I noticed that debates on free trade and free movement should form important features in the order of projected Congress. Why you should seek to discuss free movement can best be answered by quoting Schiller's famous distich:

"For years I've been using my nose to smell;
Who questions my right to my nose, pray tell?"

Free trade and free movement are matters which in a lawmaking body, are quietly decreed without debating.

The German workingmen surely have no desire to repeat the foolish spectacle of assemblages whose chief enjoyment seems to be to applaud aimless long speeches. Surely the earnest resolution of the worker will spare us the exhibition of all such pitiable weaknesses.

You want to found savings banks, invalid and sick-help societies; institutions whose relative but subordinate importance I readily recognize. Let us, however, try to distinguish between two questions which have nothing to do with each other.

Is it merely your aim to ameliorate the condition of the worker guarding him against the results of recklessness, sickness, age, and accidents; the unguarded affects of which press individuals below the ordinary condition of their class? If so, the establishment of such institutions will be fully equal to meet your aims. A movement of such magnitude as the universal agitation of the workingmen of the nation, however, would be far from finding its reward in accomplishing so little when so much could be done. It would but suggest the old saying: "The mountain labored, and brought forth a mouse."

So limited and subordinate an aim might be quietly left to local associations, they being quite equal to the attainments of such desiderati.

The aim of this movement has a wider scope than establishing beneficiary institutions for the afflicted individual. It is rather to raise the status of the class in the nation, redeeming it from the degradation of its present level.

Is not that the ultimate sought in this great movement? If so, then is the sharp line of distinction called for which I have drawn between the merely beneficiery idea and the larger scope of national interferences with the present order of society. The two features must not be confused. The institution of the first is powerless to the attainment of the second; making it imperative that the former shall be regarded as altogether outside of and apart from effort to accomplish the latter.

Allow me here to give you the testimony of a fellow workman, Professor Huber, a man whose strictly conservative and royalistic tendencies would be likely to preclude from his writings any confessions in favor of the working-class proper; but whose candor and impartial judgment make him incapable of giving an unwarrantable complexion to truth. I delight to give the evidence of this man—and in the course of this letter will do it again and again—and for the reason that, standing as he does on a different elevation from mine, what ever of suspicion might attach of my regarding what he would say as of smaller importance, through prejudice on my part, might be avoided. His views, politically as well as economically, are different from mine; but he possesses in an eminent degree the frankness to truthfully discuss, on national and economic grounds, the questions forced by the Liberal School; pointing to what, in his judgment, might mislead and disappoint the workingman.

In his *Concordia*, Professor Huber says: "Without, then, overlooking the relative benefit as far as it really goes, of savings, help and sick societies, I insist that these good things can bring with them great negative hindrances, standing as they may, in the way of something better."

And surely these negative hindrances alluded to never could take place to a greater degree as obstacles in the way of something better than with the forces of the workingmen's movement concentrated upon, or even shared with these projects.

But you should—say the newspapers—and this your own letter to me mentions as strongly recommended by many—take into consideration the organizations of Schulze Delitzsch—his Land and Credit Associations, his Raw Material and Consumers Associations—in order to better the condition of the working class.

Let us examine this a little more closely: Schulze Delitzsch can be regarded in three relations:

In his politics he belongs to the Progressive Party already alluded to.

Secondly, he has claims as a national economist; standing as such upon the ground occupied by the Liberal School; sharing alike their errors, their mistakes, and their blindness. The lectures he has given before the workingmen afford too convincing proofs of that charge; making his efforts a bundle of distorted presentations with conclusions having no connection whatever with the premises. However, it is neither your desire nor yet my aim to give a criticism of the theory of the National Economists or of the lectures of Delitzsch in particular, to prove how wide of the mark and self-blinding are the arguments used by the school of philosophers. My duty to you, however, forces me to dwell more at large on their doctrines.

The third relation alluded to, in which Delitzsch stands, is his peculiar individuality, which has the effect of forcing him beyond his theory as an economist of the National School. Of him it can be said that, of his party, he is the only one who has really benefitted the people. Although standing alone, and at a time of unusual business depression, by his untiring activity, he became the father and founder of the German Cooperative Societies; giving them a push forward which will give a wide and spreading effect to that beneficent movement; and for which, although his opponent in theory, I now, while writing, in spirit shake hands with him. Truth and Justice, even to an opponent, ought to be the first lesson as well as the first duty of all men.

That, at this day, in the German movement the question is already discussed, whether the associations are to be taken up in his sense or mine, which is to a great part his true merit—a merit, we must admit we cannot too highly estimate. In the face of the warmth with which I recognize this merit, however, I shall insist on regarding with critical sharpness the question: Are the Schultze Delitzsch associations—the Credit, Loan, Raw Material, and Consumers Associations able, effectively, to better the condition of the working class? To which I reply, and with emphasis, No! And here I briefly state my reasons for my decided negative.

In regard to the Loan and Raw Material Associations, they assist him only who has a small business for himself. For the journeymen or workers in the factory, men having no business strictly of their own, those institutions are as if they did not really exist. This feature you must never lose sight of, that from the beginning, the aim of the being of these societies was to be serviceable only to small industries; not for the elevation of the whole. They will help employers with a capital, but are not intended to reach the workingmen. In this connection you must impress yourselves with two pressing points:

First, it is in the nature of the industrial movement to give the factory, with its immense productive power, an extraordinary advantage over the small industries; so much so as to dwarf all efforts of the smaller producer. Wholesale and mass-production are daily more and more taking the place of production on a small scale.

England and France, nations ahead of us in economic development, show this in a much greater degree than with us. Germany, however, is making mighty progress on the same road. Your daily experience will be sufficient to corroborate this.

There follows, then, from these Delitzsch Loan and Raw Material Associations, allowing they did help the small tradesmen, that owing to the necessarily expanding tendencies of our industries, which are constantly developing into rich firms and corporate institutions, the small tradesmen's influence would all the while be lessening; the large firms and corporations are gradually absorbing the lesser tradesmen, the recipients of the Associations' benefits, are gradually becoming sunk in the ranks of the purely working-class: an absorption the inevitable result of our peculiar modern culture.

The other point alluded to is still more important:

Notwithstanding the fact that a few tradesmen so assisted, are enabled to carry on a small business in living competition with the larger concerns, the confession of Professor Huber is adverse to the Credit and Raw Material Associations as a successful means to ends. He says, "Unfortunately, despite our favorable perceptions that competition between dwarf-production and corporative industry was possible, we have to say that it is not satisfactorily so."

But the inherent defects of the system, and which, at the first, became developed in my mind, will, I am convinced, be still more conclusive.

How far, as an assistant to the small tradesman, can the Loan Association go? Only so far as enabling him to have good and cheap raw material—no further; placing him on an equality with his competing neighbor who had already capital of his own with which to purchase. At best it is but lengthening the lease which, in time, must expire; yielding to the larger capitalist, whose mass-production, with its smaller profits and other advantages, stock and rule the markets. The principle sways civilization: the inferior corporation yielding to the larger.

It may be urged that the small tradesman who carries on his trade helped by the Raw Material Association has advantages over the capitalist who uses his own money, and is therefore better able to endure the strain of his heavy competition. We must bear in mind, however, that the wholesale price feature is but one of a series of advantages of cheapness which inheres in industries conducted on a large scale.

But even between the master who carries on business with the help of the Raw Material Association and the one who conducts his work on his own capital, the advantages are very nearly balanced.

The latter has no interest to calculate upon, and can at all times place himself in connection with the best markets in the purchase of needed articles, giving him business chances the Raw Material Association cannot develop; particularly the knowledge which enables him to select minor articles.

The association spoken of can only lengthen out the unavoidable death struggle of the business life of the small tradesman, he is doomed to make way for the large concerns; the products of our increasing and changing culture. To seek to perpetuate the struggles of the smaller traders is but uselessly to obstruct the inevitable, while leaving the great body of the working class, employed in the larger works, entirely unreached by assistance.

We shall now look at the Consumers Associations.

The whole body of the working class would be embraced by the Consumer's Associations. But even these associations are powerless in any degree to better the condition of the worker.

Three reasons will be ample to prove this.

The disadvantages which lie upon the working class (as the two following subdivisions of the economic law will show,) strike him as a producer and not as a consumer. It is surely a false step to assist the working class as consumers, when it is apparent that we ought to help them as producers; for it is as producers the shoe pinches. As consumers, we stand today, in general, quite equal. As before the *gens d'armes* all citizens stand alike, so, in presence of the shopkeeper, the customer has no superior claims; all paying equally as well.

It is true that from this small paying ability on the part of the poor, certain special minor evils follow to the injury of the working class; the disadvantages forcing him to become prey to the usury of shopkeepers. Against this economic feature the Consumers Association is a great protection. But without mentioning how long this association can last and where it must stop, I contend that this assistance only makes the condition of the working class for the moment more endurable: I say that it must not be confused with the methods to better the condition of the working class, which is the aim of the workingmen's movement to accomplish.

The merciless economic rule, under which the present system

fixes the rate of wages, in obedience to the so-called law of supply and demand for labor is this: that the average wages always remain reduced to that rate which in a people as barely necessary for existence and propagation; a matter governed by the customary manner of living of each people. That is the inexorable point about which the real wages always gravitate, never keeping long above or below it. Were it to remain for any length of time above it, there would be an increase of marriages from which would flow a greatly increased number of the working element, which would invariably bring down the wages below its former rate.

The wages also cannot fall with anything like permanence below the ordinary rate of living; as from it would flow emigration, celibacy, restraint in the number of births; circumstances in the end lessening the number of laborers. An equilibrium is thus secured, keeping wages generally uniform, the wages being at all times in obedience to the vibrations. There is no gain saying the assurance that the wages of a people are regulated by their ordinary habits of living, those habits conforming to the limits of existence and propagation. This is the cruel, rigorous law that governs wages under the present system.

The truthfulness of this standard no man can question. I could call in support of my assertions names famous in national economic science even from the Liberal School; for, truth to tell, it was the Liberal Economic School which discovered and proved the law.

Gentlemen, this cruel inflexible law you must at all times have before you, impressing your souls with its terrible truth, and in all your thinking you must start with it as a perpetual presence.

And here I can give you and the whole body of the working people an infallible test by which all mistakes and errors can be avoided in your dealings with would-be leaders.

To every one who speaks of ameliorating the condition of the worker, you must put the question: Does he recognize this law?

If he does not, at once say to yourself, he either desires to mislead, or he has a pitiful degree of inexperience in national economic science. It is a fact that there is not, even in the Liberal School, one noteworthy national economist who denies this: Adams, Smith, Say, Ricardo, Mathews, Bastiat, and John Stuart Mill; all of them unanimously acknowledged it; so, too, do all men of science.

And then, when he who speaks to you about the condition of

the workingman, and returns in answer to your question that he does recognize this law, ask farther: How would he abolish this condition?

And if he gives you no answer upon this, quietly turn your back to him. He is, be assured, an empty talker who wishes to mislead you; or is himself a victim to hollow phrases. Let us for a moment look nearer at the effect and nature of the law. It is in other words substantially this: From the amount produced there is only so much taken and divided among the workingmen, as is necessary to their existence (wages), the entire surplus of the amount produced falling to the share of him who undertakes the enterprise.

It is therefore a consequence of the cruel, heartless law that you—who for that reason I have in my labor pamphlet called the class of the disinherited—are barred out from the increased productiveness brought about by the progress of civilization. For you comes a bare existence; the undertaker of the enterprise takes all that is produced.

Owing to the great increase of the productiveness of labor in modern times, many of the products falling to the minimum of cheapness, it becomes possible for you to have a certain degree of advantage from the excess of productiveness of labor—not as producers, but as consumers. It, however, does not change the quota or share of the amount produced; affecting you only in your condition as consumers. It likewise affects the condition of the undertaker as a consumer, as well as all who do not take part in the production; benefitting them indeed, to a much greater degree than it does the workingman.

But this advantage which does not occur to you as laborers, but as human beings, vanishes again in course of time through this cruel and relentless law which lowers the wages to the measure of consumption necessary to a bare existence.

Now, it can happen to you that through increased productiveness of labor and the consequent appearance of the minimum of cheapness in many products, together with a lengthened period for increased demand for labor, disproportionally cheap products are taken up and regarded as customary necessities for a bare existence of the people.

Thus it is then that laborers and wages at all times dance upon the outer circle of the conditions constituting a bare existence—sometimes a little above, sometimes a little below, but seldom if ever changing.

This outer circle may change at different periods through the conjunction of the above given circumstances. And it is by comparing different periods with each other that the condition of the working classes in the later century and generation seems to be superior to that of former centuries and generations; and the whole history on the minimum amount necessary for an existence has arisen.

Gentlemen, I was forced to make this small detour, distant though it may appear from my real object, because this trifling little benefit in course of centuries and generations is always the point upon which all who desire to throw dust into your eyes, after the manner of Bastiat, do so; which amounts to nothing but the hollowest declamation.

Remember my words. The time may arrive when the mimimum necessary to sustain the laboring classes will, as compared with the amount of former generations, appear greater.

Whether it is really so that, in the flow of the centuries, the general condition of the working class has continuously been bettering, involves a very grave and entangling discussion, embracing much patient research. An amount of investigation, indeed, altogether too great for ordinary persons to take the trouble to master: necessitating endless inquiries about the prices of calico in one year as compared with the others, and how much you now consume, with such-like commonplace detail—items which can be found in any commercial compendium.

I shall not go into this investigation, but will confine myself to what is absolutely firm and also easily proven.

We will grant that the mimimum amount thought necessary for an existence increases in the course of generations, and along with it comes a betterment of the condition of the working classes.

But you will be made to find, by a little effort on my part, that, with these commonplaces, they play the real question out of your hands, making it an entirely different one.

They mislead, they blind you.

Gentlemen, when you speak of the condition of the working class and how it is to be bettered, you mean the condition of your fellow beings of the present time compared with the standard of life's necessities enjoyed by other classes at the same time.

They answer you by assuming comparisons of your conditions with that of workingmen in former centuries. But the real question is, Do you stand better today because the minimum of necessities has risen over that of the workingmen of eighty, two hundred, or three hundred years ago? If so, how can it effect you any more than when told the settled fact that your condition today is superior to that of the Botokudes and man-eating savages?

All human enjoyment and contentment depend upon the proportion of the means of satisfaction of the customary necessities of the wants of life of the period. Or, which is the same, the surplus of the means of satisfaction and contentment over the lowest line of life's wants, customary and necessary at the time. An increased minimum of life's wants will bring with it sorrows and hardships which a former period knew nothing about.

It is no hardship to the Botokude that he can buy no soap; neither is it a hardship to the nauseating savage that he does not sport a respectable coat. What possible uneasiness was it to the workingman, before the discovery of America, that there was no tobacco to be had? Or before the era of printing, that no desirable book could be got?

All human hardships and sorrows depend, then, only upon the proportion of the means of contentment to the, at the time, present wants and customs of life. We measure our sorrows and hardships, our contentment and blessings, by the conditions of other classes at the period. It is because, at different periods of progress, added wants have sprung into existence, bringing desires formerly unknown into demand, that sorrows and hardships appeared.

Human conditions have ever been the same: dancing about upon the lowest circle of what, in every period, is customary and necessary to a bare existence—sometimes a little above, sometimes a little below it.

The standard has, at all times, remained substantially the same. The condition of man cannot be measured by the natural relations of the animals of the primal forest, nor yet the negro in Africa, nor the serf during the Middle Ages, nor even the workingman of two hundred or eighty years ago; but only through the relation of the condition of his fellow workers to the condition of the other classes of the same time.

Instead of stating views about this, and discussing how this relation may be bettered, and how that cruel law may be changed, which holds you constantly upon the outer circle of the wants in every period, they amuse themselves by distorting the question beneath your very nose. Entertaining you with problematical views of history, of culture, and the condition of the working class in former times: views all the more problematical with those products of industry falling to a minimum of cheapness, belonging, in a very marked degree, to the articles consumed by the workingman; while the food which chiefly forms this consumption, not at all governed by the same tendency to an ever increasing cheapness. Such views would only have value when the conditions of the entire working class, during the different periods, would be investigated in all directions, and from every point. Investigations of the gravest nature, and to be carried to a degree of completeness for which those who present them have not the requisite qualities, such duties to be performed only by the really learned.

Let us now return from our necessary detour, to the question, What influence can the Consumers Associations have upon the condition of the working class, after the law of Political Economy, formulate in Sub-Division 2?

The answer will be simple enough.

As long as only single circles of workingmen combine for a Consumers Association, so long the general wages will not be affected by it. And just so long will these Consumers Associations, through cheaper consumption, exert a subordinate influence, lightening the downtrodden conditions of the worker—a tendency I have already viewed and admitted.

It will be most important here to bear in mind that, so soon as the Consumers Associations more and more embrace the whole working class, it will be seen, as a necessary consequence, that wages, owing to the cheapness of the necessaries of life, the result of the Consumers Association, will fall in precise proportion.

These Consumers Associations never can help the whole working class; while to the single circles of workingmen who form them, they can only give slight help, so long as their example does not find imitators. While these Consumers Associations spread themselves, embracing larger masses, in that degree dwindles the trifling benefit which, under the most advantageous relations can accrue from them, until, embracing the large majority, it sinks to zero.

Can it be earnestly proposed that the workingmen should fix their eyes upon a means by which, as a class, they cannot be benefitted? Which, in fact, can only assist a few, while the larger class stand by. And which, as soon as the majority seek to benefit by, at once is of no help to any one?

The German working classes, allowing themselves to begin with a treadmill round, will find that any betterment of their condition will be in the very distant future.

I have now analyzed all the Schultze Delitzsch organizations, showing you that they are not now, nor ever can be, of permanent service to you.

The question now is, Cannot the principle of free, individual association be applied so as to better the condition of the working class?

To that I reply, Without doubt it can. But only through applying it in the massed and concentrated form of the factory, with its enormous advantage of productivity.

The working class must become itself a monster employer: the whole a series of gigantic enterprises. By this means and by this alone, can amelioration come, and the iron and cruel law governing wages be abolished.

Once the wages class becomes its own employer, the division between wages and profits of enterprise at once is removed: the wage disappears, and in its stead comes the certain and satisfying reward of labor honestly performed. The whole production of labor becomes the claim of the worker, unaffected by any employer.

This method of the abolition of the profits of enterprise is peaceful, legal, and withal, simple. Through free associations, the working classes organize themselves as their own employers. And by the simple act emancipate themselves from the system which gave the working class wages, at all times but a small part of the entire product: not more than is barely sufficient to support life, while the surplus falls to the share of the employing class, making them rich. Be assured that this is the only true method of release for the working class, all others being specious and illusory.

But how is the change to be affected? Throwing a glance upon the railroads, the dry docks, the cotton spinneries, the calico factories, and suchlike formidable institutions; then, dwelling for a moment on the enormous amount of capital needed, you will see in your empty pockets nothing but mockery of the suggested design. Where, you exclaim, are the millions to come from to inaugurate this projected system of the future? You stand appalled at the threshhold of your enterprise. To you nothing more can be apparent than your helplessness. If left to yourselves, you are indeed without help.

For this very reason, it is the duty and becomes the business of the state to come to your rescue, to enable you to expedite and give form and vitality to the scheme so promising of betterment to the working class of the nation. The state ought to regard it as its holiest duty to assist in making certain the possibility of your self-organization and association; for in your elevation lies the secret of the grandeur and completeness of the state.

And here do not allow yourselves to be misled by the cries of those who say that all interventions of the state must necessarily weaken social self-help. It does not follow that I hinder a man from reaching a certain elevation in climbing a steeple because I reach him a ladder or a rope to assist him. Shall it be said that the state seeks to surpress self-effort in study because it establishes schools, hires teachers, and opens libraries to facilitate instruction? Can I be excused of putting impediments in the way of a man who seeks to cultivate a farm by lending him a modern plow? And surely it cannot be said that I am anxious to defeat an enemy when I put weapons into the hands of others for the destruction of that enemy.

I admit that single individuals have educated themselves without teachers, schools, or libraries; it is true that people have been known to climb steeples without the aid of ladders or ropes. It is true the peasantry of Vendée, in the Revolutionary war, defeated their enemies without weapons. All these exceptions, however, do not weaken the rule; they but strengthen it. Neither does it affect the rule that under certain circumstances, single circles of workingmen in England, through organizations founded solely by their own exertions, have bettered their conditions in a small degree. In the face of these exceptions there remains to be accomplished the real improvement of the condition of labor embracing the entire class, and which can only be done through help advanced by the state.

Do not allow yourselves to be affected and misled by the affected contempt of those who decry socialism and communism; such cheap talk cannot permanently affect your demands, and is used only by such as desire to mislead you or who do not know what they are talking about.

Nothing can be farther apart from communism than is this demand of the workingmen to the state. It will not affect the individual freedom of the citizen in any manner whatever; each retaining in all essential particulars, his present relations to the community. His personal manner of life undergoes no change, save in the difference of his remuneration, the result of his changed conditions by his new relations to the state—advancing him capital; or, in other words, necessary credit.

Really and truly this is the mission of the state: to expedite and assure the advance of culture. For this the state exists, and for this only. It has already given abundant evidence that this is its characteristic work—its canals, its highways, its post offices, its boat lines, its telegraphs, its national banks. Without the intervention of the state such institutions could not exist; or, if existing, they would be productive of ceaseless wrangles by competition.

I give you an example that outweighs hundreds that might be presented; an example, too, dating from our own times: When railroads began to be built, it was found necessary in Germany, as well as in many other countries, for the state to intervene in one way or another, guaranteeing the payment of interest on stock; and in some countries much greater responsibilities were assumed.

It would be well here to mention that the English, who are always pointed to as a people opposed to state interferences, boast with commendable pride of the intervention of the state in abolishing slavery; an act of parliament authorizing the expenditure of twenty million pounds sterling ($100,000,000) for that purpose. To free an unlimited majority of its own nation from the cruel law that governs wages in their country ought surely be expected to interest them still more than freeing a strange race in a strange land.

In this connection I would also point to the example of the United States, presenting with such unexampled liberality by subsidies of land to forward railroad enterprise.

The guarantee of the interest alluded to above, so forcibly reminding one of the phrase, "the lion's share," amounted to neither more nor less than this: Should the new enterprise prove unprofitable, the state must bear the loss; that is, you, the taxpayers, shall pay the deficit. If, on the other hand, the thing should be a success, the dividends no matter how heavy, shall accrue to the rich stockholders. In some countries, particularly Prussia, this feature is sought to have a modified appearance given to it by reserving certain assumed advantages to be derived in the very far future; advantages which can only become such through the workingmen associating for ameliorative purposes, and being felt as a factor in the politics of the nation.

Without the intervention on the part of the state—of which it may be said the guarantee of payment of the interest was the smallest feature—it is extremely likely we should have had no railroads on this continent today. In any case, this fact is not to be disputed, that the government, in guaranteeing the interest, was a reliable inducement to the rich property holders who control capital, to take hold. It was clearly a case of state assistance to the bourgeoise; and if extended to one class why not to another equally willing to honorably profit by it.

How was it that no cry arose against the interest guarantee as an improper intervention of the state? Why was it not declared that the guarantee of the state was not denounced as undue interference of self-help on the part of the rich stock companies? Above all, why was not the guarantee of the state stamped as socialism and communism? The question is readily answered: The intervention was in the interest of the rich, the property holding class of society, deference to whom has always been regarded as correct. It can only be when the intervention is sought to be in favor of the poverty-stricken that communism is raised as a mad dog cry.

Let what I have said, then, answer for those who speak to you of the impropriety of state intervention, condemning it as threatening the principle of self-help and favoring socialism and communism, which they say underlies the demand. Give them to understand that, having lived so long in socialism—as proved by guaranteeing the interest on the railroad and other instances hastily touched upon, we desire to benefit by its advantages in a still greater degree.

It may be added that great though the progress of culture was made manifest by the introduction of railroads, it would sink into insignificance compared to the advance civilization would show in the same space of time by the elevation of the working class through their industrial association by state aid.

For, what do all the heaped-up riches and all the fruits of civilization benefit the community when they are used by only a few? Leaving unlimited humanity the Tantalus of the ages, reaching in vain for what forever eludes the grasp: worse, indeed than Tantalus, for he had not assisted in cultivating the fruits for which his thirsting tongue was damned to long for. The elevation of the working class ought to be regarded as the grandest achievements of culture, therefore warranting the highest efforts of the state in the accomplishment.

It is to be added that the state, through the agency of the ordinary credit and money circulating institutes (the banks) may, in the easiest possible manner, perform the needed duties of assistants to the government in its new relation to us, and without taking upon themselves any greater responsibility than was assumed in accepting guarantees for the payment of the interest of railroads.

How easily the necessary capital, or, credit, rather, might be procured for the gradual association of the entire working class, cannot be further shown here, as it would involve explanations of the theoretical, financial, and social functions of money and credit. Furthermore, such an explanation of the method as would be necessary, would be superfluous, because not called for. Not till it can have a practical value by initiating the realization of the demands will this become a duty.

From the nature of things, these associations can only gradually, and in process of time, embrace the entire working class. They would have to begin in such districts and localities where certain occupations center, where the density of the population and the known disposition for association would be likely to forward such.

As soon as a number of such associations would be formed, securing the aid of the state, their existence would make it easier to introduce them to other branches of industry, which, when combined, would form a chain of credit with relation to one another. Beside this credit association, an insurance association might embrace the different cooperative associations, equalizing all business losses and making them but scarcely felt. The state would be in no case forced to play dictator to these societies; its duties ceasing after supplying the stability needed through statutory enactments; all control being vested in the organizations themselves; thereby conducting the business exclusively by the members; so insuring safety.

The ordinary journeyman's wages would be paid weekly, while the whole business profits of the association would be distributed in the form of dividends. The practicability and the lucrative productivity of such associations can be questioned only by those who are totally ignorant of the fact that workingmen's associations already numerously exist in England and France; sprung into being, it is true, under adverse circumstances and solely by the isolated exertions of the working men, yet having attained a high degree of prosperity. Already, in the county of Lancashire—passing by the so called pioneers of Rochdale—there existed thirty-three such associations organized on the plan of the factory method of production.

And although but lately founded, they have declared a dividend of 30 to 40 percent on the capital invested. There are besides, associations of *ouvriers macons* in Paris, who presented a business exhibit in 1856 to 1857, showing a profit of 56 percent on their capital. In 1858 the business profit was 130,000 francs; of which 30,000 francs were added to the reserve and the surplus 100,000 francs divided as a dividend. Furthermore, 60 percent of this fell to the share of labor, and 40 percent to the share of the capitalist. (This association has *associés non travailleurs* who each invest at least 10,000 francs.) A like prosperity is exhibited by the *ouvriers lampistes,* also by the *ouvriers en meubles* and others. See a history of workingmen's associations in the works of Professor Huber, Cochut, Lemercier *(Etudes sur les Associations Ouvrièrs.)* The statutes and rules of these cooperative shops also contribute valuable information concerning the internal economy of these associations. Regarded from the standpoint of the philosopher, these societies are the promises of the future; the work of hard-palmed, clear souled men who through the dim vista of the coming generations saw humanity's possibilities. If so much, then, can be accomplished, not only unaided, but in the face of immense opposition and ridicule, it becomes an easy task by the aid of the state, to achieve the entire redemption and permanent elevation of the working class. And to that complexion it must come at last. Blind indeed must that man be who fails to see in the history and development of the years the unswerving swing of humanity toward the conditions aimed at by these associations.

Gentlemen as a finale, let us now consider the question: What is the state?

In response, I ask you to cast a glance at the official statistics published by the government—for I do not purpose to appear with my own calculations merely.

The official statistical bureau of the kingdom of Prussia, superintended by the King's secret councillor, Professor Dieterici, published in 1857, founded upon the official tax list, shows how the population was divided in regard to income (Professor Dieterici's *Statistical Bureau,* year 1851, vol. IV, p. 262; compare vol. III, p. 243.)

I place the results of this calculation before you with the exact words and figures.

As there exhibited, one-half percent of the population of Prussia has an income of 1,000 thalers.

Three and one-fourth percent from 400 to 1,000.

Seven and one-fourth percent from 200 to 400.

Sixteen and three-fourths percent from 100 to 200.

Seventy-two and one-fourth percent below 100.

And this income falls upon the heads of the taxable portion of the population who, according to Dieterici, represent upon the average a family of five persons or at least three persons.

And naturally the same analogy must exist in all the other German states.

These dumb official figures, if they do not claim mathematical exactness (every one, as you know, belittling his income before the tax gatherer—a matter of no importance in this relation, it not in the least degree giving grounds for difference) will speak to you more distinctly than would whole volumes.

Seventy-two and one-fourth percent of the population with an income below 100 thalers; showing them, as a consequence, to be in the most miserable condition.

Another sixteen and three-fourths percent of the population, with an income of from 100 to 200 thalers a few degrees above misery. Another, seven and one-fourth percent with an income of 200 to 400 thalers still in cramped conditions. Three and one-half percent with an income of 400 to 1000 thalers, in a comparatively comfortable position; and finally one-half percent in all possible degrees of wealth. The two lowest classes who are in the wretched, downtrodden condition form eighty-nine percent of the whole population, and if we must add the seven and one-fourth percent, of the third class, still in a cramped condition, comparatively without means, we find ninety-six and one-fourth percent of the entire number helpless and poverty stricken.

Now, gentlemen, remember this: It is to you, you the suffering, the patient, and enduring class, that the state belongs; not to us of the higher classes; *for the state is the consolidated people.* I asked you what was the state, and you have found through a few figures, a more comprehensive answer than many books could give; I repeat it, you, the people, make the state.

I now emphatically ask, why should not your large associations develop and guide to fruition the smaller circles of associations?

This question you also will discuss with those who twaddle to you about the impropriety of state interference, and of the socialism and the communism inherent in the demand.

Finally, if you desire an especial clause to prove the impossibility of bettering the condition of the entire working class, except through the cooperation of the state, aiding the free associations, look at England, the country upon which the other side chiefly rely for proof of their assertion that it is possible to bring about this improvement by limited numbers of individuals in cooperative efforts, independent of outside aid.

It seems to be regarded that England, for many reasons rooted in its peculiar conditions, is the best fitted to successfully try this experiment—the fact, however, not proving the possibility of other countries to do the same.

The especial proof referred to with reference to England, points distinctly to the workingmen's associations which, up to this time, have been given as so conclusive. I mean the pioneer movement of Rochdale. Existing since 1844, this consumer association founded a spinnery and weaving mill, with a capital of £5,500, in 1858. In the statutes of this cooperative association, an equal share of the business profits or dividend, besides the local market price for labor (wages,) was assured to all the workingmen busied in the factory, whether stockholders in the association or not; it having been decided that the yearly dividends should be equally divided, and apportioned to labor price or wages, as upon the capital stock.

Here let me say that the number of stockholders in the factory amounted to 1,600 while the number of workingmen busied in it were only 500. There was, therefore, quite a number of stockholders who were not at the same time working in the factory; at the same time all the workingmen were not stockholders. In 1861, an agitation arose from those who were merely stockholders, backed by some who were both stockholders and workingmen, against the rule that the workingmen who were not stockholders should receive a share of the business profit—the product of labor.

From the side of the stockholder, the argument advanced openly, and simply, was, that according to the universal custom in the industrial world, labor was fully paid with the wages alone; and that this wage was fixed by the law of supply and demand. (We have seen above by what law.) "This fact," says Professor Huber, in the report which he gives of the circumstances, "from the beginning was presented as the necessary, natural state of things, needing no further motive nor strengthened claim of legitimacy." True, up to this time, the custom in the factory was strictly according to the statutes, but was regarded as exceptional, impulsive. Bravely but without clear reasons, arguments founded mainly on the feelings, the sensibilities, this motion was battled for by the founders and Trustees of the association. True to the instincts of the possessor, a majority of five-eighths of the workingmen stockholders voted to change the statutes—acting precisely as would the bourgeoisie in a similar enterprise. The defeat was only for the present, however, as a majority of three-fourths of the votes was necessary.

"But nobody," further reports Professor Huber, "flatters himself that the thing has been settled. On the contrary, violent, internal struggles are in the future of such associations; doubtless, occasion will lead to discussion of the motion next year; the opposition being resolved to make its influence felt in the election for officers, where a majority vote decides, and where the domineering tendencies of the Trustees are likely to capture the opposition."

Professor Huber further reports of this: "A majority of the manufacturing productive associations have, from the beginning, conformed to the universal custom, and undoubtedly without regard to the doctrine involved. A very few, indeed, have adopted the cooperative principle in favor of labor." And Professor Huber must confess, however against his will, and with a heavy heart—for he is a disciple of the idea that association should come only through the individual efforts of workingmen: that it is a question which will, doubtless, soon come to be discussed and decided in all other associations for production, where the opposition of capital and labor exists, and where is felt the competition eternally reproduced in the industrial microcosm (the organized world,) and as represented by the workingmen's associations on a small scale.

You see, gentlemen, that when you reflect upon these facts, you find great questions are, at all times, solved in a great manner, never by inferior agencies. So long as the general wages are governed by the above law, so long the small associations of workingmen will be unable to resist its influence. Where is the gain to the workingman in working for either fellow workmen or bourgeoisie? There is none. In what can be possibly benefit by changing his employer? Nothing. You have merely changed the claimants to the results of your labor. You are in no wise freed. Where is the gain to be seen? There is no gain—unless gain is to be seen in the added depravity which changes the workingman in the associated form into the worst form of master. The person engaged in the enterprise alone has changed, the system has undergone no alteration; labor, the source of all wealth, being confined to the old status of wages; barely sufficient to keep a man alive. It is easy, under certain conditions, for the understanding to become confused; as witness the greed under the influence of this law, making workingmen, on becoming stockholders, not employed in the factory, unwilling to recognize the fact that they are enjoying the advantages of the labor of others; opposed, even, to allowing them a share apart from the gain of their own labor, even to grudging them that upon which labor has a just claim.

Workingmen with means of labor and having a greed of enterprise! This is the disgusting caricature into which the stockholding laborer has been changed.

Finally, for a last, decided proof in this discussion:

You saw that in this factory of the pioneers, 500 workingmen were busied, and that 1,600 stockholders had an interest in it. This much will also be apparent to you, that unless we can succeed in mocking ourselves with the delusion of all laborers, being rich, that the number of workingmen employed in a factory never will succeed, out of their own profits, to furnish the principle stock or capital necessary for a factory. They will find it impossible to resist the conclusion, that the admission of a greater number of stockholders, not employed in the factory, would be imperatively called for.

The proportion in this relation in the factory of the pioneers—1,600 stock-holding workingmen out of the factory, against 500 workingmen engaged in the factory—as three to one, is most favorable, and indeed rarely so: quite as small as could possibly be found to be. And is explained partly by the exceptionally comfortable condition of the organization, and partly through the fact that their peculiar branch of industry does not belong to those demanding a large amount of capital and also, because the factory does *not* belong to a mammoth, productive institution, in which case it would be very different. Finally, there is to be added, that, through the development of industry itself, and the progress of civilization, this proportion must continue to increase every day. It must be evident to every one, that the progress of industry consists in the application of more force and more machinery put in the place of human labor, and that through this is the amount of capital stock made to increase over human labor. When, then, in this factory of the pioneers, 1,600 workingmen stockholders were needed to contribute the necessary amount of capital to employ 500 workers, making a proportion of 1 to 3, then by the workingmen in other branches, and in the larger institutions of production, together with the daily progress of civilization, the proportion would vary—as 1 to 4, 1 to 5, to 6, to 8, to 10, to 20, and so on. But let us remain at the proportion of 1 to 3. To found a factory in which 500 workmen find employment, there are needed 1,600 stockholders to furnish the necessary capital.

This is well enough, so long as I wish to found only a few factories. Gentlemen, in the imaginative process there is no trouble. I can tripple and quadruple the number and still go on while I have workingmen stockholders to help me. But when I extend these associations till the whole body of workingmen of the nation are embraced, where shall I find three, four, five, ten, twenty times the number of workingmen stockholders who are to stand behind the laborers employed in the factories and furnish the capital?

It will be easy to perceive that it becomes a mathematical impossibility to free the working class through the efforts of its members; and that all argument used to prove the contrary are mere illusions—phantasms of the brain. It will be equally apparent that the only road to successful abolishment of the law which governs wages, and which regulates as with a rod of iron, is the progress and development of free individual labor associations through the helping hand of the state.

The labor movement, founded upon the purely atomic isolated strength of working individuals has had its value, and an immense one it is, to unmistakably show the way how the emancipation may take place. Practical proofs removing all doubts, real or assumed, of the practicability of the idea; so compelling the state to see its duty in upholding by its assistance, the higher interests of the nation through the culture of its members.

At the same time I have proven to you that the state is really the great organization and association of the workingmen, the central point of help and protection, holding the smaller associations in hand by a series of functionaryism. This is the natural and legitimate purpose of the state: operating the supervision over each subordinate association as each subordinate association does toward its members.

But how enable the state to make this intervention?

The answer is clear: It is possible only through universal and direct suffrage.

When the lawmaking body of Germany owes its existence to the popular vote, then, and only then will you be able to control the government in the interest of labor.

When this element of popular power shall have been introduced and the lawmaking power be the result, then the necessary forms and measures of the intervention may be discussed; and, backed by reason and science, men who understand your condition, and who are devoted to your cause will defend your interests. Then, too, the class without means will have to ascribe all disastrous elections to themselves, finding their representatives in the minority.

Universal and direct suffrage, as has been shown is the foundation of your political and social life: the basic principle of all self-help and without which the condition of the workingmen cannot be bettered.

Now, how to succeed in securing universal and direct suffrage.

Cast a glance at England! For more than five years did the English people agitate against the corn laws; and so earnest and general was the agitation that they were abolished even by a Tory ministry.

In like manner you workingmen of Germany must organize as a universal workingmen's association, peacefully but untiringly demanding continual agitation for the introduction of the universal and direct right of suffrage throughout all German countries. And mark my words: at the moment this combined movement reaches 100,000 members, it will be an acknowledged power in the land and already a factor affecting the legislative bodies. Raise this cry in every workshop, in every village, in every hut. Let the city workingmen with their deeper insight and culture, pour into the ear of their brethren of the rural districts, by debates and speeches their knowledge and experience, till mechanic and agricultural laborer, joining in the chorus of demands, compel the government to grant the right insisted on.

By debate and discussion, daily, and without cessation, was the great English agitation a success; by the same means alone will universal suffrage be gained in Germany. The more the echo of your voices is heard, the less will be the opposition to the pressure. And as auxilliary to your movement, found treasuries to which every member of the association must contribute to defray expenses of plans of organization.

Along with these treasuries—which, despite the smallness of the contribution, will form a power for agitation purposes, enabling you to have the daily papers to repeat the same demands, proving the rightfulness of your claims to deliverance from our present social condition.

Spread with the same means pamphlets. Also pay agents to carry the same views into every corner of the nation that the cry may reach the heart of every workingman, every householder, every agricultural laborer. Pay out of these means to all such workingmen who may suffer persecution and injury because of their activity in the cause. Let your voices continually be heard; in season and out of season; perpetual, never tiring; in place and out of place, a continual presence, compelling men to listen. The more repeated the more it will spread, and become mighty in the land.

All the art of practical success is contained in the secret to concentrate force at one spot, the vital and important point. In your propaganda look neither to the left side nor to the right. Be deaf to all but universal and direct suffrage or that which is connected with it and that leads to it.

When you have really established in the national mind this demand, and which in a few years you may succeed in doing through the 89 to 96 percent of the population which constitutes the proportion of the poorer classes in society, then will your wishes no longer be sought to be withheld. The government may quarrel and struggle over political rights with the Bourgeoisie. They may even refuse you political rights; deny you even under the ordinary pressure felt in political legislation, the right of suffrage. But a question brought before Parliament backed by 89 to 96 percent of the people clamoring for its passage as a bill: a question affecting the national life: a question of stomach and brains, and hot with the vitalities of both, no power can long withstand. Gentlemen, no authority can resist this.

Universal and direct suffrage!

This is the sign and symbol by which you conquer. There is no other for you.

> With Greeting and Hand Grip,
> Ferdinand Lassalle.

Berlin, March 1, 1863.

Translated by John Ehrmann and Frederick Bader

Franz Mehring

The Law against the Socialists

One Year of Bewilderment

The modern German labor movement is free from all romanticism. Nothing falls into the lap of the proletariat without effort; step-by-step it has to struggle for everything, be it small or big; only after repeated ups and downs does its path lead to the desired end. The Law against the Socialists has placed German social democracy before a completely new task; probing and searching, it has had to look for new ways, and has not always found the right way immediately. However, as it began to attain a higher level of development, the stages of its enlightenment became correspondingly shorter; no longer a decade, but a single year of inner bewilderment stands at the threshold of its second great period of existence.

The Law against the Socialists was published in the *Imperial Gazette* on October 21, 1878, and immediately the social democratic newspapers, journals, and associations began to be put down. The series of prohibitions was first applied to Leopold Jacoby's anthology *Es werde Licht* (Let there be light); this almost made it seem as if the Chief of Police, von Madai, in charge of the implementation of the law for all of Germany, wanted to play some kind of joke on himself. Of the forty-seven political newspapers of the party, only two—one in Nuremberg and the other in Offenbach—managed to survive. They had changed their names in good time and were written with great restraint; with other papers, even such measures failed. The attempt to publish insipid papers in place of the blacklisted ones did not succeed everywhere, particularly not in

Berlin. At the same time all of the numerous workers' associations—which had come into existence after the liquidation of the party organization—were closed down by law except when they decided to liquidate themselves at the last moment; the same applied to all the unions, with few exceptions such as the well-known and already sorely tried printers' union. As the unions disappeared so did their publications. The main blows fell right away during the first weeks; *Der Vorwaerts, Die Freie Berliner Presse* and *Das Hamburg-Altona Volksblatt,* the three best-known newspapers with approximately 45,000 subscribers, fell victim already during the first days. Another and still more thorough cleansing took place during the next months; by June 30, 1879, 217 associations, 5 provident funds, 127 periodicals, and 278 other publications had been banned.

The brutality of this mass murder reflected its perfidy. However little one might think of the narrow-mindedness of the National Liberals, who let themselves be deceived by the words of Bismarck and Eulenburg about the "loyal application" of the law, this was, of course, no excuse for the government's breach of promise. It trampled on all its promises and half-promises, repressed not only the "publicly dangerous endeavors" of social democracy, but everything associated with it; it did not spare the scientific literature of socialism, nor the trade unions with their registered provident funds, and brushed away the "precautionary measures" of the National Liberals as if they were spiderwebs. The Imperial Commission, whose "judicial guarantees" were argued about for weeks, proved to be nothing but a play of shadows on the wall. It lifted only 6 of the 627 prohibitions issued by the middle of 1879 of which at least three-quarters were unacceptable even according to the spirit and letter of this law itself. The lifting of this prohibition mainly affected bourgeois literature, such as "The Quintessence of Socialism" by Schäffle and one issue of a progressive paper; of all the noteworthy works of socialist literature, it only released the text of Lassalle's speech at the assizes in 1849.

While the Law against the Socialists was still under deliberation, the question had already been raised within the Social Democratic Party as to what was to be done after its enactment. Violent resistance against the disenfranchisement of the rights of the workers would have been sheer madness, but the obvious corollary of establishing a secret organization was also immediately rejected once and for all. A broadly based and powerful popular movement could not resort to an illegal secret existence, and had it nevertheless attempted to do so, it would have played right into the hands of the police. All that could be done for the moment was to wait and see how the law would be applied. On the day of its publication, the *Vorwaerts* declared that it would accept the "hard and bitter task" of writing in compliance with the style required by one of the provisions of the law.

The actual behavior of the police however proved to be far worse than expected. The champions of "sacred" private property forthwith gave an inspiring example of how to destroy private property. In the sixteen cooperative printing offices, 400 people were employed as printers, compositors, dispatchers, and editors, while more than 2,500 workers and craftsmen participated with their meager savings and—due to joint liability—with all their assets. The Berlin cooperative printing office, barred from printing even the most insipid papers including *Die Zukunft,* was forced to liquidate immediately. Given that it had managed to sell nearly all of its stock of printed matter, the members of the cooperative got away with only the loss of their contributions. For most cooperative printing offices, immediate liquidation would have been meant bankruptcy, and it was not really in the interest of the party to give up these positions immediately. The effort to find some kind of adjustment to the Law against the Socialists had to be carried through to the very end; if the shortsightedness of the opponent put an end to any of the milder methods of fighting, then a tougher method applying more pressure could be used all the more effectively. Many party members believed that once the first storm had died down, it would again become possible to proceed more actively; until such a time, they hoped that the insipid newspapers helping to keep the printing cooperatives going, would serve as "a sign of recognition and proof of identity" for knowledgeable comrades.

All the same, an element of discouragement prevailed throughout this time. After the heated struggles of the last years and particularly of the last months in which every nerve had become taut, a natural sense of fatigue took over. This was reinforced by the feeling of a complete deprivation of rights, compounded by the persisting state of emergency, the continuing regulatory and oppressive measures. Not all the leaders, who had previously proved their mettle, were capable of coping with this new and ever more difficult situation, and the host of informers, who were put at their heels, forced even the most resolute of them to become very cautious. On October 19, the Hamburg central electoral committee dissolved itself, and as a result of various personal relationships, it ended up exposing more of its connections than was perhaps necessary or certainly desirable. Geib was fatally ill; a heart ailment, which his lively nature might otherwise have been able to resist, rapidly worsened under the terrible strain of the antisocialist hunt, which daily perturbed this thoughtful and refined man. Auer had already been sent to Berlin a long time ago so as to put the precarious editorial situation at the *Berliner Freie Presse* in order. Hartmann, who would soon completely break faith with the party, lacked the necessary firmness and good judgment. Thus, there was no leadership while blows were falling on the party from all sides. Was it surprising then that feelings of insecurity and confusion began to seep into its ranks?

The first turn for the better came when Bismarck decided to strike the final crushing blow against social democracy. On November 28, shortly before the return to Berlin of the recently wounded but now recovered Kaiser, the minor state of siege—pursuant to paragraph 28 of the Law against the Socialists—was proclaimed in this city and the inner districts of Charlottenburg and Potsdam, as well as in the outer districts of Teltow, Niederbarnim, and Osthavelland. This was done through the application of two of its four provisions: the most ridiculous one that prohibited the carrying of weapons without a permit and that gave rise to all kinds of odd incidents, and the ugliest one that gave the police the right to expel all persons considered undesirable. Within the next few days sixty-seven party members, with Auer and Fritzsche in the lead, received printed orders of expulsion. Most of them had to comply within two days, some within one day and just a few were given a deadline of three days; all requests for further delay were rejected by Madai with utmost roughness. Some of those expelled had withdrawn from political involvement many years ago, many owned small businesses and all but one were family men. They bade their fellow party members farewell in an honorably written leaflet, which was immediately prohibited and yet circulated in thousands of copies. They affirmed what they had always been saying: no acts of violence, observe the law, and defend your rights within the framework of the law. In a similar way, they now demanded: Keep quiet; don't let yourselves be provoked; through our adherence to the law, we shall bring down our enemies. And at the end, a request: We can only leave our families enough provisions for a few days; remember our wives and children! Many of those expelled went to Hamburg and Leipzig; others settled down in the towns bordering the area under siege in order to stay as near as possible to their families.

Of all the promises that Bismarck broke so disdainfully, the proclamation of the minor state of siege was the most despicable. The National Liberals had only accepted paragraph 28 of the Law against the Socialists for the direst emergencies; if a district were to become so undermined by social democratic propaganda that the outbreak of violence became imminent, then the paragraph was to be implemented so as to avoid the declaration of a real state of siege. None of this applied to Berlin at the time. The hard provisions of the Law against the Socialists had been carried out without any attempt of resistance at all; it never occurred to even one single Berlin worker to play into Bismarck's hands by provoking an assassination attempt or a revolt. Even the bourgeois press agreed that none of the necessary prerequisites under which paragraph 28 could be applied were present. Only the reactionary papers mouthed some embarrassed stock phrases about the "noble head" of the kaiser, and how it had to be protected. Count Eulenburg also hid behind this pretext when the Progressives in the Prussian Chamber of Deputies questioned him. Had it been more than mere pretext, the minister of police would indeed have appeared to be suffering from a shortsightedness unworthy of his position. To suspect men like Auer and Fritzsche of assassination by treachery and to unlawfully ruin sixty-seven lives would seem to be actions more suited to nipping assassination attempts in the bud than promoting them. But all that talk about the "noble head" was nothing but pretext. Soon after, Bismarck himself admitted in the Reichstag that he had actually intended to proclaim the minor stage of siege throughout all the centers of social democratic propaganda. From his indications, it appears that the other governments drew back from this evil act; in any case, he himself did not try to hide the fact that he had intended to lead the Reichstag astray with regard to paragraph 28.

If it was the most despicable among all his despicable acts of broken promise, then the proclamation of the minor state of siege was also the most foolish of all his foolish acts of brute force. He very clearly convinced the social democratic party of the fact that it would be given no rest, that the fight against it was one of life and death. Wherever party members had slackened for a minute, they now were all flocking back to their old posts. Collections for the expelled and their families forged the first links for setting up a new organization; in fact, the exiles themselves, and even more so their starving wives and children, became agitators of a kind that the class-conscious proletariat had never known before. Gray-haired veterans, who had spent years in jail without blinking used often to say that none of the other trials and tribulations of repression had filled them with such rage as the expulsion, the arbitrary destruction of their human existence at its roots. In spite of all the suffering endured by individual party members, a major advantage that the party was to gain from this state of siege was that the people at large gradually let go of the moral disapproval that they had felt for the party since the time of the assassination attempts.

This boorish act of brute force of Bismarck's had another important result. Karl Hirsch was expelled from Paris, where he had lived for some time. When it came to doing such little services aimed against the social democrats, the official "arch-enemies" on the Seine and on the Spree liked doing favors for one another. Hirsch had intended to return to Berlin when news about the expulsion made him change his mind. He went to Brussels instead and founded *Die Laterne,* a small weekly paper similar in form and style to Rochefort's *Lantern.* Then on December 9, Most was released from Ploetzensee and immediately expelled from Berlin. He moved to London, where with the help of the Communist Workers' Educational Association, he also began publishing a weekly paper, *Die Freiheit. Die Laterne* was issued in mid-December 1878, and *Die Freiheit* in the beginning of January 1879.

So in one fell swoop, German social democracy had two foreign-based publications that—so to speak—had grown like wildflowers from soil nourished by the reactionaries. Both papers represented the interest of the party as openly as was permitted under freedom of the press abroad. At first, it was difficult to smuggle them into Germany, but the speed with which Bismarck sought to destroy these new weapons of social democracy gave full proof of how much he feared them. The postmaster general had to issue a decree, which in effect brought postal officials down to the level of accomplices of the political police, and which strongly clashed with the constitutionally guaranteed protection against tampering with the mail. This, however, was not at all surprising in Germany—the classic land of secret councillors. In March, Karl Hirsch was expelled by the Belgian ministry. Even so, Bismarck's worries did not end there because Hirsch moved to England and continued to publish *Die Laterne* there. It was wittier and better written than *Die Freiheit* but more in the nature of a political pamphlet. *Die Freiheit* had to a greater degree the qualities of a party paper, but due to the personality of its editor, it was far more subjective in tone than *Die Laterne*. Most's eccentric character had already caused the party many pains even before the passing of the Law against the Socialists. But after ten years of putting up with manipulations by the judicial system and the police, he had reached a level of bitterness and nervous tension, which—albeit understandable from a psychological point of view—diminished strongly his sense of political responsibility. In his volatile and hasty way, he had considered it superfluous to reach an agreement with the German party leadership about the publication of *Die Freiheit*. His excuse that there was no such party leadership was really not to the point; the social democratic faction in the Reichstag still had a party organization, and Most—as a former deputy—should have felt it to be doubly important to consult them.

The dilemma now faced by the German party was what position to take with regard to these two publications. *Die Laterne* was careful to refrain from committing or criticizing the party; *Die Freiheit*, however, continuously insisted on a revolutionary strategy, perhaps not yet in "pitched forks" style, but rather in a form of propaganda as had been used before the Law against the Socialists. Most wanted to write and edit *Die Freiheit* in the same vein as *Der Volksstaat* and *Der Vorwaerts* had been in the past. Despite Most's vexing behavior, a basic agreement could have been reached with him, and needless to state, with Karl Hirsch as well. But leading party circles in Germany did not want to have anything to do with the two newspapers. They concentrated their main efforts on combating as carefully as possible the unnatural hate of social democracy that had been nurtured in the politically uncommitted sector of the nation, and they feared that this feeling would be revived by the reckless language of the foreign newspapers. Bismarck was perceived as thriving on these assassination attempts and as being pushed to capitulation in case they ceased. It was not that the eventual need for and usefulness of a foreign newspaper was questioned, but that it was felt that the time for it was by no means ripe yet. Its first consequences were sure to be further persecution, and the considerably shrunken resources of the party were already insufficient for the relief needed by its expelled and disciplined members. After years of exhausting political action the comrades could certainly have used a breathing space. Socialist propaganda was still in ample supply as a result of innumerable tracts thrown at the proletariat without ever having been properly read or fully understood.

In February of 1879, this point of view no longer seemed as justified as it had been in October of 1878. When the Reichstag met on February 12, Bismarck immediately proposed a number of motions aimed at the complete crushing of social democracy. Bismarck was asking for more than the Philistines' senseless hatred of socialism; and therefore, social democracy was definitely going to employ other weapons than the moral support of politically uncommitted observers. In fact, the masses were once more pressing forward onto the battlefield, where they could meet the enemy face-to-face. On February 5, by-elections were held for the deceased Progressive Burgers in the western electoral district of Breslau where the Silesian aristocracy and plutocrats resided. Despite police repression against all campaigning, despite the suppression of all leaflets and breaking up of all meetings, despite the unjustified arrest of their candidate Kracker, the workers came up with 5,175 votes. Kracker managed to get on the second ballot and though he was defeated, the votes for him increased to 7,544. A similar striking result was obtained on February 27 in a by-election in the Saxonian electoral district of Waldheim-Doebeln, in which the social democratic candidate obtained 4,322 votes.

Up to the Easter recess, discussions in the Reichstag continued to echo the debates on the Law against the Socialists, Bismarck wanted to make up for what he had failed to achieve before ousting social democracy from the Reichstag. He tried to kill two birds with one stone; first the Reichstag was to pass the proposed motions that Fritsche and Hasselmann, who—though exiled—had returned for the Reichstag debate, should legally be prosecuted for infraction of their banishment, and further that the disciplinary power of the Reichstag should be expanded so as to exclude members for making improper speeches, indeed deprive them of their eligibility and even have improper speeches erased from the stenographic records. The Reichstag did not go along with either of these proposals; even the National Liberal speakers found strong words to reject this degree of self-degradation. However, in this they were acting much more in their own interest than out of principle or in the interest of mistreated social democracy; in another matter, they soon after demonstrated what a cheap commodity bourgeois sympathy was. A yearly report had to be given to the Reichstag on the practical application of paragraph 28; but also this "protective measure" soon went up in smoke. A social democrat was allowed to speak; but then not only the National Liberals but also all of the Progressives and the Ultramontanes voted for a conservative final motion. During the questioning period in the Prussian Chamber of Deputies, Virchow had actually shown a bit more daring when he remarked that the police should not toss "good revolutionaries" into the same pot with "regicides." But by then Bismarck had unleashed his officious pack on the "revolutionary" Progressive party, and even the most persistent among them were now careful to keep very quiet about the most severe abuses of the Law against the Socialists so as to appear as the "most conservative of all the parties" for a change.

Of the social democratic delegates, Bebel spoke on March 4 on the so-called muzzling law, Liebknecht on March 17 about the proclamation of the minor state of siege in Berlin. Bebel managed to put the noble Bismarck in his place: Bismarck—because of "presumed offense" to his person—had thousands of people, even old women, on welfare put in jail by means of his printed petitions for criminal proceedings, and yet he was now complaining that as a member of the Federal Council, he had to be very cautious because he did not enjoy the constitutional freedom of speech held by the delegates. How admirably did an appeal to such a basic common right suit a man who not only held an unlimited right to indulge in libel but also used it in such a way that, whenever one of his victims sued him in court, he could beat a quick and heroic retreat by hiding behind his officer's uniform. Liebknecht's speech was tailored to the strategy of the German party leaders. He was pitiless in pulling to pieces the empty wording of the report, and then went on to say that it would be cowardly of him to disassociate himself from the writings of party members abroad, but that the party had absolutely nothing to do with all of this, and that furthermore many of the most influential party members had disapproved of the establishment of *Die Freiheit* and *Die Laterne*. The party would observe the Law against the Socialists because it is a reform party in the strictest sense of the word and the idea of revolution by force is in itself absurd; that Bracke's snapping his finger at the law had not meant that the party would not adhere to the law, but had only established the historical truth that the party could not be suppressed by this law; that afterwards Bracke had felt sorry for having made his remarks in such an unparliamentary manner and that he—Liebknecht—did not want to endorse them either.

This speech by Liebknecht gave rise to a memorandum—designed not by Most but by Mielke, an old party member—issued by the Communist Worker Educational Association in London, wherein it was stated: "What is needed and feasible is a skillful strategy against the law, not a prudent strategy under the law. Fortunately, some countries still permit free speech, and as yet no wall has been built around the German Empire. The bold and determined will manage to scale any such walls. If all means of propaganda are suppressed within the country, then propaganda by the printed word is still possible. Other parts of the memorandum were much more dubious and could actually be interpreted as recommendations for a conspiracy after the model of the Russian nihilists and complete abstention from parliamentary participation. *Die Laterne* immediately objected to this, while at the same time endorsing the memorandum in many other aspects. In response to the protest of *Die Laterne, Die Freiheit* declared that it neither wanted to recommend a secret organization nor abstention from parliamentary politics, yet its words seemed to head in that direction. Most began to talk of a "new party" and attacked the parliamentary representatives of German democracy in such a way as to gradually exclude any possibility of an understanding.

Yet it became increasingly necessary to reach an understanding on current strategy. After the Easter recess, the Reichstag began to work on the scheduled "financial and economic reform." In fact, it was turned into a stock exchange, where Bismarck traded with the big industrialists and landowners for the pound of flesh that each of these three noble associates could cut from the mass of the consumers. After long and repugnant haggling, the big industrialists got their desired protectionist duties on iron and textiles, the big landowners theirs on grain and cattle, and Bismarck had his financial tariffs in his pocket while the people at large paid for this hocus-pocus with price increases for all foodstuffs and 130 million marks in new taxes. All of this was accompanied by a thorough shifting of party alliances. The National Liberals—now in disarray—allowed their members to vote independently on all economic issues; partly, they stayed with the Progressives under the banner of free trade, partly, they went over to the protectionists. Still, they were determined to hold on to their "constitutional guarantees"; they did not want to relinquish completely the right of the Reichstag to make appropriations; thus Bismarck had to come to an agreement with the Ultramontanes, who were content with "federal guarantees," namely the transfer of all the surpluses to the individual states, and—as a pleasant addition—with the dismissal of the minister of culture, Falk, who had been in the forefront of the Kulturkampf. This did not seem to worry a lofty soul like Bismarck one bit. When it came to pocketing such large amounts of money, he found it not only worthwhile to take a trip to Canossa but also to make a bow to separatism.

Neither the faceless papers now appearing nor the old propaganda tracts could help the workers find their way out of this disorder. Even the floor of the assembly proved to be an inadequate medium. In the long weeks when the protective tariffs were debated, the social democratic deputies could barely get a word in edgeways despite their numerous requests for the floor. They had no chance whatever to develop their concepts adequately. Their position was further complicated by the fact that Kayser* began to feel enthusiastic about some of the industrial tariffs. At the same time, working masses from the big cities were pushing forward with ever-increasing force. When Reinders—who had represented the eastern district in Breslau—died on May 22, he was given a big funeral by the Breslau workers, who then went on to elect Hasenclever in his place in two electoral fights. Five times within the course of a few months, the Breslau proletariat had shown the most energetic signs of life; there was no doubt that the workers in Berlin, in Hamburg, in Leipzig— in short, the workers in the major centers of the movement—would also have reacted in the same way if they had been given the same opportunities. In contrast, a by-election in the electoral district of Kottbus-Spremberg showed a considerable decline in social democratic votes. The danger of a split began to loom ahead; the more advanced sections of the proletariat might have succumbed to the unpredictability of *Die Freiheit*, the less-progressive elements might have been bogged down by the insipid newspapers.

*Max Kayser (1853–88), Social Democrat deputy, imprisoned in the beginning of the period of the Law against the Socialists, later tending toward Bismarck's policy of protective tariffs.

Die Laterne now also started to become more aggressive. Although in contrast to Most, it had never wavered in its adherence to the party line; it had to admit that the developments in London would never have been possible if bad mistakes had not been made in Germany. The paper said: no organization without its own publications, if the foreign papers are no good, then publish new ones, but don't delay any longer; time is running out. It lashed out against Kayser for his protectionist tariff caper, and convincingly proved the overall harmfulness of the new customs duty. It printed a letter by Liebknecht where, as a rebuttal to Most, he stated that the choice was between taking up the fight against or remaining on the legal ground of the Law against the Socialists, and that there was no third way. It also printed a letter signed "From Berlin," which said that it was a charade to believe that social democracy was so deeply rooted in the masses so as to be able to survive years of outward inactivity and to do without any real contacts. But there was in fact a third alternative, an energetic posture, defensive and offensive, taking into account the conditions inside and outside the German Empire.

Finally, Marx and Engels stepped in to clear up these mixed-up matters. Höchberg had proven to be a loyal friend of the party before as well as after the enactment of the Law against the Socialists; he gave help and support wherever he could; he put his own wealth at the service of the party. But he could not go against his nature; he kept hoping that through information and appeal to their sense of justice, members of the ruling class could be won over for social democracy. He wanted the party to make it easier for such elements to join its membership, to give greater emphasis to its economic program and push its political-revolutionary message into the background. Thus, by Easter of 1879 he had ten thousand copies of Schäffle's *Quintessenz des Socialismus* (Quintessence of socialism) sent from Brussels to civil servants, jurists, and teachers in Germany; and, in the same spirit, as replacements for the banned paper *Die Zukunft,* he founded several new scholarly journals, the *Staatswirtschaftliche Abhandlungen* (Dissertations on economics) under the pseudonym of Dr. R. F. Seyfferth in Leipzig and *Das Jahrbuch fuer Sozialwissenschaft und Sozialpolitik* (Yearbook for social science and social politics) under the pseudonym of Dr. Ludwig Richter in Zurich. The Leipzig journal, which appeared at irregular intervals, managed to escape the clutches of the Law against the Socialists. It dealt mainly with questions of practical social politics and pitted the idea of the fallacious protective tariff as a safeguard of national labor against that of an international protective labor legislation as the real interest of the workers. Not so lucky, the *Yearbook* in Zurich was immediately forbidden in spite of its very cautious stand. The first biannual edition, which appeared in the summer of 1879, contained a few essays by Greulich and Vollmar, a number of reviews, and a series of reports on the socialist movement in the modern developed countries. Most of them were excellent pieces and represented a considerable improvement over the approach that *Die Zukunft* had usually taken.

However, this edition also contained one particular essay "Retrospective Views of the Socialist Movement in Germany," posing as "Critical Aphorisms." The authors were Höchberg and C. A. Schramm. Eduard Bernstein, who had moved to Switzerland as Höchberg's literary assistant and who was considered the third author, had actually contributed nothing more than a few lines of minor importance. For social democracy to engage in constructive self-criticism at the time of the greatest repression was in itself a dubious and difficult task, which this essay failed to achieve in even a tolerably satisfactory manner. Political activism up to this date was criticized in a bitter, not always befitting, and let alone tactful way. It warned against "pointless debates about a future state," but not in the sense of revolutionary action excluding all utopias, but only in the sense of a practical implementation of bourgeois reforms. Finally, it emphasized the need to win over more followers among the propertied and educated classes if political struggles that had claimed so many sacrifices in strength and family well-being were to lead to tangible results. Against this, Marx and Engels protested in a circular letter to Bebel, Bracke, and others. They demanded that such opinions were not to be expressed by leading party figures, if they were to be tolerated by the party at all.

Obviously, the Zurich *Yearbook* was never called upon to lead the party, but next to *Die Laterne* and *Die Freiheit*, it had now begun to present a third tactical direction and still the authoritative voice remained silent. The need for an official paper—appearing abroad—could no longer be denied. This fact was even recognized by Geib, who had held out against this idea most persistently. Yet he was not to see the appearance of the new paper. His sufferings came to an end on August 1. His coffin was followed by an impressive procession of Hamburg workers, estimated by the bourgeois press at thirty-thousand. At his grave side, his old friends vowed that they would never cease from striving forward in the spirit of this unforgettable man.

Zurich was chosen as the point of publication for the party paper. There the Swiss labor movement had a printing press of their own. Also, other favorable conditions for the successful execution of this enterprise were present. *Die Laterne* had already gone out of circulation at the end of June because Karl Hirsch himself had realized that the form he had chosen for it failed to meet the needs of the party. Given all its past problems, *Die Freiheit* was a still less suitable candidate as official paper since Most got increasingly lost in senseless revolutionary schemes. On September 28, *Der Sozialdemokrat, Internationales Organ der Sozialdemokratie deutscher Zunge* (The social democrat, international journal of German-speaking social democrats) published its trial issue there.

It considered itself to be an offspring of the Law against the Socialists. In spite of some merits, the insipid newspapers now being published in Germany by party members would never be able to replace the former party press; not only were they obliged to avoid the slightest criticism of capitalist society, but only under imminent danger of being banned could they permit themselves a fraction of the frankness with which the traditional press might at times comment on social and official institutions. In matters of principle and strategy, *Der Sozialdemokrat* stood by the Gotha program. As the mouthpiece of German social democracy, now as before a revolutionary party in the best sense of the word, it would strive for the gradual enlightenment and organization of the masses. It would fight all revolutionary posturings, which seemingly promised quick solutions but in actual fact were foolish and harmful. Although not in the domain of the German and Austrian party, the paper intended to avoid—inasfar as possible—any infraction of common law, a fact that would in no way reduce its overall determination.

Hence, a grievous ban was broken and once again the old time-tested battle cry swept through the ranks of the party: Forward march altogether!

The End of the Law against the Socialists

The Law against the Socialists outlasted its begetter by half a year, but during this time it gave hardly any signs of life. Actually,

February 20 was the day on which a new period of the history of the German Empire as well as of the German Social Democratic Party began, a period which has not come to an end yet and which—until it does so—cannot be seen from a historical perspective. But, the termination of the Law against the Socialists—begun by the party during the last months of its being in force and completed one year after its expiration—still fits into the framework of this presentation.

It is not possible to draw up an exhaustive report on the victims claimed by the Law against the Socialists. After the law had been in force for ten years, *Der Sozialdemokrat* tried to bring out a commemorative issue, which would not only have supplied exact statistics of all prohibitions but would also have listed the names of all those expelled from their hometowns and made public the names of all those whose livelihood had been destroyed, put its finger on all house searches, arrests, condemnations with all their pertinent details, and have told the full story of all the contrived schemes involving spies and informers. But even at that time, carrying out this project had run into insurmountable difficulties. The most enthusiastic members in the major party strongholds were soon worn out by this endeavor, and the results thereof would have been so voluminous that they could not possibly have been turned into a readable publication of more or less manageable proportions.

According to rough estimates, 1,300 periodicals and other kinds of publications and 332 different types of workers' organizations were banned under the Law against the Socialists. Orders of expulsion from areas under state of siege were issued against 900 persons, of whom over 500 were family providers—293 in Berlin, 311 in Hamburg, 164 in Leipzig, 71 in Frankfurt, 53 in Stettin, 1 in Spremberg; in Offenbach, the Hessian government contented itself with the expelling of those citizens of the empire who had no right of domicile in the locality. The length of the legally decreed terms of imprisonment amounted to approximately one-thousand years, distributed among 1,500 persons. Not only did these figure fail to provide a proper estimate of what really happened, in no way did they manage to give a true picture of the havoc wrought in terms of human happiness and human lives, of the innumerable martyrs who—driven from hearth and home into the penuries of exile by dint of capitalistic or police-state harassment—were sent to an early grave.

But unlike the dead of March 18 [1848] who had been able to

speak through the mouth of their poet, the victims of the Law against the Socialists were able to say of themselves: the price was high but the results were real. None of the true and brave, who were mown down by the scythe of the Law against the Socialists, suffered in vain: the avengers would rise from the vestiges of those who had perished and fallen to dust in the dark. At the time the Law against the Socialists was passed, the party had 437,158 votes and forty-two political papers; the trade union organizations had 50,000 members and fourteen publications; at the time of the expiration of the Law against the Socialists, the party could count 1,427,298 votes and sixty political papers and the trade union organizations numbered 200,000 members and forty-one publications. In the three years since the party convention in St. Gallen, the party had collected 325,000 marks, and when the struggle had finally ended, the war chest of the party was still well filled—with almost 172,000 marks.

But neither the losses nor the gains of the Law against the Socialists can be measured by a few figures, however impressive these may be. True to the well-known law of dialectics, at a certain point quantity had suddenly turned into quality. During the twelve years of struggle, not only had the party grown in size and strength but its very essence had become more fully developed. It had not only fought and won, it had also worked and learned. It had not only given proof of strength but also of its spirit. These were priceless attainments that could no more be expressed in figures than could the consciousness of invincibility that had permeated the party since it had victoriously withstood a twelve-year war waged against it with all the powerful weapons of a modern state. The masses had become the hero of the proletarian heroic age. This was the party's peculiar greatness and distinction.

In vain did the bourgeois parties try to prove that the ruling classes had freely let go of the Law against the Socialists, and that the party—without this voluntary surrender by their opponents—would simply have had to go on bearing this yoke. This point of view was not shared by all the ruling class. For those who did so, it was only to the extent that they accepted their defeat "voluntarily." They were now relinquishing their allegiance to the Law against the Socialists due to the fact that the class-conscious proletariat had turned the tables on its creators. Obviously, the ruling classes could have gone on maintaining the Law against the Socialists, but only at the cost of a general decay, which would have made it possible for the Holy Roman Empire of the German nation to look down disdainfully on the new German Empire. Clearly, any sensible general would withdraw his troops from a battle that was being hopelessly lost in order to prevent them from being decimated, but only a fool would regard such a general as a victor and—let alone—as a victor "by his own free will."

Just as ludicrous was the bourgeois mockery insinuating that it had been unreasonable for social democracy to fight the Law against the Socialists so fiercely when it had turned out to have been so useful to the party. In a certain sense, the saying "the crazier, the better," does sometimes ring true. But the German Social Democratic Party has never thought along these lines, nor does it have any intention of ever doing so. The class-conscious proletariat is confident of its future and is most willing to give its opponents precedence when it comes to carrying things to the extremes by force. We have all heard the apocryphal tale of the Battle of Fontenoy, when an English officer called out to a French officer: "Let your people shoot!" only to get back the reply: "We never fire first." This was also how social democracy chose to respond to the provocations of their opponents. It did not do so out of high-sounding gallantry, but by means of well-considered tactics used in its struggle for emancipation: only when the opponents are using force in carrying things to extremes can the party make use of the political strategy of "the crazier, the better" for its own purposes in the most profitable way, as was done during the days of the Law against the Socialists.

The party went into the fight as an adolescent with dangling limbs and a head full of dreams and ideas. When it returned home, it had turned into a muscular and toughened man—determined, mature, clear, and grown to its full height in every way.

Translated by Irene Schmied

Eduard Bernstein

The Most Pressing Problems of Social Democracy

"And what she is, that dares she to appear."
—SCHILLER, *Maria Stuart.*

The tasks of a party are determined by a multiplicity of factors: by the position of the general, economic, political, intellectual and moral development in the sphere of its activity, by the nature of the parties that are working beside it or against it, by the character of the means standing at its command, and by a series of subjective, ideologic factors, at the head of them, the principal aim of the party and its conception of the best way to attain that aim. It is well known what great differences exist in the first respect in different lands. Even in countries of an approximately equal standard of industrial development, we find very important political differences and great differences in the conceptions and aspirations of the mass of the people. Peculiarities of geographical situation, rooted customs of national life, inherited institutions, and traditions of all kinds create a difference of mind which only slowly submits to the influence of that development. Even where socialist parties have originally taken the same hypothesis for the starting point of their work, they have found themselves obliged in the course of time to adapt their activity to the special conditions of their country. At a given moment, therefore, one can probably set up general political principles of social democracy with a claim that they apply to all countries, but no program of action applicable for all countries is possible.

As shown above, democracy is a condition of socialism to a much greater degree than is usually assumed, *i.e.,* it is not only the means but also the substance. Without a certain amount of democratic institutions or traditions, the socialist doctrine of the present time would not indeed be possible. There would, indeed, be a workers' movement, but no social democracy. The modern socialist movement—and also its theoretic explanation—is actually the product of the influence of the great French Revolution and of the conceptions of right which through it gained general acceptance in the wages and labor movement. The movement itself would exist without them as, without and before them, a communism of the people was linked to primitive Christianity.

But this communism of the people was very indefinite and half mythical, and the workers' movement would lack inner cohesion without the foundation of those organizations and conceptions of law which, at least to a great part, necessarily accompany capitalist evolution. A working class politically without rights, grown up in superstition and with deficient education, will certainly revolt sometimes and join in small conspiracies, but never develop a socialist movement. It requires a certain breadth of vision and a fairly well developed consciousness of rights to make a socialist out of a workman who is accidentally a revolter. Political rights and education stand indeed everywhere in a prominent position in the socialist program of action.

So much for a general view. For it does not lie in the plan of this work to undertake an estimation of individual points of the socialist program of action. As far as concerns the immediate demands of the Erfurt program of the German social democracy, I do not feel in any way tempted to propose changes with respect to them. Probably, like every social democrat, I do not hold all points equally important or equally expedient. For example, it is my opinion that the admistration of justice and legal assistance free of charge, under present conditions, is only to be recommended to a limited degree, that certainly arrangements should be made to make it possible for those without means to seek to have a chance of getting their rights; but that no pressing need exists to take over the mass of the property law suits today and put the lawyers completely under the control of the state. Meanwhile, although legislators of today will hear nothing of such a step, as a socialist legislature cannot be achieved without a full reform of the legal system, or only according to such newly created legal institutions, as, for example, exist already in arbitration courts for trade disputes, the said demand may keep its place in the program as an indication of the development striven after.

I gave a very definite expression to my doubt as to the expediency of the demand in its present form as early as in 1891, in an essay on the draft scheme of the program then under discussion, and I declared that the paragraph in question gave "too much and too little." The article belongs to a series which Kautsky and I then drew up jointly on the program question, and of which the first three essays were almost exclusively the mental work of Kautsky, whilst the fourth was composed by me. Let me here quote two sentences from it which indicate the point of view which I upheld at that time with regard to the action of social democracy, and which will show how much or how little my opinions have changed since then:

"To demand simply the maintenance of all those without employment out of the state money means to commit to the trough of the state not only everyone who cannot find work but everyone that will not find work. . . . One need really be no anarchist in order to find the eternal heaping of duties on the state too much of a good thing. We will hold fast to the principle that the modern proletarian is indeed poor but that he is no pauper. In this distinction lies a whole world, the nature of our fight, the hope of our victory."

"We propose the formula: 'Conversion of the standing armies to citizen armies' because it maintains the aim and yet leaves the party a free hand today (when the disbanding of standing armies is utterly impossible) to demand a series of measures which narrow as much as possible the antagonism between army and people as, for example, the abolition of special military courts of justice, lessening of time of service, etc."

But has social democracy, as the party of the working classes and of peace, an interest in the maintenance of the fighting power? From many points of view it is very tempting to answer the question in the negative, especially if one starts from the sentence in the *Communist Manifesto:* "The proletarian has no fatherland." This sentence might, in a degree, perhaps, apply to the worker of the forties without political rights, shut out of public life. Today, in spite of the enormous increase in the intercourse between nations, it has already forfeited a great part of its truth and will always forfeit more, the more the worker, by the influence of socialism, moves from being a proletarian to a citizen. The workman who has equal rights as a voter for state and local councils, and who thereby is a fellow owner of the common property of the nation, whose children the community educates, whose health it protects, whom it secures against injury, has a fatherland without ceasing on that account to be a citizen of the world, just as the nations draw nearer one another, without, therefore, ceasing to lead a life of their own.

The complete breaking up of nations is no beautiful dream, and in any case is not to be expected in the near future. But just as little as it is to be wished that any other of the great civilized nations should lose its independence, just as little can it be a matter of indifference to German social democracy whether the German nation, which has indeed carried out, and is carrying out, its honorable share in the civilizing work of the world, should be repressed in the council of the nations.

In the foregoing is shown in principle the point of view from which the social democracy has to take its position under present conditions with regard to questions of foreign politics. If the worker is still no full citizen, he is not without rights in the sense that national interests can be indifferent to him. And if also social democracy is not yet in power, it already takes a position of influence which lays certain obligations upon it. Its words fall with great weight in the scale. With the present composition of the army and the complete uncertainty as to the changes in methods of war, etc., brought about by the use of guns of small bore, the Imperial Government will think ten times before venturing on a war which has social democracy as its determined opponent. Even without the celebrated general strike social democracy can speak a very important, if not decisive, word for peace, and will do this according to the device of the International as often and as energetically as it is necessary and possible. It will also, according to its program, in the cases when conflicts arise with other nations and direct agreement is not possible, stand up for settling the difference by means of arbitration. But it is not called upon to speak in favor of renunciation of the preservation of German interests, present or future, of or because English, French, or Russian chauvinists take umbrage at the measures adopted. Where, on the German side, it is not a question merely of fancies or of the particular interests of separate groups which are indifferent or even detrimental to the welfare of the nation, where really important national interests are at stake, internationalism can be no reason for a weak yielding to the pretensions of foreign interested parties.

This is no new idea, but simply the putting together of the lines of thought which lie at the bottom of all the declarations of Marx, Engels, and Lassalle on the questions of foreign politics. It is also no attitude endangering peace which is here recommended. Nations today no longer lightly go to war, and a firm stand can under some circumstances be more serviceable to peace than continuous yielding.

The doctrine of the European balance of power seems to many to be out of date today, and so it is in its old form. But in a changed form the balance of power still plays a great part in the decision of vexed international questions. It still comes occasionally to the question of how strong a combination of powers supports any given measure in order that it may be carried through or hindered. I consider it a legitimate task of German Imperial politics to secure a right to have a voice in the discussion of such cases. And to oppose, on principle, proper steps to that end, I consider, falls outside the domain of the tasks of social democracy.

To choose a definite example. The leasing of the Kiauchow Bay at the time was criticized very unfavorably by the socialist press of Germany. As far as the criticism referred to the circumstances under which the leasing came about, the social democratic press had a right, nay, even a duty, to make it. Not less right was it to oppose in the most decided way the introduction of or demand for a policy of partition of China because this partition did not lie at all in the interest of Germany. But if some papers went still further and declared that the party must under all circumstances and as a matter of principle condemn the acquisition of the Bay, I cannot by any means agree with it.

It is a matter of no interest to the German people that China should be divided up and Germany be granted a piece of the Celestial Empire. But the German people has a great interest in this—that China should not be the prey of other nations; it has a great interest in this—that China's commercial policy should not be subordinated to the interest of a single foreign power or a coalition of foreign powers—in short, that in all questions concerning China, Germany should have a word to say. Its commerce with China demands such a right to protest. In so far as the acquisition of the Kiauchow Bay is a means of securing this right to protest, and it will be difficult to gainsay that it does contribute to it, there is no reason in my opinion for the social democracy to cry out against it on principle. Apart from the manner in which it was acquired and the pious words with which it was accompanied, it was not the worst stroke of Germany's foreign policy.

It was a matter of securing free trade with and in China. For there can be no doubt that without that acquisition China would have been drawn to a greater degree into the ring of the capitalist economy, and also that without it Russia would have continued its policy of encircling, and would have occupied the Manchurian harbours. It was thus only a question as to whether Germany should look on quietly whilst, by the accomplishment of one deed after another, China fell ever more and more into dependence on Russia, or whether Germany should secure herself a position on the ground that she also, under normal conditions, can make her influence felt at any time on the situation of things in China, instead of being obliged to content herself with belated protests. So far ran and runs the leasing of the Kiauchow Bay, a pledge for the safeguarding of the future interests of Germany in China, be its official explanation what it may, and thus far could social democracy approve it without in the least giving away its principles.

Meanwhile, owing to the want of responsibility in the management of the foreign policy of Germany, there can be no question of positive support from the social democracy, but only of the right foundation of its negative attitude. Without a guarantee that such undertakings should not be turned to account over the heads of the people's representative House for other aims than those announced, say as a means to achieve some temporary success which might surrender the greater interests of the future, without some such pledge social democracy can take upon itself no share in the measures of foreign policy.

As can be seen the rule here unfolded for the position regarding questions of foreign policy turns on the attitude observed hitherto in practice by social democracy. How far it agrees in its fundamental assumptions with the ruling mode of viewing things in the party, does not lie with me to explain. On the whole tradition plays a greater part in these things than we think. It lies in the nature of all advanced parties to lay only scanty weight on changes already accomplished. The chief object they have in view is always that which does not change—quite a justifiable and useful tendency towards definite aims—the setting of goals. Penetrated by this, such parties fall easily into the habit of maintaining longer than is necessary or useful opinions handed down from the past, in assumptions of which very much has been altered. They overlook or undervalue these changes; they seek for facts which may still make those opinions seem valid, more than they examine the question whether in the face of the totality of the facts appertaining to it, the old opinion has not meanwhile become prejudice.

Such political *à priori* reasoning often appears to me to play a part in dealing with the question of colonies.

In principle it is quite a matter of indifference today to socialism, or the workmen's movement, whether new colonies should prove unsuccessful or not. The assumption that the extension of colonies will restrict the realization of socialism, rests at bottom on the altogether outworn idea that the realization of socialism depends on an increasing narrowing of the circle of the well-to-do and an increasing misery of the poor. That the first is a fable was shown, and the misery theory has now been given up nearly everywhere, if not with all its logical conclusions and outright, yet at least by explaining it away as much as possible.

But even if the theory were right, the colonies about which there is now an interest in Germany are far from being in the position to react so quickly on social conditions at home, that they could only keep off a possible catastrophe for a year. In this respect the German social democracy would have nothing to fear from the colonial policy of the German Empire. And because it is so, because the development of the colonies which Germany has acquired (and of those which it could perhaps win, the same holds good) will take so much time that there can be no question for many a long year of any reaction worth mentioning on the social conditions of Germany. Just from this reason the German social democracy can treat the question of these colonies without prejudice. There can even be no question of a serious reaction of colonial possessions on the political conditions of Germany. Naval chauvinism, for example, stands undoubtedly in close connection with colonial chauvinism, and draws from it a certain nourishment. But the first would also exist without the second, just as Germany had her navy before she thought of the conquest of colonies. It must nevertheless be granted that this connection is the most rational ground for justifying a thorough resistance to a colonial policy.

Otherwise, there is some justification during the acquisition of colonies to examine carefully their value and prospects, and to control the settlement and treatment of the natives as well as the other matters of administration; but that does not amount to a reason for considering such acquisition beforehand as something reprehensible.

Its political position, owing to the present system of government, forbids social democracy from taking more than a critical attitude to these things, and the question whether Germany today needs colonies can, particularly in regard to those colonies that are still to be obtained, be answered in the negative with good authority. But the future has also its rights for us to consider. If we take into account the fact that Germany now imports yearly a considerable amount of colonial produce, we must also say to ourselves that the time may come when it will be desirable to draw at least a part of these products from our own colonies. However speedy socialists may imagine the course of development in Germany towards themselves to be, yet we cannot be blind to the fact that it will need a considerable time before a whole series of other countries are converted to socialism. But if it is not reprehensible to enjoy the produce of tropical plantations, it cannot be so to cultivate such plantations ourselves. Not the whether but the how is here the decisive point. It is neither necessary that the occupation of tropical lands by Europeans should injure the natives in their enjoyment of life, nor has it hitherto usually been the case. Moreover, only a conditional right of savages to the land occupied by them can be recognized. The higher civilization ultimately can claim a higher right. Not the conquest, but the cultivation, of the land gives the historical legal title to its use.

According to my judgment these are the essential points of view which should decide the position of social democracy as regards the question of colonial policy. They also, in practice, would bring about no change worth mentioning in the vote of the party; but we are not only concerned, I repeat, with what would be voted in a given case, but also with the reasons given for the vote.

There are socialists to whom every admission of national interests appears as chauvinism or as an injury to the internationalism and class policy of the proletariat.

It must be admitted that it is not always easy to fix the boundary where the advocacy of the interests of one's nation ceases to be just and to pass into pseudopatriotism; but the remedy for exaggeration on this side certainly does not lie in greater exaggeration on the other. It is much more to be sought in a movement for the exchange of thought between the democracies of the civilized countries and in the support of all factors and institutes working for peace.

Of greater importance today than the question of raising the demands already standing on the program is the question of supplementing the party's program. Here practical development has placed a whole series of questions on the orders of the day which at the drawing up of the program were partly considered to be lying away too far in the future for social democracy to concern itself specially with them, but which were also partly not sufficiently considered in all their bearings. To these belong the agrarian question, the policy of local administration, cooperation, and different matters of industrial law. The great growth of social democracy in the eight years since the drawing up of the Erfurt Program, its reaction on the home politics of Germany as well as its experiences in other lands, have made the more intimate consideration of all these questions imperative, and many views which were formerly held about them have been materially corrected.

Concerning the agrarian question, even those who thought peasant cultivation doomed to decay have considerably changed their views as to the length of time for the completion of this decay. In the later debates on the agrarian policy to be laid down by the social democracy, certainly many differences of opinion have been shown on this point, but in principle they revolved round this—whether, and in a given case to what limit, social democracy should offer assistance to the peasant as an independent farmer against capitalism.

The question is more easily asked than answered. The fact that the great mass of peasants, even if they are not wage earners, yet belong to the working classes, *i.e.* do not maintain existence merely on a title to possessions or on a privilege of birth, places them near the wage-earning class. On the other side they form in Germany such an important fraction of the population that at an election in very many constituencies their votes decide between the capitalist and socialist parties. But if social democracy would not or will not limit itself to being the party of the workers in the sense that it is only the political completion of trade unionism, it must be careful to interest at least a great part of the peasants in the victory of its candidates. In the long run that will only happen if social democracy commits itself to measures which offer an improvement for the small peasants in the immediate future. But with many measures having this object the legislature cannot distinguish between the small and the middle class peasants, and on the other hand they cannot help the peasant as a citizen of the state or as a worker without supporting him at least indirectly as an "undertaker."

This is shown with other things in the program of socialist agrarian policy which Kautsky sketched at the end of his work on the agrarian question under the heading *The Neutralization of the Peasantry*. Kautsky shows most convincingly that even after a victory for social democracy no reason will exist for the abolition of peasants' holdings. But he is at the same time a strong opponent of such measures, or the setting up of such demands, as aim at forming a "protection for peasants" in the sense that they would retain the peasant artificially as an undertaker. He proposes quite a series of reforms, or declares it admissible to support them, which result in relieving the country parishes and in increasing their sources of income. But to what class would these measures be a benefit in the first instance? According to Kautsky's own representation, to the peasants. For, as he shows in another passage of his work, in the country, even under the rule of universal suffrage, there could be no question of an influence of the proleteriat on the affairs of the parish worth mentioning. For that influence is, according to him, too isolated, too backward, too dependent on the few employers of labor who control it. "A communal policy other than one in the interest of the landowner is not to be thought of." Just as little can we think today "of a modern management of the land by the parish in a large cooperative farming enterprise controlled by the village community." But, so far, and so long, as that is so, measures like "amalgamation of the hunting divisions of the great landowners in the community," "nationalization of the taxes for schools, roads, and the poor," would obviously contribute to the improvement of the economic position of the peasants and therewith also to the strengthening of their possessions. Practically, then, they would just work as protection for the peasants.

Under two hypotheses the support of such protection for the peasants appears to me innocuous. First a strong protection of agricultural laborers must go hand in hand with it, and secondly democracy must rule in the commune and the district. Both are assumed by Kautsky. But Kautsky undervalues the influence of agricultural laborers in the democratized country parish. The agricultural laborers are as helpless as he describes them in the passage quoted, only in such districts as lie quite outside commercial intercourse; and their number is always becoming smaller. Usually the agricultural laborer is today tolerably conscious of his interests and with universal suffrage would even become more so. Besides that, there exist in most parishes all kinds of antagonisms among the peasants themselves, and the village community contains, in craftsmen and small traders, elements which in many respects have more in common with the agricultural laborers then with the peasant aristocracy. All that means that the agricultural laborers, except in a very few cases, would not have to make a stand alone against an unbroken "reactionary mass." Democracy has, in the country districts, if it is to exist, to work in the spirit of socialism. I consider democracy in conjunction with the results of the great changes in the system of communication, of transport, a more powerful lever in the emancipation of agricultural laborers than the technical changes in peasant farming.

I refrain from going through all the details of Kautsky's program with which, as I have already remarked, I agree thoroughly in principle; but I believe that a few observations on it ought not to be suppressed. For me, as already observed, the chief task which social democracy now has to fulfil for the agricultural population can be classified under three heads, namely: (1) *The struggle against all the present remnants and supports of feudal landowners, and the fight for democracy in the commune and district.* This involves a fight for the removal of entail, of privileged estate parishes, hunting privileges, etc., as laid down by Kautsky. In Kautsky's formulation "the fullest self-government in the parish and the province," the word "fullest" does not seem to me well chosen, and I would substitute for it the word "democratic." Superlatives are nearly always misleading. "Fullest self-government" can apply to the circle of those entitled to have a say, what it means can be better expressed by "democratic self-government"; but it can also denote the administrative functions, and then it would mean an absolutism of the parish, which neither is necessary nor can be reconciled with the demands of a healthy democracy. The general legislature of the nation stands above the parish, apportioning its definite functions and representing the general interests against its particular interests.

(2) *Protection and relief of the working classes in agriculture.* Under this heading falls the protection of laborers in the narrower

sense: Abolition of regulations for servants, limitation of hours of labor in the various categories of wage earners, sanitary policy regulations, a system of education, as well as measures which free the small peasant as a taxpayer.

(3) *Measures against the absolutism of property and furthering cooperation.* Hereunder would fall demands like "limitation of the rights of private property in the soil with a view to promoting (1) the suppression of adding field to field (2) the cultivation of land (3) prevention of disease" (Kautsky); "reduction of exorbitant rents by courts of justice set up for the purpose" (Kautsky); the building of healthy and comfortable workmen's dwellings by the parish; "facilities for cooperative unions by means of legislation" (Kautsky); the right of the parish to acquire land by purchase or expropriation and to lease it at a cheap rent to workmen and workmen's associations.

This latter demand leads to the question of cooperation. After what has been said in the chapter on the economic possibilities of cooperative associations I need say little here. The question today is no longer whether cooperative associations ought to exist or not. They exist and will exist whether the social democracy desires it or not. By the weight of its influence on the working classes, social democracy certainly can retard the spread of workmen's cooperative societies, but it will not thereby do any service for itself or the working class. The hard-and-dry Manchesterism which is often manifested by sections of the party in regard to cooperation and is grounded on the declaration that there can be no socialist cooperative society within a capitalist society is not justified. It is, on the contrary, important to take a decided position and to be clear which kind of associations social democracy can recommend, and can morally support.

We have seen what an extraordinary advance associations for credit, purchasing, dairy farming, working and selling, make in all modern countries. But these associations in Germany are generally associations of peasants, representatives of the "middle class movement" in the country. I consider it incontrovertible that they, in conjunction with the cheapening of the rate of interest which the increased accumulation of capital brings with it, could indeed help much towards keeping peasant enterprises capable of competing with large enterprises. Consequently, these peasant associations are in most cases the scene of the action of anti-socialist elements, of *petits bourgeois* liberals, clericals, and anti-semites. So far as social democracy is concerned, they can today be put out of reckoning nearly everywhere—even if in their ranks there are here and there small peasants who are nearer to the socialist than to other parties. The middle class peasant takes the lead with them. If social democracy ever had a prospect of winning a stronger influence on the class of the country population referred to by means of cooperation, it has let the opportunity slip.

But if the social democratic party has not the vocation of founding cooperative stores, that does not mean it should take no interest in them. The dearly-loved declaration that cooperative stores are not socialist enterprises, rests on the same formalism which long acted against trade unions, and which now begins to make room for the opposite extreme. Whether a trade union or a workmen's cooperative store is or is not socialistic, does not depend on its form but on its character—on the spirit that permeates it. They are not socialism, but as organizations of workmen they bear in themselves enough of the element of socialism to develop into worthy and indispensable levers for the socialist emancipation. They will certainly best discharge their economic tasks if they are left completely to themselves in their organization and government. But as the aversion and even enmity which many socialists formerly felt against the trade union movement has gradually changed into friendly neutrality and then into the feeling of belonging together, so will it happen with the stores—so has it already happened in some measure.

Those elements, which are enemies not only of the revolutionary, but of every emancipation movement of the workers, by their campaign against the workmen's cooperative stores have obliged the social democracy to step in to support them. Experience has also shown that such fears, as that the cooperative movement would take away intellectual and other forces from the political movement of the workers, were utterly unfounded. In certain places that may be the case temporarily, but in the long run exactly the opposite takes place. Social democracy can look on confidently at the founding of workingmen's cooperative stores where the economic and legal preliminary conditions are found, and it will do well to give it its full good-will and to help it as much as possible.

Only from one point of view could the workmen's cooperative store appear something doubtful in principle—namely, as the good which is in the way of the better, the better being the organization of the purchase and the distribution of commodities through the municipality, as is designed in nearly all socialist systems. But first of all the democratic store, in order to embrace all members of the place in which it is located, needs no alteration in principle, but only a broadening of its constitution, which throughout is in unison with its natural tendencies (in some smaller places cooperative stores are already not far from counting all the inhabitants of the place as their members). Secondly, the realization of this thought still lies such a long way off, and assumes so many political and economic changes and intermediate steps in evolution, that it would be mad to reject with regard to it all the advantages which the workers can draw today from the cooperative store. As far as the district council or parish is concerned we can only through it today provide clearly defined, general needs.

With that we come now to the borough or municipal policy of social democracy. This also for a long time was the stepchild of the socialist movement. It is, for example, not very long ago that in a foreign socialist paper (which has since disappeared), edited by very intellectual folk, the following idea was rejected with scorn as belonging to the *petit bourgeois,* namely, the using of municipalities as the lever of the socialist work of reform without, on that account, neglecting parliamentary action, and the beginning through the municipality of the realization of socialist demands. The irony of fate has willed it that the chief editor of that paper was only able to get into the Parliament of his country on a wave of municipal socialism. Similarly in England, social democracy found in the municipalities a rich field of fruitful activity before it succeeded in sending its own representatives to parliament. In Germany the development was different. Here social democracy had long obtained Parliamentary civil rights before it gained a footing to any extent worth mentioning in the representative bodies of the communes. With its growing extension its success also increased in the elections for local bodies, so that the need for working out a socialist municipal program has been shown more and more, and such has already been drawn up in individual states or provinces. What does social democracy want for the municipality, and what does it expect from the municipality?

With regard to this the Erfurt Program says only "Self-government of the people in empire, state, province, and municipality; election of officials by the people," and demands for all elections the direct right to vote for all adults. It makes no declaration as to the legal relation of the enumerated governing bodies to one another. As shown farther back, I maintain that the law or the decree of the nation has to come from the highest legal authority of the community—the state. But that does not mean that the division line between the rights and powers of the state and the municipality should always be the same as today.

Today, for example, the municipal right of expropriation is very limited, so that a whole series of measures of an economic-political character would find in the opposition, or exaggerated demands, of town landlords a positively insurmountable barrier. An extension of the law of expropriation should accordingly be one of the next demands of municipal socialism. It is not, however, necessary to demand an absolutely unlimited law of expropriation. The municipality would always be bound to keep to the regulations of the common law which protect the individual against the arbitrary action of accidental majorities. Rights of property which the common law allows must be inviolable in every community so long as, and in the measure in which, the common law allows them. To take away lawful property otherwise than by compensation, is confiscation, which can only be justified in cases of extreme pressure of circumstances—war, epidemics.

Social democracy will thus be obliged to demand for the municipality, when the franchise becomes democratic, an extension of the right of expropriation (which is still very limited in various German states) if a socialist policy of local government is to be possible. Further, demands respecting the creation of municipal enterprises and of public services, and a labor policy for the municipality, are rightly put into the forefront of the program. With respect to the first, the following demand should be set up as essential, that all enterprises having a monopolist character and being directed towards the general needs of the members of the municipality must be carried out under its own management, and that, for the rest, the municipality must strive constantly to increase the area of the service it gives to its members. As regards labor policy, we must demand from the municipalities that they, as employers of labor, whether under their own management or under contract, insert as a minimum condition the clauses for wages and hours of labor recognized by the organizations of such workmen, and that they guarantee the right of combination for these workmen. It should, however, be observed here that if it is only right to endeavor to make municipalities as employers of labor surpass private firms with regard to conditions of labor and arrangements for the welfare of the workers, it would be a shortsighted policy for municipal workmen to demand such conditions as would place them, when compared with their fellow workers in the same trades, in the position of an unusually privileged class, and that the municipality should work at a considerably higher cost than the private employer. That would, in the end, lead to corruption and a weakening of public spirit.

Modern evolution has assigned to municipalities further duties: the establishment and superintendence of local sick funds, to which perhaps at a not very distant epoch the taking over of insurance against invalidity will be added. There has further been added the establishment of labor bureaus and industrial arbitration courts. With regard to the labor bureaus the social democracy claims as its minimum demand that their character should be guaranteed by their being composed of an equal representation of workmen and employers; that arbitration courts should be established by compulsion and their powers extended. Social democracy is skeptical of, even if it does not protest against, municipal insurance against unemployment, as the idea prevails that this insurance is one of the legitimate duties of trade unions and can best be cared for by them. But that can only hold good for well organized trades which unfortunately still contain a small minority of the working population. The great mass of workers is still unorganized, and the question is whether municipal insurance against unemployment can, in conjunction with trade unions, be so organized that, so far from being an encroachment on the legitimate functions of the latter, it may even be a means of helping them. In any case it would be the duty of the social democratic representatives of the municipality, where such insurance is undertaken, to press with all their energy for the recognition of the unions.

From its whole nature, municipal socialism is an indispensable lever for forming or completely realizing what I, in the last chapter, called "the democratic right of labor." But it is and must be patchwork where the franchise of the municipality is class franchise. That is the case in more than three-fourths of Germany. And so we stand here, as we do with reference to the diets of the federal states, on which the municipalities depend to a great extent, and to the other organs of self-government (districts, provinces,, etc.), face to face with the question: how will social democracy succeed in removing the existing class franchise and in obtaining the democratization of the electoral systems?

Social democracy has today in Germany, besides the means of

propaganda by speech and writing, the franchise for the Reichstag as the most effective means of asserting its demands. Its influence is so strong that it has extended even to those bodies which have been made inaccessible to the working class owing to a property qualification, or a system of class franchise; for parties must, even in these assemblies, pay attention to the electors for the Reichstag. If the right to vote for the Reichstag were protected from every attack, the question of treating the franchise for other bodies as a subordinate one could be justified to a certain extent, although it would be a mistake to make light of it. But the franchise for the Reichstag is not secure at all. Governments and government parties will certainly not resolve lightly on amending it, for they will say to themselves that such a step would raise amongst the masses of the German workers a hate and bitterness, which they would show in a very uncomfortable way on suitable occasions. The socialist movement is too strong, the political self-consciousness of the German workers is too much developed, to be dealt with in a cavalier fashion. One may venture, also, to assume that a great number even of the opponents of universal suffrage have a certain moral unwillingness to take such a right from the people. But if under normal conditions the curtailing of the franchise would create a revolutionary tension, with all its dangers for the governing classes, there can, on the other hand, be no doubt as to the existence of serious technical difficulties in the way of altering the franchise so as to allow, only as an exception, the success of independent socialist candidatures. It is simply political considerations which, on this question, determine the issue.

On this and other grounds it does not seem advisable to make the policy of social democracy solely dependent on the conditions and possibilities of the imperial franchise. We have, moreover, seen that progress is not so quickened by it as might have been inferred from the electoral successes of 1890 and 1893. Whilst the socialist vote in the triennial period from 1887 to 1890 rose 87 percent, and from 1890 to 1893, 25 percent, in the five years from 1893 to 1898 it only rose 18 percent—an important increase in itself, but not an increase to justify extraordinary expectations in the near future.

Now social democracy depends not exclusively on the franchise and Parliamentary activity. A great and rich field exists for it outside Parliaments. The socialist working class movement would exist even if Parliaments were closed to it. Nothing shows this better than the gratifying movements among the Russian working classes. But with its exclusion from representative bodies the German working class movement would, to a great extent, lose the cohesion which today links its various sections; it would assume a chaotic character, and instead of the steady, uninterrupted forward march with firm steps, jerky forward motions would appear with inevitable back-slidings and exhaustions.

Such a development is neither in the interest of the working classes nor can it appear desirable to those opponents of social democracy who have become convinced that the present social order has not been created for all eternity but is subject to the law of change, and that a catastrophic development with all its horrors and devastation can only be avoided if in legislation consideration is paid to changes in the conditions of production and commerce and to the evolution of the classes. And the number of those who recognize this is steadily increasing. Their influence would be much greater than it is today if the social democracy could find the courage to emancipate itself from a phraseology which is actually outworn and if it would make up its mind to appear what it is in reality today: a democratic, socialistic party of reform.

It is not a question of renouncing the so-called right of revolution, this purely speculative right which can be put in no paragraph of a constitution and which no statute book can prohibit, this right which will last as long as the law of nature forces us to die if we abandon the right to breathe. This imprescriptible and inalienable right is as little touched if we place ourselves on the path of reform as the right of self-defense is done away with when we make laws to regulate our personal and property disputes.

But is social democracy today anything beyond a party that strives after the socialist transformation of society by the means of democratic and economic reform? According to some declarations which were maintained against me at the congress in Stuttgart this might perhaps appear to be the case. But in Stuttgart my letter was taken as an accusation against the party for sailing in the direction of Blanquism, whilst it was really directed against some persons who had attacked me with arguments and figures of speech of a Blanquist nature and who wanted to obtain from the congress a pronouncement against me.

Even a positive verdict from the Stuttgart Congress against my declaration would not have diverted me from my conviction that the great mass of the German social democracy is far removed from fits of Blanquism. After the speech at Oeynhausen I knew that no other attitude of the congress was to be expected than the one which it in fact adopted.

The Oeynhausen speech has since then shared the fate of so many other speeches of extraordinary men, it has been semi-officially corrected. And in what sense has the party expressed itself since Stuttgart? Bebel, in his speeches on the attempts at assassination, has entered the most vigorous protests against the idea that social democracy upholds a policy of force, and all the party organs have reported these speeches with applause; no protest against them has been raised anywhere. Kautsky develops in his *Agrarian Question* the principles of the agrarian policy of social democracy. They form a system of thoroughly democratic reform just as the Communal Program adopted in Brandenburg is a democratic program of reform. In the Reichstag the party supports the extension of the powers and the compulsory establishment of courts of arbitration for trades disputes. These are organs for the furtherance of industrial peace. All the speeches of their representatives breathe reform. In the same Stuttgart where, according to Clara Zetkin, the "Bernstein-iade" received the finishing stroke, shortly after the Congress, the social democrats formed an alliance with the middle class democracy for the municipal elections, and their example was followed in other Wurttemberg towns. In the trade union movement one union after another proceeds to establish funds for out-of-work members, which practically means a giving up of the characteristics of a purely fighting coalition, and declares for municipal labor bureaus embracing equally employers and employees; whilst in various large towns—Hamburg, Elberfeld—cooperative stores have been started by socialists and trade unionists. Everywhere there is action for reform, action for social progress, action for the victory of democracy. "People study the details of the problems of the day and seek for levers and starting points to carry on the development of society in the direction of socialism." Thus I wrote a year ago, and I see no reason to induce me to delete a word of it.

Translated by Edith C. Harvey

Rosa Luxemburg

Reform or Revolution?

At present, the trade union struggle and parliamentary practice are considered to be the means of guiding and educating the proletariat in preparation for the task of taking over power. From the revisionist standpoint, this conquest of power is at the same time impossible and useless. And therefore, trade union and parliamentary activity are to be carried on by the party only for their immediate results, that is, for the purpose of bettering the present situation of the workers, for the gradual reduction of capitalist exploitation, for the extension of social control.

So that if we do not consider momentarily the immediate amelioration of the workers' condition—an objective common to our party program as well as to revisionism—the difference between the two outlooks is, in brief, the following. According to the present conception of the party, trade union and parliamentary activity are important for the socialist movement because such activity prepares the proletariat, that is to say, creates the *subjective* factor of the socialist transformation, for the task of realizing socialism. But according to Bernstein, trade unions and parliamentary activity gradually reduce capitalist exploitation itself. They remove from capitalist society its capitalist character. They realize *objectively* the desired social change.

Examining the matter closely, we see that the two conceptions are diametrically opposed. Viewing the situation from the current standpoint of our party, we say that as a result of its trade union and parliamentary struggles, the proletariat becomes convinced of the impossibility of accomplishing a fundamental social change through such activity and arrives at the understanding that the conquest of power is unavoidable. Bernstein's theory, however, begins by declaring that this conquest is impossible. It concludes by affirming that socialism can only be introduced as a result of the trade union struggle and parliamentary activity. For as seen by Bernstein, trade union and parliamentary action has a socialist character because it exercises a progressively socializing influence on capitalist economy.

We tried to show that this influence is purely imaginary. The relations between capitalist property and the capitalist State develop in entirely opposite directions, so that the daily practical activity of the present social democracy loses, in the last analysis, all connection with work for socialism. From the viewpoint of a movement for socialism, the trade-union struggle and our parliamentary practice are vastly important in so far as they make socialistic the *awareness,* the consciousness, of the proletariat and help to organize it as a class. But once they are considered as instruments of the direct socialization of capitalist economy, they lose not only their usual effectiveness but cease being means of preparing the working class for the conquest of power. Eduard Bernstein and Konrad Schmidt suffer from a complete misunderstanding when they console themselves with the belief that even though the program of the party is reduced to work for social reforms and ordinary trade-union work, the final objective of the labor movement is not thereby discarded, for each forward step reaches beyond the given immediate aim and the socialist goal is implied as a tendency in the supposed advance.

That is certainly true about the present procedure of the German social democracy. It is true whenever a firm and conscious effort for the conquest of political power impregnates the trade-union struggle and the work for social reforms. But if this effort is separated from the movement itself and social reforms are made an end in themselves, then such activity not only does not lead to the final goal of socialism but moves in a precisely opposite direction.

Konrad Schmidt simply falls back on the idea that an apparently mechanical movement, once started, cannot stop by itself, because "one's appetite grows with eating," and the working class will not supposedly content itself with reforms till the final socialist transformation is realized.

Now the last mentioned condition is quite real. Its effectiveness is guaranteed by the very insufficiency of capitalist reforms. But the conclusion drawn from it could only be true if it were possible to construct an unbroken chain of augmented reforms leading from the capitalism of today to socialism. This is, of course, sheer fantasy. In accordance with the nature of things as they are, the chain breaks quickly, and the paths that the supposed forward movement can take from that point on are many and varied.

What will be the immediate result should our party change its general procedure to suit a viewpoint that wants to emphasize the practical results of our struggle, that is, social reforms? As soon as "immediate results" become the principal aim of our activity, the clear-cut, irreconcilable point of view, which has meaning only in so far as it proposes to win power, will be found more and more inconvenient. The direct consequence of this will be the adoption by the party of a "policy of compensation," a policy of political trading, and an attitude of diffident, diplomatic conciliation. But this attitude cannot be continued for a long time. Since the social reforms can only offer an empty promise, the logical consequence of such a program must necessarily be disillusionment.

It is not true that socialism will arise automatically from the daily struggle of the working class. Socialism will be the consequence of (1) the growing contradictions of capitalist economy and (2) of the comprehension by the working class of the unavoidability of the suppression of these contradictions through a social transformation. When, in the manner of revisionism, the first condition is denied and the second rejected, the labor movement finds itself reduced to a simple corporative and reformist movement. We move here in a straight line toward the total abandonment of the class viewpoint.

This consequence also becomes evident when we investigate the general character of revisionism. It is obvious that revisionism does not wish to concede that its standpoint is that of the capitalist apologist. It does not join the bourgeois economists in denying the existence of the contradictions of capitalism. But, on the other hand, what precisely constitutes the fundamental point of revisionism and distinguishes it from the attitude taken by the social democracy up to now, is that it does not base its theory on the belief that the contradictions of capitalism will be suppressed as a result of the logical inner development of the present economic system.

We may say that the theory of revisionism occupies an intermediate place between two extremes. Revisionism does not expect to see the contradictions of capitalism mature. It does not propose to suppress these contradictions through a revolutionary transformation. It wants to lessen, to attenuate, the capitalist contradictions. So that the antagonism existing between production and exchange is to be mollified by the cessation of crises and the formation of capitalist combines. The antagonism between capital and labor is to be adjusted by bettering the situation of the workers and by the conservation of the middle classes. And the contradiction between the class state and society is to be liquidated through increased state control and the progress of democracy.

It is true that the present procedure of the social democracy does not consist in waiting for the antagonisms of capitalism to develop and in passing on, only then, to the task of suppressing them. On the contrary, the essence of revolutionary procedure is to be guided by the direction of this development, once it is ascertained, and inferring from this direction what consequences are necessary for the political struggle. Thus the social democracy has combatted tariff wars and militarism without waiting for their reactionary character to become fully evident. Bernstein's procedure is not guided by a consideration of the development of capitalism, by the prospect of the aggravation of its contradictions. It is guided by the prospect of the attenuation of these contradictions. He shows this when he speaks of the "adaptation" of capitalist economy.

Now when can such a conception be correct? If it is true that capitalism will continue to develop in the direction it takes at present, then its contradictions must necessarily become sharper and more aggravated instead of disappearing. The possibility of the attenuation of the contradictions of capitalism presupposes that the capitalist mode of production itself will stop its progress. In short, the general condition of Bernstein's theory is the cessation of capitalist development.

This way, however, his theory condemns itself in a twofold manner.

In the first place, it manifests its *utopian* character in its stand on the establishment of socialism. For it is clear that a defective capitalist development cannot lead to a socialist transformation.

In the second place, Bernstein's theory reveals its *reactionary* character when it is referred to the rapid capitalist development that is taking place at present. Given the development of real capitalism, how can we explain, or rather state, Bernstein's position?

We have demonstrated in the first chapter the baselessness of the economic conditions on which Bernstein builds his analysis of existing social relationships. We have seen that neither the credit system nor cartels can be said to be "means of adaptation" of capitalist economy. We have seen that not even the temporary cessation of crises nor the survival of the middle class can be regarded as symptoms of capitalist adaptation. But even though we should fail to take into account the erroneous character of all these details of Bernstein's theory, we cannot help but be stopped short by one feature common to all of them. Bernstein's theory does not seize these manifestations of contemporary economic life as they appear in their organic relationship with the whole of capitalist development, with the complete economic mechanism of capitalism. His theory pulls these details out of their living economic context. It treats them as the *disjecta membra* (separate parts) of a lifeless machine.

Consider, for example, his conception of the adaptive effect of *credit*. If we recognize credit as a higher natural stage of the process of exchange and, therefore, of the contradictions inherent in capitalist exchange, we cannot at the same time see it as a mechanical means of adaptation existing outside of the process of exchange. It would be just as impossible to consider money, merchandise, capital as "means of adaptation" of capitalism.

However, credit, like money, commodities, and capital, is an organic link of capitalist economy at a certain stage of its development. Like them, it is an indispensable gear in the mechanism of capitalist economy and at the same time, an instrument of destruction, since it aggravates the internal contradictions of capitalism.

The same thing is true about cartels and the new, perfected means of communication.

The same mechanical view is presented by Bernstein's attempt to describe the promise of the cessation of crises as a symptom of the "adaptation" of capitalist economy. For him, crises are simply derangements of the economic mechanism. With their cessation, he thinks, the mechanism could function well. But the fact is that crises are not "derangements" in the usual sense of the word. They are "derangements" without which capitalist economy could not develop at all. For if crises constitute the only method possible in capitalism—and therefore the normal method—of solving periodically the conflict existing between the unlimited extension of production and the narrow limits of the world market, then crises are an organic manifestation inseparable from capitalist economy.

In the "unhindered" advance of capitalist production lurks a threat to capitalism that is much graver than crises. It is the threat of the constant fall of the rate of profit, resulting not from the contradiction between production and exchange, but from the growth of the productivity of labor itself. The fall in the rate of profit has the extremely dangerous tendency of rendering impossible any enterprise for small and middle-sized capitals. It thus limits the new formation and therefore the extension of placements of capital.

And it is precisely crises that constitute the other consequence of the same process. As a result of their periodic *depreciation* of capital, crises bring a fall in the prices of means of production, a paralysis of a part of the active capital, and in time the increase of profits. They thus create the possibilities of the renewed advance of production. Crises therefore appear to be the instruments of rekindling the fire of capitalist development. Their cessation—not temporary cessation, but their total disappearance in the world market— would not lead to the further development of capitalist economy. It would destroy capitalism.

True to the mechanical view of his theory of adaptation, Bernstein forgets the necessity of crises as well as the necessity of new placements of small and middle-sized capitals. And that is why the constant reappearance of small capital seems to him to be the sign of the cessation of capitalist development though, it is, in fact, a symptom of normal capitalist development.

It is important to note that there is a viewpoint from which all the above mentioned phenomena are seen exactly as they have been presented by the theory of "adaptation." It is the viewpoint of the isolated (single) capitalist, who reflects in his mind the economic facts around him just as they appear when refracted by the laws of competition. The isolated capitalist sees each organic part of the whole of our economy as an independent entity. He sees them as they act on him, the single capitalist. He therefore considers these facts to be simple "derangements" of simple "means of adaptation." For the isolated capitalist, it is true, crises are really simple derangements; the cessation of crises accords him a longer existence. As far as he is concerned, credit is only a means of "adapting" his insufficient productive forces to the needs of the market. And it seems to him that the cartel of which he becomes a member really suppresses industrial anarchy.

Revisionism is nothing else than a theoretic generalization made from the angle of the isolated capitalist. Where does this viewpoint belong theoretically if not in vulgar bourgeois economics?

All the errors of this school rest precisely on the conception that mistakes the phenomena of competition, as seen from the angle of the isolated capitalist, for the phenomena of the whole of capitalist economy. Just as Bernstein considers credit to be a means of "adaptation" so vulgar economy considers money to be a judicious means of "adaptation" to the needs of exchange. Vulgar economy, too, tries to find the antidote against the ills of capitalism in the phenomena of capitalism. Like Bernstein, it believes that it is possible to regulate capitalist economy. And in the manner of Bernstein, it arrives in time at the desire to palliate the contradictions of capitalism, that is, at the belief in the possibility of patching up the sores of capitalism. It ends up by subscribing to a program of reaction. It ends up in a utopia.

The theory of revisionism can therefore be defined in the following way. It is a theory of standing still in the socialist movement, built, with the aid of vulgar economy, on a theory of a capitalist standstill.

*　*　*

Bernstein's socialism offers to the workers the prospect of sharing in the wealth of society. The poor are to become rich. How will this socialism be brought about? His articles in the *Neue Zeit (Problems of Socialism)* contain only vague allusions to this question. Adequate information, however, can be found in his book.

Bernstein's socialism is to be realized with the aid of these two instruments: labor unions—or as Bernstein himself characterizes them, economic democracy—and cooperatives. The first will suppress industrial profit; the second will do away with commercial profit.

Cooperatives—especially cooperatives in the field of production constitute a hybrid form in the midst of capitalism. They can be described as small units of socialized production within capitalist exchange.

But in capitalist economy exchange dominates production.* As a result of competition, the complete domination of the process of

---

*That is, production depends to a large extent on market possibilities.

production by the interests of capital—that is, pitiless exploitation—becomes a condition for the survival of each enterprise. The domination of capital over the process of production expresses itself in the following ways. Labor is intensified. The work day is lengthened or shortened according to the situation of the market. And, depending on the requirements of the market, labor is either employed or thrown back into the street. In other words; use is made of all methods that enable an enterprise to stand up against its competitors in the market. The workers forming a cooperative in the field of production are thus faced with the contradictory necessity of governing themselves with the utmost absolutism. They are obliged to take toward themselves the role of the capitalist entrepreneur—a contradiction that accounts for the usual failure of production cooperatives which either become pure capitalist enterprises or, if the workers' interests continue to predominate, end by dissolving.

Bernstein has himself taken note of these facts. But it is evident that he has not understood them. For, together with Mrs. Potter-Webb, he explains the failure of production cooperatives in England by their lack of "discipline." But what is so superficially and flatly called here "discipline" is nothing else than the natural absolutist regime of capitalism, which, it is plain, the workers cannot successfully use against themselves.*

Producers' cooperatives can survive within capitalist economy only if they manage to suppress, by means of some detour, the capitalist contradiction between the mode of production and the mode of exchange. And they can accomplish this only by removing themselves artifically from the influence of the laws of free competition. And they can succeed in doing the last only when they assure themselves beforehand of a constant circle of consumers, that is, when they assure themselves of a constant market.

It is the consumers' cooperative that can offer this service to its brother in the field of production. Here—and not in Oppenheimer's distinction between cooperatives that purchase and cooperatives that sell—is the secret sought by Bernstein: the explanation for the invariable failure of producers' cooperatives functioning independently and their survival when they are backed by consumers' organizations.

---

*The cooperative factories of the laborers themselves represent within the old form the first beginnings of the new, although they naturally reproduce, and must reproduce, everywhere in their actual organization all the shortcomings of the prevailing system.—*Capital,* vol. III, p. 521.

If it is true that the possibilities of existence of producers' cooperatives within capitalism are bound up with the possibilities of existence of consumers' cooperatives, then the scope of the former is limited, in the most favorable of cases, to the small local market and to the manufacture of articles serving immediate needs, especially food products. Consumers', and therefore producers' cooperatives, are excluded from the most important branches of capital production—the textile, mining, metallurgical and petroleum industries, machine construction, locomotive and shipbuilding. For this reason alone (forgetting for the moment their hybrid character), cooperatives in the field of production cannot be seriously considered as the instrument of a general social transformation. The establishment of producers' cooperatives on a wide scale would suppose, first of all, the suppression of the world market, the breaking up of the present world economy into small local spheres of production and exchange. The highly developed, wide-spread capitalism of our time is expected to fall back to the merchant economy of the Middle Ages.

Within the framework of present society, producers' cooperatives are limited to the role of simple annexes to consumers' cooperatives. It appears, therefore, that the latter must be the beginning of the proposed social change. But this way the expected reform of society by means of cooperatives ceases to be an offensive against capitalist production. That is, it ceases to be an attack against the principal bases of capitalist economy. It becomes, instead, a struggle against commercial capital, especially small and middle-sized commercial capital. It becomes an attack made on the twigs of the capitalist tree.

According to Bernstein, trade unions too, are a means of attack against capitalism in the field of production. We have already shown that trade unions cannot give the workers a determining influence over production. Trade unions can neither determine the dimensions of production nor the technical progress of production.

This much may be said about the purely economic side of the "struggle of the rate of wages against the rate of profit," as Bernstein labels the activity of the trade union. It does not take place in the blue of the sky. It takes place within the well defined framework of the law of wages. The law of wages is not shattered but applied by trade-union activity.

According to Bernstein, it is the trade unions that lead—in the general movement for the emancipation of the working class—the real attack against the rate of industrial profit. According to Bernstein, trade unions have the task of transforming the rate of industrial profit into "rates of wages." The fact is that trade unions are least able to execute an economic offensive against profit. Trade unions are nothing more than the organized *defense* of labor power against the attacks of profit. They express the resistance offered by the working class to the oppression of capitalist economy.

On the one hand, trade unions have the function of influencing the situation in the labor-power market. But this influence is being constantly overcome by the proletarianization of the middle layers of our society, a process which continually brings new merchandise on the labor market. The second function of the trade unions is to ameliorate the condition of the workers. That is, they attempt to increase the share of the social wealth going to the working class. This share, however, is being reduced, with the fatality of a natural process, by the growth of the productivity of labor. One does not need to be a Marxist to notice this. It suffices to read Rodbertus's *In Explanation of the Social Question*.

In other words, the objective conditions of capitalist society transform the two economic functions of the trade unions into a sort of labor Sisyphus,* who is, nevertheless, indispensable. For as a result of the activity of his trade unions, the worker succeeds in obtaining for himself the rate of wages due to him in accordance with the situation of the labor-power market. As a result of trade union activity, the capitalist law of wages is applied and the effect of the depressing tendency of economic development is paralyzed, or to be more exact, is attenuated.

However, the transformation of the trade union into an instrument for the progressive reduction of profit in favor of wages presupposes the following social conditions; first, the cessation of the proletarianization of the middle strata of our society; secondly, a stoppage of the growth of productivity of labor. We have in both cases *a return to precapitalist conditions*.

Cooperatives and trade unions are totally incapable of transforming the *capitalist mode of production*. This is really understood by Bernstein though in a confused manner. For he refers to cooperatives and trade unions as a means of reducing the profit of the capitalists and thus enriching the workers. In this way, he renounces

---

*The mythological king of Corinth who in the lower world was condemned to roll to the top of a hill a huge stone, which constantly rolled back again, making his task incessant.

the struggle against the *capitalist mode of production* and attempts to direct the socialist movement to struggle against "capitalist distribution."* Again and again, Bernstein refers to socialism as an effort toward a "just, juster and still more just" mode of distribution (*Vorwaerts*, March 26, 1899).

It cannot be denied that the direct cause leading the popular masses into the socialist movement is precisely the "unjust" mode of distribution characteristic of capitalism. When the social democracy struggles for the socialization of the entire economy, it aspires therewith also to a "just" distribution of the social wealth. But, guided by Marx's observation that the mode of distribution of a given epoch is a natural consequence of the mode of production of that epoch, the social democracy does not struggle against distribution in the framework of capitalist production. It struggles instead for the suppression of capitalist production itself. In a word, the social democracy wants to establish the mode of socialist distribution by suppressing the capitalist mode of production. Bernstein's method, on the contrary, proposes to combat the capitalist mode of distribution in the hope of gradually establishing, in this way, the socialist mode of production.

What, in that case, is the basis of Bernstein's program for the reform of society? Does it find support in definite tendencies of capitalist production? No. In the first place, he denies such tendencies. In the second place, the socialist transformation of production is for him the effect and not the cause of distribution. He cannot give his program a materialist base, because he has already overthrown the aims, and the means of the movement for socialism, and therefore its economic conditions. As a result, he is obliged to construct himself an idealist base.

"Why represent socialism as the consequence of economic compulsion?" he complains. "Why degrade man's understanding, his feeling for justice, his will?" (*Vorwaerts*, March 26, 1899). Bernstein's superlatively just distribution is to be attained thanks to man's free will, man's will acting not because of economic necessity, since this will itself is only an instrument, but because of man's comprehension of justice, because of man's *idea of justice*.

We thus quite happily return to the principle of justice, to the old war horse on which the reformers of the earth have rocked for ages,

---

*The term used by Bernstein to describe the allocation of the total social wealth to the several sections of capitalist society.

for the lack of surer means of historic transportation. We return to that lamentable Rosinante on which the Don Quixotes of history have galloped toward the great reform of the earth, always to come home with their eyes blackened.

The relation of the poor to the rich, taken as a base for socialism, the principle of cooperation as the content of socialism, the "most just distribution" as its aim, and the idea of justice as its only historic legitimation—with how much more force, more wit, and more fire did Weitling defend that sort of socialism fifty years ago. However, that genius of a tailor did not know scientific socialism. If today the conception torn into bits by Marx and Engels a half century ago is patched up and presented to the proletariat as the last word of social science, that, too, is the art of a tailor, but it has nothing of genius about it.

Trade unions and cooperatives are the economic points of support for the theory of revisionism. Its principal political condition is the growth of democracy. The present manifestations of political reaction are to Bernstein only "displacements." He considers them accidental, momentary, and suggests that they are not to be considered in the elaboration of the general directives of the labor movement.

To Bernstein, democracy is an inevitable stage in the development of society. To him, as to the bourgeois theoreticians of liberalism, democracy is the great fundamental law of historic development, the realization of which is served by all the forces of political life. However, Bernstein's thesis is completely false. Presented in this absolute form, it appears as a petty-bourgeois vulgarization of the results of a very short phase of bourgeois development, the last twenty-five or thirty years. We reach entirely different conclusions when we examine the historic development of democracy a little closer and consider at the same time the general political history of capitalism.

Democracy has been found in the most dissimilar social formations: in primitive communist groups, in the slave states of antiquity, and in the medieval communes. And similarly absolutism and constitutional monarchy are to be found under the most varied economic orders. When capitalism began, as the first production of commodities, it resorted to a democratic constitution in the municipal communes of the Middle Ages. Later, when it developed to manufacturing, capitalism found its corresponding political form in the absolute monarchy. Finally, as a developed industrial economy, it brought into being in France the democratic republic of 1793, the absolute monarchy of Napoleon I, the nobles' monarchy of the Restoration period (1815–1830), the bourgeois constitutional monarchy of Louis-Philippe, then again the democratic republic, and again the monarchy of Napoleon III, and finally, for the third time, the Republic. In Germany, the only true democratic institution—universal suffrage—is not a conquest won by bourgeois liberalism. Universal suffrage in Germany was an instrument for the fusion of the small States. It is only in this sense that it has any importance for the development of the German bourgeoisie, which is otherwise quite satisfied with a semi-feudal constitutional monarchy. In Russia, capitalism prospered for a long time under the regime of Oriental absolutism, without having the bourgeoisie manifest the least desire in the world to introduce democracy. In Austria, universal suffrage was above all a safety line thrown to a foundering and decomposing monarchy. In Belgium, the conquest of universal suffrage by the labor movement was undoubtedly due to the weakness of the local militarism, and consequently to the special geographic and political situation of the country. But we have here a "bit of democracy" that has been won not by the bourgeoisie but *against* it.

The uninterrupted victory of democracy, which to our revisionism, as well as to bourgeois liberalism, appears as a great fundamental law of human history and, especially of modern history, is shown, upon closer examination, to be a phantom. No absolute and general relation can be constructed between capitalist development and democracy. The political form of a given country is always the result of the composite of all the existing political factors, domestic as well as foreign. It admits within its limits all variations of the scale, from absolute monarchy to the democratic republic.

We must abandon, therefore, all hope of establishing democracy as a general law of historic development, even within the framework of modern society. Turning to the present phase of bourgeois society, we observe here, too, political factors which, instead of assuring the realization of Bernstein's schema, lead rather to the abandonment by bourgeois society of the democratic conquests won up to now.

Democratic institutions—and this is of the greatest significance—have completely exhausted their function as aids in the development of bourgeois society. Insofar as they were necessary to bring about the fusion of small states and the creation of large modern states

(Germany, Italy), they are no longer indispensable at present. Economic development has meanwhile effected an internal organic cicatrization.

The same thing can be said concerning the transformation of the entire political and administrative state machinery from feudal or semi-feudal mechanism to capitalist mechanism. While this transformation has been historically inseparable from the development of democracy, it has been realized today to such an extent that the purely democratic "ingredients" of society, such as universal suffrage and the republican state form, may be suppressed without having the administration, the state finances, or the military organization find it necessary to return to the forms they had before the March Revolution (of 1848–*eds.*).*

If liberalism as such is now absolutely useless to bourgeois society, it has become, on the other hand, a direct impediment to capitalism from other standpoints: Two factors dominate completely the political life of contemporary states: world politics and the labor movement. Each is only a different aspect of the present phase of capitalist development.

As a result of the development of the world economy and the aggravation and generalization of competition on the world market, militarism and the policy of big navies have become, as instruments of world politics, a decisive factor in the interior as well as in the exterior life of the great states. If it is true that world politics and militarism represent a *rising* tendency in the present phase of capitalism, then bourgeois democracy must logically move in a descending line.

In Germany, the era of great armament, begun in 1893, and the policy of world politics, inaugurated with the seizure of Kiao-Cheou, were paid for immediately with the following sacrificial victim: the decomposition of liberalism, the deflation of the Center party, which passed from opposition to government. The recent elections to the Reichstag of 1907, unrolling under the sign of the German colonial policy were at the same time the historical burial of German liberalism.

If foreign politics push the bourgeoisie into the arms of reaction, this is no less true about domestic politics—thanks to the rise of the working class. Bernstein shows that he recognizes this when he

---

*The German revolution of 1848, which struck an effective blow against the feudal institutions in Germany.

makes the social democratic "legend," which "wants to swallow everything"—in other words, the socialist efforts of the working class—responsible for the desertion of the liberal bourgeoisie. He advises the proletariat to disavow its socialist aim, so that the mortally frightened liberals might come out of the mouse hole of reaction. Making the suppression of the socialist labor movement an essential condition for the preservation of bourgeois democracy, he proves in a striking manner that this democracy is in complete contradiction with the inner tendency of development of the present society. He proves at the same time that the socialist movement is itself a *direct product* of this tendency.

But he proves, at the same time, still another thing. By making the renouncement of the socialist aim an essential condition of the resurrection of bourgeois democracy, he shows how inexact is the claim that bourgeois democracy is an indispensable condition of the socialist movement and the victory of socialism. Bernstein's reasoning exhausts itself in a vicious circle. His conclusion swallows his premises.

The solution is quite simple. In view of the fact that bourgeois liberalism has given up its ghost from fear of the growing labor movement and its final aim, we conclude that the socialist labor movement is today the *only* support for that which is not the goal of the socialist movement—democracy. We must conclude that democracy can have no other support. We must conclude that the socialist movement is not bound to bourgeois democracy, but that, on the contrary, the fate of democracy is bound with the socialist movement. We must conclude from this that democracy does not acquire greater chances of life in the measure that the working class renounces the struggle for its emancipation, but that, on the contrary, democracy acquires greater chances of survival as the socialist movement becomes sufficiently strong to struggle against the reactionary consequences of world politics and the bourgeois desertion of democracy. He who would strengthen democracy should want to strengthen and not weaken the socialist movement. He who renounces the struggle for socialism renounces both the labor movement and democracy.

* * *

Bernstein began his revision of social democracy by abandoning the theory of capitalist collapse. The latter, however, is the cornerstone of scientific socialism. Rejecting it, Bernstein also rejects the whole doctrine of socialism. In the course of his discussion, he abandons one after another of the positions of socialism in order to be able to maintain his first affirmation.

Without the collapse of capitalism the expropriation of the capitalist class is impossible. Bernstein therefore renounces expropriation and chooses a progressive realization of the "cooperative principle" as the aim of the labor movement.

But cooperation cannot be realized within capitalist production. Bernstein, therefore, renounces the socialization of production, and merely proposes to reform commerce and to develop consumers' cooperatives.

But the transformation of society through consumers' cooperatives, even by means of trade unions, is incompatible with the real material development of capitalist society. Therefore, Bernstein abandons the materialist conception of history.

But his conception of the march of economic development is incompatible with the Marxist theory of surplus-value. Therefore, Bernstein abandons the theory of value and surplus-value and, in this way, the whole economic system of Karl Marx.

But the struggle of the proletariat cannot be carried on without a given final aim and without an economic base found in the existing society. Bernstein, therefore, abandons the class struggle and speaks of reconciliation with bourgeois liberalism.

But in a class society, the class struggle is a natural and unavoidable phenomenon. Bernstein, therefore, contests even the existence of classes in society. The working class is for him a mass of individuals, divided politically and intellectually, but also economically. And the bourgeoisie, according to him, does not group itself politically in accordance with its inner economic interest, but only because of exterior pressure from above and below.

But if there is no economic base for the class struggle and, if, consequently, there are no classes in our society, not only the future, but even the past struggles, of the proletariat against the bourgeoisie appear to be impossible and the social democracy and its successes seem absolutely incomprehensible, or they can be understood only as the results of political pressure by the government—that is, not as the natural consequences of historic development but as the fortuitous consequences of the policy of the Hohenzollern; not as the legitimate offspring of capitalist society, but as the bastard children of reaction. Rigorously logical in this respect, Bernstein passes from the materialistic conception of history to the outlook of the *Frankfurter Zeitung* and the *Vossische Zeitung*.

After rejecting the socialist criticism of capitalist society, it is easy for Bernstein to find the present state of affairs satisfactory—at least in a general way. Bernstein does not hesitate. He discovers that at the present time reaction is not very strong in Germany, that "we cannot speak of political reaction in the countries of Western Europe," and that in all the countries of the West "the attitude of the bourgeois classes toward the socialist movement is at most an attitude of defense but not one of oppression" (*Vorwaerts*, March 26, 1899). Far from becoming worse, the situation of the workers is getting better. Indeed, the bourgeoisie is politically progressive and morally sane. We cannot speak either of reaction or oppression. It is all for the best in the best of all possible worlds. . . .

Bernstein thus travels in logical sequence from A to Z. He began by abandoning the *final aim* and supposedly keeping the movement. But as there can be no socialist movement without a socialist aim, he ends by renouncing the *movement*.

And thus Bernstein's conception of socialism collapses entirely. The proud and admirable symmetric construction of socialist thought becomes for him a pile of rubbish, in which the debris of all systems, the pieces of thought of various great and small minds, find a common resting place. Marx and Proudhon, Leon von Buch and Franz Oppenheimer, Friedrich Albert Lange and Kant, Herr Prokopovitch and Dr. Ritter von Neupauer, Herkner and Schulze-Gaevernitz, Lassalle and Professor Julius Wolff: all contribute something to Bernstein's system. From each he takes a little. There is nothing astonishing about that. For when he abandoned scientific socialism, he lost the axis of intellectual crystallization around which isolated facts group themselves in the organic whole of a coherent conception of the world.

His doctrine, composed of bits of all possible systems, seems upon first consideration, to be completely free from prejudices. For Bernstein does not like talk of "party science," or to be more exact, of class science, any more than he likes to talk of class liberalism or class morality. He thinks he succeeds in expressing human, general, abstract science, abstract liberalism, abstract morality. But since the society of reality is made up of classes, which have diametrically opposed interests, aspirations and conceptions, a general human science in social questions, an abstract liberalism, an abstract morality, are at present illusions, pure utopia. The science, the democracy, the morality, considered by Bernstein as general, human, are merely the dominant science, dominant democracy, and dominant morality, that is, bourgeois science, bourgeois democracy, bourgeois morality.

When Bernstein rejects the economic doctrine of Marx in order to swear by the teachings of Bretano, Boehm-Bawerk, Jevons, Say, and Julius Wolff, he exchanges the scientific base of the emancipation of the working class for the apologetics of the bourgeoisie. When he speaks of the generally human character of liberalism and transforms socialism into a variety of liberalism, he deprives the socialist movement (generally) of its class character, and consequently of its historic content, consequently of all content; and conversely, recognizes the class representing liberalism in history, the bourgeoisie, as the champion of the general interests of humanity.

And when he wars against "raising of the material factors to the rank of an all-powerful force of development," when he protests against the so-called "contempt for the ideal" that is supposed to rule the social democracy, when he presumes to talk for idealism, for morals, pronouncing himself at the same time against the only source of the moral rebirth of the proletariat, a revolutionary class struggle—he does no more than the following: preach to the working class the quintessence of the morality of the bourgeoisie, that is, reconciliation with the existing social order and the transfer of the hopes of the proletariat to the limbo of ethical simulacra.

When he directs his keenest arrows against our dialectic system, he is really attacking the specific mode of thought employed by the conscious proletariat in its struggle for liberation. It is an attempt to break the sword that has helped the proletariat to pierce the darkness of its future. It is an attempt to shatter the intellectual arm with the aid of which the proletariat, though materially under the yoke of the bourgeoisie, is yet enabled to triumph over the bourgeoisie. For it is our dialectical system that shows to the working class the transitory character of this yoke, proving to the workers the inevitability of their victory, and is already realizing a revolution in the domain of thought. Saying good-bye to our system of dialectics, and resorting instead to the intellectual see-saw of the well-known "on one hand—on the other hand," "yes—but," "although—however," "more—less," etc., he quite logically lapses into a mode of thought that belongs historically to the bourgeoisie in decline, being the faithful intellectual reflection of the social existence and political activity of the bourgeoisie at that stage. The political "on one hand—on the other hand," "yes—but" of the bourgeoisie of today resembles in a marked degree Bernstein's manner of thinking, which is the sharpest and surest proof of the bourgeois nature of his conception of the world.

But, as it is used by Bernstein, the word "bourgeois" itself is not a class expression but a general social notion. Logical to the end he has exchanged, together with his science, politics, morals and mode of thinking, the historic language of the proletariat for that of the bourgeosie. When he uses, without distinction, the term "citizen" in reference to the bourgeois as well as to the proletarian, intending, thereby, to refer to man in general, he identifies man in general with the bourgeois, and human society with bourgeois society.

* * *

Bernstein's book is of great importance to the German and the international labor movement. It is the first attempt to give a theoretic base to the opportunist currents common in the social democracy.

These currents may be said to have existed for a long time in our movement, if we take into consideration such sporadic manifestations of opportunism as the question of subsidization of steamers. But it is only since about 1890, with the suppression of the antisocialist laws, that we have had a trend of opportunism of a clearly defined character. Vollmann's "state socialism," the vote on the Bavarian budget, the "agrarian socialism" of South Germany, Heine's policy of compensation, Schippel's stand on tariffs and militarism, are the high points in the development of our opportunist practice.

What appears to characterize this practice above all? A certain hostility to "theory." This is quite natural, for our "theory," that is, the principles of scientific socialism, impose clearly marked limitations to practical activity—insofar as it concerns the aims of this activity, the means used in attaining these aims, and the method employed in this activity. It is quite natural for people who run after immediate "practical" results to want to free themselves from such limitations and to render their practice independent of our "theory."

However, this outlook is refuted by every attempt to apply it in reality. State socialism, agrarian socialism, the policy of compensation, the question of the army, all constituted defeats to our opportunism. It is clear that, if this current is to maintain itself, it must try to destroy the principles of our theory and elaborate a theory of its own. Bernstein's book is precisely an effort in that direction. That is why at Stuttgart all the opportunist elements in our party immediately grouped themselves about Bernstein's banner. If the opportunist currents in the practical activity of our party are an entirely natural phenomenon which can be explained in light of the special conditions of our activity and its development, Bernstein's theory is no less natural an attempt to group these currents into a general theoretic expression, an attempt to elaborate its own theoretic conditions and to break with scientific socialism. That is why the published expression of Bernstein's ideas should be recognized as a theoretic test for opportunism, and as its first scientific legitimation.

What was the result of this test? We have seen the result. Opportunism is not in a position to elaborate a positive theory capable of withstanding criticism. All it can do is to attack various isolated theses of Marxist theory and, just because Marxist doctrine constitutes one solidly constructed edifice, hope by this means to shake the entire system, from the top to its foundation.

This shows that opportunist practice is essentially irreconcilable with Marxism. But it also proves that opportunism is incompatible with socialism (the socialist movement) in general, that its internal tendency is to push the labor movement into bourgeois paths, that opportunism tends to paralyze completely the proletarian class struggle. The latter, considered historically, has evidently nothing to do with Marxist doctrine. For, *before Marx* and independently from him, there have been labor movements and various socialist doctrines, each of which, in its way, was the theoretic expression, corresponding to the conditions of the time, of the struggle of the working class for emancipation. The theory that consists in basing socialism on the moral notion of justice, on a struggle against the mode of distribution, instead of basing it on a struggle against the mode of production, the conception of class antagonism as an antagonism between the poor and the rich, the effort to graft the "cooperative principal" on capitalist economy—all the nice notions found in Bernstein's doctrine—already existed before him. And these theories were, *in their time,* in spite of their insufficiency, effective theories of the proletarian class struggle. They were the children's seven-league boots, thanks to which the proletariat learned to walk up on the scene of history.

But after the development of the class struggle and its reflex in its social conditions had led to the abandonment of these theories and to the elaboration of the principles of scientific socialism, there could be no socialism—at least in Germany—outside of Marxist socialism, and there could be no socialist class struggle outside of the social democracy. From then on, socialism and Marxism, the proletarian struggle for emancipation and the social democracy, were identical. That is why the return to pre-Marxist socialist theories no longer signifies today a return to the seven-league boots of the childhood of the proletariat, but a return to the puny worn-out slippers of the bourgeoisie.

Bernstein's theory was the *first*, and at the same time, the *last* attempt to give a theoretic base to opportunism. It is the last, because in Bernstein's system, opportunism has gone—negatively through its renunciation of scientific socialism; positively through its marshalling of every bit of theoretic confusion possible—as far as it can. In Bernstein's book, opportunism has crowned its theoretic development (just as it completed its practical development in the position taken by Schippel on the question of militarism), and has reached its ultimate conclusion.

Marxist doctrine cannot only refute opportunism theoretically. It alone can explain opportunism as an historic phenomenon in the development of the party. The forward march of the proletariat, on a world historic scale, to its final victory is not, indeed, "so simple a thing." The peculiar character of this movement resides precisely in the fact that here, for the first time in history, the popular masses themselves, *in opposition to* the ruling classes, are to impose their will, but they must effect this outside of the present society, beyond the existing society. This *will* the masses can only form in a constant struggle against the existing order. The union of the broad popular masses with an aim reaching beyond the existing social order, the union of the daily struggle with the great world transformation, that is the task of the social democratic movement, which must logically grope on its road of development between the following two rocks: abandoning the mass character of the party or abandoning its final aim, falling into bourgeois reformism or into sectarianism, anarchism or opportunism.

In its theoretic arsenal, Marxist doctrine furnished, more than half a century ago, arms that are effective against both of these two extremes. But because our movement is a mass movement and because the dangers menacing it are not derived from the human brain but from social conditions, Marxist doctrine could not assure us, in advance and once for always, against the anarchist and opportunist tendencies. The latter can be overcome only as we pass from the domain of theory to the domain of practice, but only with the help of the arms furnished us by Marx.

"Bourgeois revolutions," wrote Marx a half century ago, "like those of the eighteenth century, rush onward rapidly from success to success, their stage effects outbid one another, men and things seem to be set in flaming brilliants, ecstasy is the prevailing spirit; but they are short-lived, they reach their climax speedily, and then society relapses into a long fit of nervous reaction before it learns how to appropriate the fruits of its period of feverish excitement. Proletarian revolution, on the contrary, such as those of the nineteenth century, criticize themselves constantly; constantly interrupt themselves in their own course; come back to what seems to have been accomplished, in order to start anew; scorn with cruel thoroughness the half-measures, weaknesses, and meannesses of their first attempts; seem to throw down their adversary only to enable him to draw fresh strength from the earth and again to rise up against them in more gigantic stature; constantly recoil in fear before the undefined monster magnitude of their own objects—until finally that situation is created which renders all retreat impossible, and conditions themselves cry out: "Hic Rhodus, hic salta!" Here is the rose. And here we must dance!

This has remained true even after the elaboration of the doctrine of scientific socialism. The proletarian movement has not as yet, all at once, become social-democratic, even in Germany. But it is becoming more social-democratic, surmounting continuously the extreme deviations of anarchism and opportunism, both of which are only determining phases of the development of the social democracy, considered as a process.

For these reasons we must say that the surprising thing here is not the appearance of an opportunist current but rather its feebleness. As long as it showed itself in isolated cases of the practical activity of the party, one could suppose that it had a serious practical base. But now that it has shown its face in Bernstein's book, one cannot help exclaim with astonishment: "What? Is that all you have to say?" Not the shadow of an original thought! Not a single idea that was not refuted, crushed, reduced into dust, by Marxism several decades ago!

It was enough for opportunism to speak out to prove it had nothing to say. In the history of our party that is the only importance of Bernstein's book.

Thus saying good-bye to the mode of thought of the revolutionary proletariat, to dialectics and to the materialist conception of history, Bernstein can thank them for the attenuating circumstances they provide for his conversion. For only dialectics and the materialist conception of history, magnanimous as they are, could make Bernstein appear as an unconscious predestined instrument, by means of which the rising working class expresses its momentary weakness but which, upon closer inspection, it throws aside contemptuously and with pride.

Translation by Integer

Karl Kautsky

The Revisionist Controversy

The Theory of Crisis (Zusammenbruchstheorie)

The attempts to monopolize trade, to eliminate competition already begin at an early stage of commodity trade. During the Reformation this was a source of universal discontent. The elimination of competition from production, the monopolization of entire branches of industry by concentrating them all into one organization. These branches of industry produce not luxury articles but products for the daily consumption of large masses; they no longer belong to one small town but to a large state, indeed to the world. This monopolization is a phenomenon which has become of economic significance only since the death of Marx in 1883. Since then it has become such a widespread phenomenon, that the economic and political life of the capitalist nations is increasingly dominated by these monopolies.

* * *

The struggle against cartels generates new cartels, as a result of which businesses of various kinds sometimes merge into one gigantic enterprise. What we are now witnessing in Germany is a struggle for control between the coal syndicates which is forcing up the price of coal and the steel industry, which retaliates by also raising its prices. At the time of writing, large iron and steel works are trying to liberate themselves from the control of the coal cartels by acquiring their own mines. But just like the coal syndicate, the cartels of the steel industry are trying to push their prices up as much as possible. In Austria the iron cartels have created enormous difficulties for all those branches of industry which require steel in great quantities. Eventually steel consumers will have to create their own associations so that they can then jointly purchase their own iron works. It is a well-known fact that large enterprises, like the railways, have their own coal mines and their own workshops.

The transformation of different businesses of the same kind into cartels and trusts on the one hand, and on the other the concentration of many enterprises of a different kind into one, are the most characteristic phenomena of contemporary economic life. This process of concentration is happening very rapidly; hardly a day passes in this period of economic development in which one does not hear of the formation of some new cartel. Moreover, the agricultural enterprises happily join in, including the sugar cartels; apparently the dairies are also thinking of creating a cartel.

This whole development spread over a period of scarcely two decades has been made possible only as a result of the concentration of capital to which in turn it again powerfully contributes. That Marx's theory of the concentration of capital is completely, and not one-sidedly, correct is sufficiently testified by the existence of cartels and trusts. But in his critique of the theory of concentration Bernstein presents as evidence to the contrary, the existence of the most insignificant forms of small property but he never discusses the emergence of entrepreneurial associations as one of the most important phenomena, apart from the agrarian crisis, since Marx's death, the study of which moreover is absolutely necessary for anyone who wants to understand Marxist economics.

When the existence of cartels proves that Marx's analyses were right, Bernstein ignores them. He only remembers to discuss them when he thinks that their existence disproves another part of Marx's theory, namely the crisis theory.

The New Middle Class

Before we turn away from the subject of the growth of the propertied classes, let us briefly examine the view that, for Bernstein, these are not capitalists, but the strata which on the basis of their income make up the middle classes. That would at any rate explain why he stresses the importance of income tax statistics, which do not in fact reflect the distribution of property. Many of his comments indicate that this is his view, even though elsewhere he is clearly referring to the growth in the number of capitalists.

We would agree with Bernstein if all he was saying is that the middle classes *[Mittelstand]* are not dying out, but are being replaced by a new class, and that the independent artisan and small tradesman are being replaced by the intelligentsia. I would like to point out that in a series of articles published in 1895 in *Neue Zeit* on "The intelligentsia and social democracy," I had already discussed the emergence of this middle class. I argued that studying the conditions for winning over this stratum of the population was one of the most important tasks of our party:

> A new, very numerous, continually increasing stratum is coming into being. Its growth may conceal the decline of small industry and hence of the middle classes.*

The growth of this stratum of society is mainly due to the fact that the functions of the dominant and exploiting classes are increasingly being taken over by paid skilled workers, who sell their services either piecemeal—like doctors, lawyers, artists—or in return for a salary, like officials of every kind. During the Middle Ages the clergy provided the scholars, doctors, artists, and some of the administrative officials; the aristocracy took care also of public administration, the law, the police, and above all the army. With the rise of the modern state and of modern science both these classes were deprived of their functions; although they survived, for the most part they lost their independence as well as their social significance.

But the functions taken from them and the labor force to carry them out grew from year to year in accordance with the tasks imposed on the state, the municipal authorities and science, by the development of society.

From the very beginning the capitalist class also began to hand its functions in trade and industry over to paid workers, tradesmen and technicians. Initially these were only assistants to the capitalist, entrusted with organizing, initiating, and supervising the labor process, with the purchase of the means of production, and the sale of products: in other words with functions which, due to the growing

*'Die Intelligenz und die Sozialdemokratie', *Neue Zeit*, XIII.2 (1895) pp. 10–16, 43–9, 74–80. Here p. 16.

demand for specialized skills, the capitalist was incapable of carrying out himself. Eventually, due to the existence of joint-stock companies, where even the management is handed over to a subordinate, the capitalist became completely superfluous. It is evident that the existence of joint-stock companies contributes to the growth of these strata—this is not, however, a result of the splitting up of capitals.

* * *

This is not the origin of the new middle class *[Mittelstand]*. Private property in the means of production is of no importance to them. Their role as independent workers—as painters, doctors, or writers—is unimportant. Where the means of production operate as capital, the 'white-collar workers' *[Kopfarbeiter]* exist as a group, as wage earners, not as capitalists.

Indeed it would be equally mistaken to think of the new middle class as forming part of the proletariat.

It has emerged from the bourgeoisie, and is connected to it through family and social ties; it holds similar values. Other sectors of the intelligentsia even more closely connected to the bourgeoisie are the directors and managers who have taken over the functions of the capitalist. They are also closer to the capitalist in terms of their outlook and in their opposition to the proletariat. Other professions within the intelligentsia require a specific political or religious stance. This is true of political journalists, many legal officials, for example, public prosecutors, policemen, the clergy, etc.: only those are employed by the state, capitalist publishers and the church who either share the outlook of their 'employers,' or who are willing to adopt an alien outlook in return for money. That is another reason why the intelligentsia is generally opposed to the proletariat.

But the greatest concern between the intelligentsia and the proletariat is generated by the fact that the former constitutes a privileged class, due to the fact that it has the privilege of education. The intelligentsia has every interest in educating the mass of the people enough so that they can grasp the significance of science and so that they will bow before it and its representatives, but they oppose every attempt to gain access to the restricted circle of professional education.

Clearly the capitalist mode of production requires a massive intelligentsia. The educational facilities of the feudal state were incapable of catering for that need. Thus the bourgeois regime has always been in favor of improving and expanding not only elementary but also higher education. This was supposed to promote not only the development of production, but also to lessen class conflict; given that higher education was a way of gaining access to the professional world, it seemed self-evident that the universal expansion of higher education would integrate the proletariat into the bourgeoisie.

But the bourgeois standard of life* only becomes a necessary correlate of higher education when the latter is a privilege. When it becomes universal, far from integrating the proletariat into the bourgeoisie, it degrades him to a "white-collar worker," to a proletarian. That too is one of the manifestations of the immiseration of the mass of people.

In countries where there has been a considerable expansion of popular education, and consequently education loses its privileged status, the intelligentsia becomes hostile to education. Thus a contradiction arises between the needs of the modern mode of production and these anti-intellectual strata. They become less progressive than the capitalists themselves and join the ranks of the reactionaries, the agrarians, and the dispossessed artisans. The strongest opposition to the education of women is expressed by university professors and students, and by the leading scientists. It is they who exclude the Jewish intelligentsia from all competition for positions in the professional world, and who go to great lengths to make higher education more expensive and hence inaccessible to the poor. Naturally this arouses the most energetic opposition and antagonism of the proletariat, which fights with the greatest determination against privilege, including education.

In spite of all obstacles, popular education continues expanding so that one stratum of the intelligentsia after another becomes proletarianized. Think of the large numbers of small businessmen at our business schools, musicians, sculptors, and draughtsmen at our music and art schools, the mechanics and chemists produced by our technical institutions every year. The concentration of capital also affects the spheres of trade, art, and the applied sciences, since the amount of capital needed to set up a viable independent business in

---

*In English in the original.

these sectors becomes increasingly larger. Since the amount of capital required to set up an independent business becomes larger, the spheres of trade, art, and the applied sciences are also affected by the concentration of capital. Thus while the number of skilled workers in these spheres grows, the possibilities for becoming independent diminish, and life-long wage labor becomes their fate. As a result of the growth of professional workers, the situation of the intelligentsia becomes increasingly hopeless, for it is no longer able to protect itself against competitors by creating artificial restrictions or through the formation of guild-like associations. Immiseration begins to affect these sectors of society as well, and it is all the more painful to those affected since the extent of their misery is directly compared with the rising standard of living of the bourgeoisie. To maintain this standard of living is a matter of life and death to white-collar workers. While the physical misery of the manual worker is manifested mainly in his living conditions, then in his clothing and only finally in the consumption of food, with the white-collar worker the order is the reverse. He begins by saving on food.

But no matter how hard they try to keep up bourgeois appearances, all these proletarianized strata of the intelligentsia eventually discover their proletarian heart, gain interest in the proletarian class struggle, and eventually participate actively in it. That applies to shop assistants, sculptors, and musicians. And the rest will follow.

When liberal economists point to the rapid growth of the intelligentsia in order to prove the capitalist mode of production creates a middle class, they do not take account of the fact that this growth is accompanied by the process of proletarianization.

Somewhere between the definitely anti-proletarian sectors which share the capitalists' orientation and the groups which definitely share the proletariat's point of view, there is a broad stratum of the intelligentsia which is indifferent, standing in its opinion above class conflicts.

What this middle stratum shares with the old petty bourgeoisie is the ambiguity of its social position. It is just as unreliable and changeable in its attitude towards the proletariat. While today it protests against the greediness of capital, tomorrow it will look down on the bad manners of the proletariat. While today it appeals to it to defend its human dignity, tomorrow it will try to preserve social peace by stabbing it in the back.

But it does differ from the old petty bourgeoisie in two aspects, one positive, the other negative. It is distinguished by the fact that it has been trained in abstract thinking and has a far greater intellectual culture. In general this social group tends to consider itself above the narrow-mindedness of class interests, to be under the idealistic illusion that it is somehow superior and not affected by momentary and particular interests, and that it alone keeps in mind and represents the interests of society as a whole.

The negative aspect of the middle class in comparison to the old petty bourgeoisie is its lack of fighting ability. While previously they were a belligerent class, capable of resisting the attempts of capital to break its back, our contemporary intelligentsia situated somewhere between the proletariat and capitalism no longer knows how to defend itself against the dominant classes. Few in number, with no unified class interests or proper form of organization, without any property but nevertheless demanding a bourgeois standard of life, the middle classes are able to fight only by joining another class which is wealthy enough to provide it with the means of fighting for its survival. The middle strata of the intelligentsia, the "cultural aristocracy" could afford as a group to be in opposition as long as the bourgeoisie itself it has become submissive and has lost its capacity and desire to fight; every progressive move, except currying favor with the powerful is rejected as immoral; in fact, it has become cowardly and byzantine.

They detest the class struggle, and according to them it should be eliminated or at least weakened. Class struggle means insurrection, rebellion, revolution; and these forces are to be rendered superfluous by social reforms.

I was not trying to polemicize against Bernstein, who was then beginning to change his views, when I stated:

> that amongst those not directly involved in capitalist exploitation, there was hardly an honest or independent intellectual left who was not concerned with the social question, i.e. concerned that "something" should be done for the workers—whatever that "something" may be. Stumm and Eugen Richter, the patriarchal-absolutist and the Manchester businessman respectively, can no longer count on any meaningful support from the intelligentsia. The condemnation of capital and solidarity with the proletariat—if not with the fighting at least with the exploited proletariat—has become fashionable, and Harcourt's words "We are all socialists now" are beginning to be true for these circles. The socialism which our poets and painters, scholars and

journalists pay homage to in their cafes and salons, in their ateliers and lecture halls is not proletarian and revolutionary socialism, but a kind of socialism which unhappily is very similar to the conception of "true socialism" contained in the *Communist Manifesto* of 1847.*

Frequently these sectors have declared that only proletarian brutality prevents them from joining the social democrats. What actually keeps them from becoming involved are not externals, but their own lack of character and insight. Even though they are by far superior to the narrow-minded capitalist, they nevertheless do not seem to understand that it is neither possible to save the given social order nor to prevent the final victory of the proletariat. They are either unaware of their impotence to alter the course of the development of society, or they simply lack the strength and courage to admit that and to break with bourgeois society.†

Very few either dare to or are able to make this break. Certainly there are some genuine supporters of the proletariat amongst the knights of the spirit, but they do not come out into the open until the proletariat is actually victorious. It cannot expect the intelligentsia to provide it with reinforcements for the struggle, but it need not fear any fierce opposition from them either.

The few indications show that the growing intelligentsia is a class which the proletariat should not ignore. It would be expecting too much to try to convert them to the proletariat, but it would be an even greater mistake to include them among the "propertied." This stratum unifies in concentrated form all the contradictions which characterize capitalist society, but nevertheless the proletarian seed is growing in this microcosm as well as in the social organism as a whole.

* * *

It is impossible to deny the growth of the middle-class intelligentsia; likewise one has to admit that there has been a rise in the standard of living of certain strata of the working classes. But none of these phenomena disproves the Marxist doctrine of the concentration of capital, of increasing exploitation of the proletariat, nor of the intensification of social conflict. It could of course be argued that the increase in the number of property owners contra-

Neue Zeit, XIII.2, pp. 76, 77.
†Ibid.

dicts the breakdown theory. Bernstein however has not been able to demonstrate that such an increase has taken place. Theory and statistical evidence have shown us that this is not the case.

Politics and Economics

Bernstein has drawn our attention to the importance of cooperatives, trade unions, and so-called municipal socialism. Without any doubt these bodies can make valuable contributions to the emancipation of the proletariat and must continue to do so. But that is now what even Bernstein's most determined opponents object to. In fact Parvus has repeatedly critized the leadership of our party for not being concerned enough with trade unions, and stated that nowhere were the consumers' cooperatives thriving so well as in Saxony, the region where Bernstein has been most ferociously attacked.

Therefore there are no disputes over that question. The differences arise when it is a question of determining what each of these bodies must undertake in order to promote the liberation struggle of the proletariat. This is where the differences begin to emerge; Bernstein has only felt them but has not expressed them clearly. Occasionally he touches upon this problem of socialism but then drops it again. The question of the effectiveness [*Leistungsfähigkeit*] of the cooperatives, the trade unions, and municipal politics is intimately connected with the question of their relation to state politics.

* * *

If the proletariat did not have economic power it would certainly never be able to achieve political rights. The basis of its economic power is the role it plays in the process of production and this does not depend on the good will of the government. Everywhere governments and capitalists are eager to expand the capitalist mode of production as quickly as possible. This means increasing the mass of the proletariat, concentrating it in specific places, training and organizing it—initially only for the purpose of production, but the organization of the factory then also influences the class struggle. The actions of governments and capitalists thus lead to a situation in which the economic life of the nation increasingly comes to be dependent on wage labor, becoming dominated by it to the extent that the proletariat becomes conscious of its power.

Everywhere the economic power of the proletariat is growing, in despotic as well as in democratic countries, in Russia as well as in Switzerland, and this constitutes the basis for the inevitable victory of the working class, the most important event of our century. If Bernstein's criticisms were right and the concentration of capital and of the proletariat did not come about in the manner described by the *Communist Manifesto,* then no matter how hard the proletariat tried to organize politically, the governments and capitalists would be strong enough to deal with them. In fact, they destroy themselves in their hopeless struggle against the enemy, which after every defeat arises more numerous, more unified, and more intransigent.

It is as a result of this power that the working class can make demands on the state for political rights, many of which it has already obtained and which it will continue to obtain.

It is quite self-evident that the working class will make use of its political rights in order to organize itself and thus increase its power even more. It is evident that nobody has ever questioned the fact that a proletariat which is well organized into unions, which has at its disposal wealthy consumers' associations, numerous printing presses, and a widely circulating press, achieves better results at elections and in parliament than a proletariat which does not have these means. The fundamental power of the proletariat, however, consists in the power which it acquires automatically as a result of economic development. And the highest form of class struggle which leaves its mark on all others, is not the struggle of particular economic organizations but the fight of the totality of the proletariat for the most powerful social organization—the state. That is the truly political struggle and, in the last instance, the most decisive one.

Of course this does not mean that the relationship between the economic and political struggle will always and under all conditions be the same, that the working class will make the greatest and the fastest progress by means of political struggle and that the struggle for and through economic organizations is of secondary importance.

The relative importance of the economic and political struggle fluctuates, similar to fluctuations of capitalist industry. The latter goes through periods of prosperity, of crisis; likewise in the sphere of politics there are periods of great struggle, rapid progress—times of political "revolution"—followed by periods of stagnation in which the development of economic organizations and social "reform" take precedence. The fluctuations in the industrial and the political sphere are not only similar but related.

Times of prosperity are naturally times in which there is least general social discontent, when the desire to work upwards through one's own effort has the greatest chance of success and the need to question the state lessens. Not only capitalists but also workers regard politics as less important, and economic organizations and enterprises which offer immediate tangible advantages as more important.

During a crisis the possibilities of purely economic advancement diminish; the most powerful economic institution, the state, has to provide assistance; it is necessary to seize the state in order to regain lost ground, there is more social discontent, contradictons become more acute and the general tendency is towards political struggle.

Of course the intensity of political struggle and its relative importance in relation to purely economic activity does not only depend on whether capitalism is going through a period of expansion or of crisis. Other factors also have an inhibiting or a stimulating effect. But in any case the economic cycle has a great deal of influence on the relationship between economics and politics.

The revolution of 1848 broke out during an economic crisis. One of the reasons why its recurrence was inconceivable once it had been defeated—apart from the bourgeoisie's fear of the proletariat, which had fought so bravely in the battle of June—was the growth of industry in 1850. Engels wrote in 1885 in his introduction to *The Revelations of the Communist Trials in Cologne*:

> The industrial crisis of 1847 which prepared the revolution of 1848 had been overcome; a new and previously unimagined period of industrial prosperity began. For anybody with eyes in their head, it was evident that the revolution of 1848 had exhausted itself.

In 1850 Marx and Engels had already declared in the review of the *Neue Rheinische Zeitung*:

> In conditions of general prosperity, when the productive forces of bourgeois society grow as is possible only in a bourgeois society, one

cannot speak of true revolution. Such a revolution is only possible where both factors, the modern productive forces, and the bourgeois relations of production, enter into contradiction with each other.

The next period of tremendous economic growth was 1871. But unlike 1850 it did not follow an unsuccessful revolution but a highly successful European revolution, brought about not by popular uprisings but by dynastic wars. The events of 1866 and 1870–1 were still in the air: the fall of Austrian absolutism and of the French Empire, the unification of Germany and the assurance of universal suffrage, finally the heroic struggle of the Commune. These events were not going to diminish workers' interest in politics, to destroy the belief in the rapid success of political struggles, and to put into the foreground economic advancement. Even less so since the period of prosperity was short and thanks to the reaction after 1849 trade union and cooperative life had scarcely begun.

Thus with the exception of England the political struggle remained in the foreground: it remained "revolutionary."

For some years now we have been witnessing a period of economic prosperity, although this particular period is lasting much longer than 1871. This is due to the fact that the underlying economic base is more developed and that we are going through a period of political stagnation, which in turn becomes more pronounced as a result of this development.

Thus we are in a similar situation to that of 1850, a situation of political reaction and industrial growth. But in the meantime there has been half a century of capitalist development, of proletarian class struggles and a generation in which the rights of free collective bargaining have been maintained. If the situation of 1850 brought about an interruption in the workers' movement on the European continent, the situation in 1899 merely indicates that the economic struggle is becoming predominant and that the workers believe that at the moment they can achieve more through the organization of trade unions and associations, than through political activity.

Bernstein's book partly derives its strength from this situation. His emphasis on small-scale practical economic work does correspond to actual existing needs; his skepticism regarding the probability of significant and rapid political transformations—catastrophes—is entirely in keeping with the experience of the last years. The "practical" people who read Bernstein's book are indifferent to his theories; all they are interested in knowing is what he says concerning the present tasks and the present conditions.

But its weaknesses are precisely due to the fact that it corresponds to a particular situation. The explicit intention of the book is not to act as a guide for the present but to act as a guide for "the way towards socialism"; it states that it is not merely concerned with contemporary tasks but with the "tasks of social democracy" in general.

When the era of prosperity began in 1850, Marx and Engels drew appropriate conclusions for their tactics for the coming period, but did not immediately set aside the results they had gained from the study of the entire development of capitalism. If all Bernstein was arguing was that in the present era of prosperity and reaction nothing much can be achieved politically, so let us devote ourselves to bringing about small partial reforms for as long as this period lasts, and work with trade unions, municipalities and cooperatives, etc., to achieve this end—then that program would certainly be accepted and supported by our party.

But according to Bernstein, the present situation is the normal condition of society. He argues that political stagnation is slow but sure progress on the road of democracy and social reform; he thinks that the prosperity we are now witnessing will be prolonged indefinitely and therefore he can have an optimistic conception of the course of development of society and of the state. This development must break down as soon as political stagnation and economic prosperity come to an end.

What appears to Bernstein as the contrast between traditional revolutionary phases and a truly reformist attitude, is in part only the contrast between the conception which is derived from the totality of the phenomena of our mode of production and one which takes only one of its phases into consideration.

He talks of "tactics for catastrophic situations." He does not reveal where these are to be found. In fact precisely because of its theoretical basis the tactics of social democracy are extremely adaptable. It is prepared for every eventuality and it is not oriented towards a particular tempo of social development. It is prepared for situations of crisis and prosperity, of catastrophes and slow peaceful development. The vitality of social democracy is in fact due to its adaptability. It does not need to elaborate tactics specifically to meet catastrophes nor in order to carry out peaceful small-scale work at all periods. Its tactics do not ignore crises, catastrophes, revolutions, nor do they speculate about them. It utilizes every situation and never commits itself in advance.

Independent or Dependent Politics

If Bernstein's writings were to have any effect at all, it should above all be to correct the confused conceptions about us spread by our opponents, and to give new vitality and depth to our analyses, a task which in fact has taken up a good portion of our life's work.

It is evident that the proletariat as an independent political party must be revolutionary not in the criminal sense *[Polizeisinn]*, but in the politico-economic sense. Bernstein proposes that the phrase "fundamental transformation of the social order" be replaced by "social transformation." but no one would claim that the latter phrase expresses the fundamental conflict between the new and the old order of society—a conflict which Bernstein himself sometimes denies. In fact his socialism seems to be the consummation of liberalism.

I willingly admit that the word "revolutionary" may be misleading, and it should not indeed be used without good cause. One should not give way to error using it wrongly. Or should we not use it at all? In order to define and analyze specific processes it is absolutely necessary as a concept. When it is a question of distinguishing between a course of social development which does not transcend the given social forms and a course of development which tends towards a higher social order of an entirely different structure, one cannot be content with using the phrase "social transformation," apart from the fact that no one who is even superficially acquainted with our party literature can have any doubt that social revolution and political insurrection are entirely different concepts. Social revolution is an objective which one can in principle aim at, while political insurrection is only a means to an end, to be evaluated only with regard to its suitability.

Insurrection differs from both social and political revolution. When not using police language, we conceive of a political revolution as a significant political crisis which intensifies and quickens the pulse of the political life of the nation in contrast to counter-revolutionary crises which have the opposite effect. Insurrection or the "extra-legal use of force" can be an episode, a very important episode during such a political crisis: it must however never be mistaken for the revolution itself. The highly legal action of summoning the Estates/Assembly is just as much an integral part of the revolution as the storming of the Bastille. No one will refer to this as the great French insurrection of 1789, and no one will refer to extra-legal violent actions, which have no repercussions on political life at all, as revolutions. For example, no one will call the illegal acts of resistance of the Indian natives against the British pest commission, revolutions.

In order "to avoid misunderstandings," Bernstein uses the word "revolution" in the sense in which it is usually used by the police and by state prosecutors who merely consider it illegal action. He does not use it in its proper scientific and political meaning.

Social revolution—not in the sense in which it is used by Bernstein—is the necessary final objective which every independent proletarian political party must necessarily strive for. Anyone who organizes the proletariat as an independent political party thereby prepares the possibility of social revolution, no matter how pacific and sober, or how sceptical in relation to the future. Conversely anyone who wants to draw the proletariat away from other parties and wants to make it politically independent, will achieve this all the more clearly the more he awakens in them the consciousness of the necessity of social revolution.

On the other hand we have seen that the politics of the social democrats involve the absorption of the proletarian to a popular party, reformism, and the elimination of revolution as our final objective.

Thus the whole question of social revolution is of eminently practical and contemporary importance. Some may think that it is a waste of time to quarrel over the question of revolution; that is to speculate about unhatched eggs. At present both currents within the workers' movement are aiming at the same thing: socio-political and democratic reforms. So it is said that one should aim at these and not break the unity with quarrels over issues which are irrelevant to the present problems. But we have seen that the question as to the final aim of our politics, whether we should aim at revolution or limit ourselves to reforms, is intimately related to the problem of the organization and the propaganda of the proletariat as a contemporary political party.

If that were not the case, then the emphasis on the revolutionary point of view would be meaningless and this applies equally to the attacks of the reformists on what they call the "revolutionary phrase." The intensity of the conflict, however, becomes comprehensible, when one sees that underlying the quarrel over ways of speaking is the struggle over a question which is a matter of life and death for social democracy as well as for bourgeois democracy, namely the question whether the proletariat should engage directly in the class struggle as an independent political organization, or whether only as part of a people's party [*Volkspartei*] which embraces all democratic strata of society.

Translated by Patrick Good

Report of the Executive Committee of the German Social Democratic Party

1. The Parliamentary Activity of the Social Democratic Group in the German Reichstag

The report we submitted in 1907 to the International Congress at Stuttgart was written under the impression that a change in the politics of the German Empire would soon take place. Prince Bülow, the then chancellor, desired to try the policy of combination. He dissolved the Reichstag in 1906 and had, according to his own opinions, obtained a success in the elections. He found that the Conservatives, National Liberals and Radicals were ready to form a "block" or combination of parties. The majority of this block, which consisted of 206 members, were Conservative and National-Liberal Agrarians. The Agrarians, however, were not at all willing to sacrifice any of their principles (which were born of purely ego-tistical motives) either for the sake of reputation, or for an individual statesman. Therefore the only policy which would possibly be pursued by this block would be such as has hitherto been followed by the Conservatives and Center.

The only persons placed in a favorable situation were the "Junkers." They formed the majority of the "block" and therefore were in a position to demand that a policy according to their views should be pursued.

If the Liberals could be induced to assist in creating a majority for Conservative motions, all would be well. If, however, the Liberals would refuse, the "Junkers" would still have at their disposal the votes of the Center and the Polish members.

The Center tries, in the industrial districts, to make out that it is their first and principal task to safeguard the rights of the Catholic Church. This party, in fact, uses all the means at the disposal of the

Church for their agitation purposes. The few industrial constituencies and the votes of the workers are merely used as a pretext to veil the policy of agrarian interests. The Center decides always in favor of the landlords in such cases where antagonism between the interests of agrarians and manufacturers, and between workers and landlords exists. This is quite natural because the Center polls more than half of its votes in rural districts, viz., in districts of less than 2,000 inhabitants and, among the 105 constituencies represented by members of the Center, there are scarcely one dozen where industrial interests prevail. The attitude of the Center depends on the program of the Unions of Christian Peasants, which stand under the leadership of Graf von Spee. These Unions try to compete with a Federation of Peasants which has been formed for Northern Germany, by upholding the most exaggerated demands.

The Junkers were thus able to look forward with an easy mind to the development of things. The "block" policy therefore was handled in the legislature only as long as such matters which did not hurt the interests of their class were handled, for instance, the vote of the Budget, the new association law, a revision of the bank laws, and so forth. Bülow had also resolved to keep out of this discussion all questions where no unity between Conservatives and Liberals was to be expected. The real conditions, however, are far more powerful than the will of the ministers. There are a good many questions that cannot be put aside at will.

There was much political agitation, when on October 28th, 1908, the *Daily Telegraph* published an interview of the Emperor Wilhelm II with an Englishman. According to this article, the Emperor had said that the great mass of the German people were not well disposed towards England and that he was in the minority in his own country, as regards his friendship towards England. The above-named article also contained other statements which called forth lively opposition on the part of the German population, with the effect that it was believed autocratic government would be abolished and the Reichstag would obtain larger constitutional rights. We profited by this favorable occasion to demand a change in the constitution of the empire, claiming full responsibility of the ministers. We also requested that the consent of the Reichstag should be necessary for a declaration of war. Our middle classes, however, live in a state of continual agitation on account of the awakening of the proletariat, and they possess very little self-confidence. An extension of the rights of the Parliament would necessarily lead to an extension of the power of social democracy. The liberal bourgeoisie prefer to content themselves with the role of train-bearer to the feudal absolutistic state, instead of defending the rights of the people side by side with social democrats. This action of the Reichstag which had been brought about by agitation of the people did not lead to any definite result.

The beautiful block-dream very soon vanished. This was brought about by the policy with regard to taxes.

The financial condition of the empire has become entirely hopeless on account of senseless armaments. The expenditure of the Empire for military purposes has increased, during the last twenty years as follows:

	1889 Mk.	1908 Mk.
Army.........................	461,036,057	855,868,451
Navy.........................	51,069,080	348,973,677
Military Pensions..............	33,711,086	107,495,775
Interest on the National Debt	37,483,500	154,784,524
Total.....	583,299,723	1,467,122,427

This increase still continues, for our military and navy bills provide for a continual increase. There are also technical improvements made daily, demanding a still further increase of these expenditures. It was believed in 1898 and 1900, when the new Navy Bills were passed and when the number of men-of-war to be built up to the year 1907 was determined, that the cost of an iron-clad would be about 20,000,000 marks. The newest type of this ship, however, requires an outlay of about 50,000,000 marks. The cost of maintenance of these ships has increased in the same proportion.

The tax-paying capabilities of the people, however, are strained to the utmost, not only by the increasing demands of the empire, the states, and the communities but also by the protective tariffs by means of which the great landlords and capitalists get thousands of millions out of the pockets of the consumers and also out of the Treasury. The amount of these sums can be easily proved by the various articles. In 1908, for instance, there has been sold in Germany 8,902,180 tons of rye and 5,674,155 tons of wheat. Every ton of rye is 50 marks dearer in Germany than abroad and every ton of wheat is 55 marks dearer than abroad. As soon as this difference between the prices disappears, then the corn is sold abroad and the exporters receive in return so-called "import certificates," i.e. checks to the amount of 50 marks for every ton of rye or 55 marks for every ton of wheat. These checks are, within the next six months, accepted as cash, by the custom offices for the payment of duties on corn, pulse, petroleum, and coffee. It follows from this that the rye consumed in Germany has been 445,000,000 marks dearer than it would have been without these corn duties, whilst the wheat has been 312,000,000 marks dearer owing to this system.

The same is the case with the other grains, pulse, and so on. The treasury pays also part of these costs which disappear into the pockets of the great landowners. The empire uses large quantities of grain for the army and the 112,000 military horses and consequently pays the exalted price brought about by the tariffs. It must be added that in years with a good harvest more import checks are given out by the customs office than money is received for duties on the above-named articles. In 1909 for instance we imported 581,987 tons of rye, whilst 1,248,814 tons have been exported. The import duties thereon amounted to 31,099,350 marks but the import checks cost the Empire 62,440,700 marks. The rye duty, therefore, brought a deficit to the customs of 31,341,350, not including the cost of management. The case is the same with manufactured articles. The big iron manufacturers, for instance, are organized in syndicates. They charge to their customers the prices of the world's market, plus customs duties. The duty on pig iron is M. 10 per ton. In 1908 Germany has consumed 13,016,135 tons of pig iron, out of which the German manufacturers have produced 12,803,782 tons. The 103 works which produced pig iron had therefore an extra income of 128,037,820 marks, through this duty on iron. This sum has been paid by the German consumers of iron.

It is obvious that it must be very difficult to find new taxes to fill the treasury in a country where the tax-paying capabilities of the people are so much abused by all sorts of customs duties, for the sole benefit of the big landowners and manufacturers. But new taxes have to be found if it is not considered desirable to limit the military expenditure. One thing was certain—the annual income was about 500,000 marks less than the annual expenditure, and the money therefore had to be provided for somehow. The Government therefore proposed new taxes of which about 400,000,000 marks had to be paid by the large masses of the population, whilst only 92,000,000 was to be derived from succession duties; however, the big landowners would also have been liable to pay these duties and therefore the Junkers opposed it. They were joined in their efforts by the Catholic agrarians of the Center party. The Liberals, however, were prepared to vote for the succession duty. It has not been found possible to get an arrangement between Liberals and Conservatives on this point, and according to Bülow's policy of the block, it ought to have been adjourned. The financial situation of the Empire, however, did not permit of such an adjournment. The block, therefore, fell to pieces and its originator vanished from the scene. Now the Catholic and Protestant agarians united fraternally to exploit the nation; [. . .]*

The industrial crisis commenced in the building trade already in 1907. The number of workers employed in these trades amounted to 1,376,208 in 1906 and to 1,297,922 in 1907, and dropped further to 1,260,270 in 1908. According to the increase of population, the number of workers in the building trades ought to have grown by 1.5 percent but instead of showing an annual increase of 206,430 workers in the building trades we find that their number has decreased by 115,938 during the last two years. All the 66 trade corporations combined reported during 1908 a decrease of 100,595 insured workers, whilst there should have been an increase of about 400,000. The total number of workers insured against accidents was 9,018,367 in 1907 and this number dropped in 1908 to 8,917,772.

The number of unemployed chiefly in the big cities and industrial centers increased rapidly in 1908; our comrades therefore addressed a question to the government in the Reichstag asking what it intended to do against unemployment.

The government could not deny the seriousness of unemployment. The large liners were lying idle in the docks, their crews having been discharged, new ships were not commenced by the shipbuilding yards, the casual wards were overcrowded. The Party and the trade unions organized a census of the unemployed in Berlin and the suburbs on February 14th, 1909, when they ascertained that the number of the unemployed was 101,300. The wages decreased, while the price of food stuffs advanced rapidly, thereby continually

---

*Illegible in original.

adding to the number of the unemployed, because, the workers necessarily had to restrict their consumption of manufactured articles, on account of their smaller income and increased expenditure for food stuffs. The price of grain reached an unexampled height in the spring of 1909. Our comrades in Parliament then asked that the institution of import checks be abolished, that the grain duties be abolished or temporarily suspended, when the price of grain should surpass those rates fixed by that famous motion Kanitz [had introduced] in the middle of the nineties.

There has never been a session with less positive result on the field of social politics than the era of Bülow. The government, compelled by the Berne Convention, introduced an amendment of the trade laws which contained a number of alterations. A special committee, which had been appointed to study this amendment, proposed a number of alterations which had not been suggested by the government, but after all only those paragraphs which had been arranged by the Berne Convention were passed at the second and third reading. This amendment became law on December 28th, 1908. It first of all did away with the word "factory" that had been used in old trade laws. The protective measures provided by this law affected hitherto only factories. The employers usually pretended that their establishments were not factories, when they were prosecuted for contravention of the protective regulations. The court frequently accepted this interpretation and discharged the defendants, and the court, in its judgments, sometimes tried to give a definition of the word "factory." On reading these definitions, one might be inclined to doubt whether factories really exist at all. This inconvenience has now disappeared, the word "factory" having been replaced by "establishment." The above-named protective regulations are now extended to all establishments with less than ten workers, as well as to all establishments with less then ten workers, when they employ elementary forces.

The hours of labor for female workers have been fixed at ten and at eight on the eves of Sunday and holidays. They, as well as males under sixteen, are debarred from labor between eight at night and six in the morning, while under the old law they were not allowed to work from half-past eight p.m. to half-past five a.m.

A bill on Chambers of Labor has recently been introduced in the Reichstag. A bill on home work has already passed the committee stage. This bill, however, only gives new powers to the various authorities. The only compulsory regulation in this bill provides that the workers shall be enabled to learn the actual rate of payment when the work is given out to them. The federal council, the federated governments and the police authorities will be empowered to extend to home industries the protective regulations existing for large industrial establishments.

A law affecting employment agencies has recently been passed by the Reichstag. It is hoped that this law will to some extent abolish the exploitation of the unemployed by the employment agencies.

A peculiar law has been passed by the Reichstag entitled the "Potash Law." This law, for the first time in the history of German legislation, deals with the question of cartels and syndicates, and what is more, this law enables a syndicate, which otherwise would have fallen to pieces, to maintain itself. The governments of Prussia, Anhalt, and Mecklenburg were especially interested in this law, because potash mines are owned by them. They had to accede to a number of protective measures, which are not found in any other German law, for the benefit of workers in those mines.

The "clou" of the German social policy is to be, according to the opinion of the bureaucracy, the new national insurance law. This bill, consisting of 1754 paragraphs, has just been laid before the Reichstag. This bill and the appended "elaboration" consisting of about 1000 pages are without doubt very interesting documents for students of political science, but their contents unfortunately are of very little value for the workers. This bill first of all tries to create a somewhat more uniform organization of the boards that are charged to survey the good working of the insurance schemes. This part of the bill is dealt with in the first 176 paragraphs. The next 386 paragraphs are on sick insurance. The old sick insurance law had only 123 paragraphs.

The wording has been changed very little and still less important are the improvements. Domestic servants, agricultural and home workers are to be included in the compulsory insurance schemes. The federal states, under the old law, had the power to extend the compulsory insurance scheme to the above-named classes by a separate statute. A number of federal states and districts had made use of this provision. If, however, under the old law the compulsory insurance scheme were extended to these classes, then they enjoyed the same privileges as other workers who were insured, while under the new law they will be under less favorable conditions. Compulsory insurance will furthermore be extended to apothecaries' assistants and apprentices, stage and orchestral members, teachers, private tutors, and the crews of vessels employed in inland navigation.

The principal alterations for those hitherto insured will be as follows:—whilst at present the employer pays one-third and the employee two-thirds of the whole subscription, in future both parties will pay an equal share. In 1907 for instance the workers paid in subscriptions 225,273,100 marks, while the employers contributed 106,262,300 marks. This apparent gain of 60,000,000 marks for the workers, however, is met on the other side by an immense loss of privileges for them.

The right of representation on the managing boards at present is divided according to the subscriptions paid. The employers elect one-third and the workers elect two-thirds of the members of the various boards. The workers have the right and the power to increase the benefits of the insurance funds above the legally provided minimum and they have made extensive use of this privilege. This will not be possible any more if the employers are soon to control one-half of the boards. Apart from some ameliorations relating to the extension of benefits to women during their confinement, the government bill contains numerous deteriorations compared with the regulations in force at present.

The much-needed uniform organization will not be achieved. The name of the inferior communal insurance fund will disappear, but still more inferior rural insurance funds will be created in its stead. The insurance funds in the building trades and of the federated states will also be abolished, whilst so many difficulties will be made concerning the voluntary Supplementary Funds that they are bound to disappear as well. In future, we will have local sick insurance funds, rural funds, staff funds, and corporation funds. No reason founded on the purpose of the sick insurance scheme could be stated for this division of forces. This division, however, is needed in order to limit the rights of the workers in the election of members to the insurance boards. The employers henceforth are to have one-half of the votes in local staff and corporation insurance funds, and they will rule the rural sick funds entirely, the workers having no representation on these funds. The workers consequently will always be in the minority.

A uniform insurance scheme which would also be in the interest of those coming within the scope of the law is also avoided in order to permit the sick insurance funds to be used against the workers for political purposes. The 653 paragraphs following are made up of the five insurance laws in force at present and their contents have suffered the least change.

Then come the laws for invalid insurance, supplemented by a so-called insurance of widows and orphans. Although the invalid insurance law has apparently been very little changed, this part of the insurance scheme has been burdened with a very important task, viz., to provide the larger part of the money necessary for the support of the widows and orphans. This indeed seems to be the chief point, because the whole insurance of widows and orphans is simply a question of finance. There is no difference of opinion as to the desirability and necessity of providing for widows and orphans.

The amount necessary for this scheme can be easily calculated according to the number of widows and orphans per 1000 inhabitants. There are on the average per 1000 inhabitants 41.75 widows and 55.22 children under fifteen years of age. According to the last census of trades and professions in every 1000 inhabitants there were 510.3 employees, workers and servants; thus every 12 of this number would have to provide for 1 widow and 1.34 children.

The main question discussed by political economists and insurance experts is how to adequately finance the scheme. The Center tried to mix up in 1902 this popular question with the very unpopular question of tariffs. They declared that the whole surplus derived from the tariff on agrarian produce would be set aside for the purposes of widows and orphans insurance, but when it came to keep this promise then only the surplus duties on rye, wheat, oats, and barley, live stock, meat, and dairy produce appeared under the promised heading, out of the total 130 articles of agrarian produce affected by tariffs. The Center calculated that the surplus of these duties would amount to 91,000,000 marks annually. This sum, as well as yearly interest, was to be accumulated for the next five years. After this time, so it was suggested, this surplus with interest as well as subscriptions to the amount of 91,000,000 mk. was to be appropriated. These propositions were passed by the committee against the expectations of the Center, and this party thereupon immediately changed its attitude withdrawing from their motion the articles oats, barley, and dairy produce, and substituting the word "surplus per head of the population" for surplus. Thus the national exchequer might reckon on an income of 1.49 marks per head of the population. The national exchequer has an increasing income according to the growth of the population. The Center also refused to support any more levying of subscriptions. This law has been in force since March 1st, 1906. Up to today it has provided the following for widows and orphans:

In 1906 Nil
" 1907 42,000,000 marks
" 1908 Nil
" 1909 Nil

By subscriptions of the employers	1,084,719,500 Mk.
" " " " workers	1,084,719,500 "
" interest....................	416,088,100 "
Total	
	2,585,527,100 Mk.

It became then obvious that the object of the law could not be achieved in this way. The government thereupon made another proposition. It suggests first of all using the funds of the invalid insurance scheme, as this branch has more money than is needed. From 1891 to 1907 the following sums have been contributed to the invalid insurance funds:—

The expenditure amounted to:
Pensions and returned subscriptions up to
   Dec. 31, 1907 .... 1,015,896,000 Mk.
Management expenses .... 165,563,400 "
                            Total 1,181,459,400 Mk.

The empire has also contributed under the form of national subsidies to these pensions and returned subscriptions, to the amount of 485,204,400 marks. The accumulated capital at the end of 1907 amounted to 1,404,067,700 marks.

The following methods are proposed as to financing the widow's and orphans' insurance scheme.

1. By far the greater proportion of the widows and orphans are

not to have a pension; for a widow will only be entitled to a pension if she is at the same time invalid, or in other words so generally incapable, physically or mentally, that she is not in a position to earn one-third of the average earnings of the women in her class.

2. Some money is to be found by simply abolishing the repayment of subscriptions. Hitherto, the women were entitled to get their subscriptions returned when they became married. Pensioners of the accident insurance funds who for this reason were not entitled to an invalid pension enjoyed the same privilege. Widows and orphans or deceased members might also claim the subscriptions of the deceased. A grand total of 77,181,600 marks has been expended for these purposes up to 1907.

3. It is proposed to increase the subscriptions from 14, 20, 24, 30, 36 pfennigs respectively per week to 16, 24, 30, 38, 40 pfennigs respectively per week. This will bring an increase of from 45 to 50 millions per year.

4. The national exchequer is to contribute as hitherto to every old age and invalid pension, and to every pension of a widow, 50 marks per year and 25 marks to every pension of an orphan.

5. The pensions of widows and orphans, however, will be so small that they can scarcely be called a pension.

6. We are of opinion, and this opinion was also held by our party's congress at Leipzig, that a reform of the social insurance scheme should have much loftier ideals. Our friends in the Reichstag will therefore propose a complete amalgamation and further extension of the social insurance schemes. This reform should begin by bringing about the unification of the sick insurance scheme. A uniform organization under the self-government of the insured must be established, including all those working for wages or salary, also all other persons with an income of not more than 5,000 marks per year. The sick and convalescent members should be entitled to free medical attendance and remedies, apart from a monetary benefit to the amount of the members' full earnings. Nursing mothers should get adequate support.

The accident insurance funds should be compelled to pay full compensation to the insured and their relatives.

The invalid insurance scheme ought to be developed in such a manner that the full income be insured and that such pensions be paid to enable decent living to the invalids. The insurance of widows and orphans ought to be improved accordingly.

Apart from these schemes an adequate unemployed insurance scheme should also be established.

A social insurance of this kind will certainly require big sums of money, but the people will be able to pay them. All those cases where we should like to give material support by means of the insurance happen whether the people are insured or not. Sickness, accidents, invalidity, and unemployment are bound to happen more frequently and for a longer period without insurance. Sickness can be prevented or otherwise, when it happens, it can be quicker and more effectively dealt with, if good therapeutic treatment is provided. Rational treatment of sickness can also prevent many cases of invalidity. One of the principal tasks of the accident insurance scheme should be to provide good safeguarding methods. If properly organized the number of accidents can be reduced to such an extent that even a full compensation would be cheaper than the present accident insurance by which at the utmost two-thirds of the loss is compensated. Unemployed insurance would enable us to get a precise view of the state of the labor market. By regulating the hours of labor it will then be possible to prevent a good deal of unemployment. The support of the unemployed would cost less than is absorbed by unemployment. Many unemployed become criminals and vagabonds on account of misery. Many a girl is driven to prostitution alone by want. Society pays more for criminals, vagabonds, and prostitutes than would be necessary to benefit the unemployed regularly.

The biggest sums will be necessary for the insurance of women in confinement, nursing mothers, widows, and orphans. There are about thirty-five births per 1000 inhabitants per year. These charges are borne at present only by the poorest families, who have the most children. The privations caused by widowhood and orphanhood at present oppress only the widows and orphans themselves.

Our principle is: sickness, invalidity, accidents, and unemployment should be prevented as much as possible, and otherwise their cost, as well as the cost derived from motherhood and the cost of supporting widows and orphans should be defrayed by the whole population. The demands of the second part of our party's official program are being upheld by our comrades in every session of the Reichstag and of the national diets in the form of initiative motions. Unfortunately we have only little opportunity of getting them discussed. The Reichstag in every session has only a few days at its disposal to discuss such motions. The succession of these motions depends on the numerical strengths of the various groups. Every group is entitled to say what motion they would like to have discussed first. It happens very seldom that more than one motion of every group is discussed at all. It has become a regular use since a number of years to introduce initiative motions in the form of resolutions when the budgets of the ministers are under discussion. The respective minister is then asked to prepare, as soon as possible, a bill in which the demands of the initiative motion are set forth. These propositions are regularly rejected by the reactional majority; if, however, they happen to be accepted, then they are thrown out by the Federal Council, who perhaps will say that the motion is to be used as material for future legislation.

2. The Political Movement

Since the national congress at Stuttgart the political life of Germany has been filled with violent struggles of the proletariat for further political rights. The suffrage question has been the center of all this agitation, i.e. the general and equal right to direct and secret voting for all the elective bodies. The diets of the various federated states are taken into consideration first for these endeavors.

We have already fully explained in our report to the International Congress at Stuttgart how this movement sprung up in November, 1905, with great vehemence, and it has received an even greater impetus since. The German proletariat has shown in mass meetings and monster street demonstrations that they will allow themselves neither peace nor rest before they have obtained general and equal right for direct and secret voting. This question has got into full swing now and even our ruling classes recognize that the present state of affairs has become unbearable.

We have universal suffrage for the Reichstag elections for all male citizens of twenty-five years of age. This so-called equality is however much injured by the growth of population in this country. The present constituencies have been defined in 1867 and nothing has been changed with respect to this division since that time, namely since forty-three years. The population has since then declined in some constituencies, for instance in the agrarian parts of Eastern Prussia. Other parts of the country, as the big cities and industrial centers, have at the same time experienced a rapid increase of their population. The constituency Angerburg-Lötzen, in Eastern Prussia, for instance numbered in 1905, 77,373 inhabitants and Ostprignitz in the province of Brandenburg had but 67,307 inhabitants, whilst the constituency Teltow-Beeskow, which includes the western and southern suburbs of Berlin, numbered 959,289 inhabitants. This number has since increased up to more than 1,000,000, but is only entitled to one member in the diet. A good many similar examples could be cited which go to prove that the results of our elections in no way give a true reflex of the political tendencies of the electorate.

Our diets have many very important questions to deal with, for instance those concerning educational matters, also the carrying out of nearly all Imperial laws. These diets are constituted on the ground of differing election systems of the various states. Some of our federated states, for instance, Bavaria, Wurttemburg, and Baden, possess the general and equal right to direct and secret voting for their diets. In Mecklenburg however this name and the privileges of a legislative body are given to a corporation which is simply a meeting of the big landowners, that is of the feudal aristocracy, and of representatives of the city councils. There is a large variety of all possible suffrage systems, so that we must refrain from further commenting on them. As one of the results of these systems we have agrarian rule in nearly all the federated states of Germany. The 1907 census shows that in Germany only 17,681,176 Inhabitants or 286.5 out of every 1,000 lived from agriculture, gardening, stock-breeding, forestry, and fishing, whilst 34,664,776 inhabitants or 561.6 out of every 1,000 are dependent on industries, mining, commercial trades, and transports. The agrarians all the same rule in nearly every federated state as well as in imperial affairs. This rule is based upon the total absence of privileges for the workers in the election for the diets and on the difference of dimensions of the various constituencies.

The Prussian diet consists of two chambers, the House of Lords, and the House of Deputies. The House of Lords is composed of 364 members, including 238 representatives of the high feudal caste, who are born members of this chamber, or have been nominated through noble families, generals and big manufacturers nominated for life, ten representatives of the universities, and fifteen mayors of the big cities.

The House of Deputies consists of 443 members which have been elected under the three-class suffrages. Any decision of this chamber only becomes law with the consent of the lords. The three classes for election purposes are made up in the following manner: every male Prussian who is twenty-four years of age has a right to a vote. If an election is forthcoming then a list of all the electors of that constituency is compiled, indicating also the amount of direct taxes paid by each elector. A fictitious sum of 3 marks is put in for all those who pay no direct taxes because they may own no land, carry on no trade liable to taxation, or have an income of less than 900 marks. The total amount of all the taxes paid by the whole electorate is thereupon ascertained and is then divided by three. Now those are picked out who pay the highest taxes and whose combined taxes amount to one-third of the total direct taxes paid by the whole electorate. These electors constitute a first class. The same thing is done with regard to those who pay the next highest taxes, who together form the second class, whilst the remainder, namely the large mass of the population, constitute a third class of electors.

In the last elections there were 7,682,721 electors on the rolls. They included 293,402 or 3.82 percent of the total number, first-class electors: 1,065,240 or 13.87 percent second-class electors: and 6,324,079 or 82.32 percent third-class electors. Every class nominates an equal number of election men or delegates and these delegates ultimately elect the deputy. Apart from these privileges of the rich, we have also the inequality in the division of the constituencies. There are rural constituencies with one member of Parliament, for less than 8,000 electors, whilst in some urban districts, a deputy is allotted to about 78,000 electors.

A similar preference system has been introduced in 1895 in Saxony with the only difference that the vote was secret, namely by ballot, whilst in Prussia we have a public vote, the elector being compelled to publicly name his candidate. The Prussian government in 1908 gave the formal promise in the king's speech that the suffrage system would be organically developed and would be organized in such a manner as would correspond to the actual necessities of the Prussian people. A bill was indeed introduced into the diet in February, 1910, which however preserved all the injustices of the present system.

The three-class system and the public vote was not to be altered. It was only proposed to substitute the direct vote for the old indirect vote. Ministers, officers, men with university education, state officials, reservists entitled to civil employment, on account of their twelve years' service, were to be elevated from the third class of electors. This bill and its consequent treatment in the diet had a most provocative effect on the population, more than the most inflammatory speeches. The diet then refused the government's proposition, adding also a great number of amendments. They have in no way improved the bill.

This agitation for the general and equal right of secret and direct voting for the various diets had since 1907 rapidly gained in vehemence. Big demonstrations in the streets and mass meetings as they had not yet occurred in Germany, nor, as we might safely say in any other country, have proved the stern determination of the proletariat. There were more than a million workers who assembled on the 10th of April, 1910, in mass meetings all over Prussia.

The old suffrage system has been changed in a number of federated states during the last few years. In the kingdom of Saxony the three-class suffrage system was sustituted by a plural system which provided for additional votes, according to age, amount of taxes paid, and so forth. The rich usually have four votes. A plural system has also been introduced in the Grand Duchy of Oldenburg, but only one additional vote is given there to all electors over forty years of age. Saxe-Weimar changed the indirect vote for the direct vote.

Late election results show a continuous growth of the socialist movement. Ten by-elections for the Reichstag have taken place during the last year. In the general elections 1907 the candidates of our party polled in these constituencies 78,656 votes out of a total vote of 294,808. In the by-elections, however, they polled 93,310 votes out of a total vote of 274,430. We thus increased our vote from 26.7 percent to 35 percent of all votes recorded.

Similar results have been obtained in the elections for the diets. General elections for the Prussian diet took place in 1908. A comparison of the vote with 1903 gives the following statistic:

	1903	1908
Socialists	314,149	598,522
Conservatives......................	324,157	354,786
Independent Conservatives	47,975	63,612
National Liberals	256,220	318,589
Liberal Association.................	16,735	21,993

cont'd.	1903	1908
Liberal People's Party	73,245	98,600
Centre	251,958	499,343
Poles, Danes and so forth	181,356	226,248
Union of Agricultural Landowners....	12,548	15,013
Union of Anti-Semites	2,880	8,959
Political attitude unknown...........	190,390	301,894
Total	1,671,613	2,507,559

In 1903 we were the second strongest party in the country. We had 18.8 percent of the total votes, but had not succeeded in getting a single seat in Parliament. Numerically we became the strongest party in 1908. We polled 23.87 percent of the total votes and got seven of our candidates elected. Four of these elections were later on declared invalid, under the pretext that the officials of the Berlin City Council had not properly compiled the register. We successfully defended three of these seats, but the fourth seat was lost.

General elections under the new plural system took place for the first time in the Kingdom of Saxony on October 21st, 1909. Altogether 634,212 electors recorded their votes; 343,296 of these voted for a social democratic candidate, whilst our opponents disposed only of 292,816 electors. These 634,212 electors had, on account of the plural system, 1,273,908 votes. The number of electors and votes recorded for every party were as follows:

	Number of	
	electors	votes
Social Democrats	311,396	492,522
Conservatives	103,517	281,804
National Liberals	125,157	236,511
Radical Liberals	41,857	100,804
Anti-Semites	20,248	55,502

Out of the ninety-one seats of that chamber, our comrades gained twenty-five.

The general elections for the diet in Baden took place on the same date. In the previous general elections in that country, our party had polled 50,431 votes. Now this number increased to 80,835 votes and they elected twenty members, instead of twelve. A similar progress in the elections for their respective legislative bodies has been made by comrades in Lübeck, Bremen, Hamburg, and Saxe-Weimar.

This movement demands great sacrifices through the present punishing power of the state. The following penalties have been inflicted on comrades of our party on account of advocating our cause, during the last three years:

In 1907: 36 years, 4 months, 2 weeks, and 1 day imprisonment and fines to the amount of 30,600 marks.

In 1908: 18 years, 8 months, and 4 day imprisonment, and fines to the amount of 33,446 marks.

In 1909: 27 years, 10 months, and 2 days imprisonment, and fines to the amount of 28,750 marks.

Lately, the movement among the juveniles is fiercely prosecuted by the authorities, who continually inflict heavy fines on the representatives of the juveniles.

3. The Organization of the Party

The organization of our Party, to which we referred at some length in previous reports, has meanwhile undergone some important changes. A new association law has come into operation on May 15th, 1908, of which a short description will be given later on. The new law also allows women to adhere to political parties, which hitherto had only been possible in some of our federated states. The social democratic women have since joined the organziation of the Party all over the country. A uniform minimum subscription for all members of the Party has been established. The parties' associations in the various constituencies will in future be entitled to representation on the parties' congresses, according to their membership.

The manner in which a member can be expelled from the Party has also been changed.

We herewith quote the more important changes that have been made in our rules:

§ 4. Organizations which include female members must allow them representation on their committee. The female committee members have to carry on special propaganda among women, in agreement with the other committee members.

§ 5. The district and national organizations may fix their rate of subscription themselves, providing that the minimum monthly subscriptions is not less than 30 pfennigs for males and 15 for females. At least 20 percent of the regular subscriptions must be forwarded to the central fund. The Party's executive committee may allow the various organizations a higher amount than 80 percent of these takings for their local expenses, if the committee of the district or the national organization agree.

§ 6. The business year for the organization of the Party extends from July 1st to June 30th. The Presidents of the social democratic societies have to report annually to the executive committee, not later than July 15th, on a list of queries prepared by the executive. They should at least give details on the form and extension of the propaganda that has been carried on, on the number of organized comrades in their respective constituency. The amount of subscriptions paid by the members, total income, and how the money at their disposal has been spent.

A similar annual report on their activity and on the way they spent the money received from the Party's executive, must be prepared by the committees of the district and national organizations.

§ 7. The Party's congress is the chief authority of the Party. Entitled to representation at the national congress are:

1. The Party's delegates of the various constituencies. The number of delegates depends on the number of members. Constituencies with but 1,500 members are entitled to but 1 delegate. Two delegates are allowed up to 3,000, 3 for up to 6,000, 4 for up to 12,000, 5 for up to 18,000, and 6 for more than 18,000. The number of members is calculated according to the number of subscriptions paid into the central fund, as provided by § 5.

   A female comrade should, if possible, be amongst the delegates wherever several delegates are elected.

2. The members of the Party's group in the Reichstag.

3. The members of the Party's executive committee, and of the control commission.

4. Special reporters invited by the executive committee.

The members of the Party's group in the Reichstag are only entitled to an advisory vote in all matters parliamentary. The same is the case with the members of the Party's executive in all questions relating to the business management of the Party. The representatives of the Party's institutions, which have been invited by the executive, are also allowed no vote.

§ 14. The number of the members of the Party's executive is fixed by Congress. The Party's executive consists of two Presidents, a treasurer, the secretaries, and three auxiliary members, the latter including a female comrade. The members of the Party's executive committee are entitled to represent each other.

The election of the President, the treasurer, the secretaries, and of the representative of the female comrades must proceed at the congress by means of voting papers, the result of the first ballot being final.

The second ballot between the two candidates with the highest number of votes must take place if none have received the absolute majority of all votes cast.

In case of an equality of votes, the result is decided by lot.

The other two auxiliary members are selected by the control commission. The executive committee has to be constituted immediately after its election, of which proper notice is to be published in the official organ of the party.

§ 23. Nobody can be a member of the party who has seriously contravened the principles of the Party's program or has been guilty of a dishonorable action. A member can furthermore be expelled for violating the interests of the Party, or for obstinate resistance to the decisions of the Party's organization.

In case of dispute, the committee has to decide as to the admissibility of a member in the district or national organization.

The expulsion of a member can only be decided by an organization of the party (local society or association covering the respective constituency). The same proposal can only be made by the committee of an organization with the consent of the accused.

The member in question will be informed of the decision by the district or national committee, which may also eventually publish the decision.

§ 24. Both parties may, if not satisfied with the decision of the district or national committee, demand that arbitrators should be appointed, if such demand is made within four weeks after they were informed of the decision.

Such an arbitration court to consist of seven members; the accused and the interested organization appointing three members each out of the membership of the district organization to which the accused belonged. A chairman is then appointed by the executive committee of the party.

The accused is considered expelled from the party if he neglects to appoint arbitrators within a term fixed by the executive committee. Four weeks at least must be allowed for this.

A written judgment will be forwarded by the executive of the Party, who is also charged to eventually publish the decision.

§ 25. Both parties may eventually lodge an appeal against the decision of the arbitrators in the next national congress of the party. This appeal must be addressed to the executive committee within four weeks after the judgment has been forwarded to the parties.

§ 26. A member can be expelled from the party on the ground of Par. 23, Section 1, only in the way prescribed in the foregoing rules.

All committees of the Party are entitled, if they do not definitely pronounce the expulsion, to temporarily exclude a member from all offices of confidence, or to pass a vote of censure. Both parties may also appeal against this decision.

The foregoing regulations shall in no way interfere with the right of the organizations to appoint an investigation committee to investigate the case of a member without proposing his expulsion.

§ 27. Membership of the Party ceases, with death, expulsion, or resignation. In such a case, all privileges that the member may have had, by virtue of his membership, with regard to the Party, the executive committee, the control commission, and the individual members, are null and void.

§ 28. A demand for readmission of an expelled member can only be addressed to the committee of the district or national association, in whose area the candidate lives.

The organization which had proposed the previous expulsion should be asked for information before a decision is rendered.

The candidate as well as this organization may appeal against that decision to the next national congress of the Party. This appeal should be lodged with the Party's executive early enough to enable its publication together with other motions to be submitted to the congress.

The associations in the various constituencies for the Reichstag form the base of our organization. A local branch of the Party may be established in every city if this constituency covers more than one city, but these societies are only considered sections of the association for the whole constituency. The associations of the various constituencies are combined into district or national federations. These federations have their own rules of management, providing they are not contradictory to the general rules of management of the whole Party. Our organization at present consists of forty-five district or national federations, at the head of each being a separate committee. Every federation has one or two permanent secretaries at its disposal. There are at present forty-seven district or national permanent secretaries in office.

The district and national federations are in constant relations with the executive committee of the Party. Their advice is always sought for in all important questions relating to their sphere of activity. Special conferences of representatives of the district and national committees are organized in cases of general importance.

The Party has gained a solid footing in nearly all constituencies, except in six purely agrarian constituencies, where we have not been successful so far. The following statement gives a review of the numerical strength of the associations in the various constituencies.

The actual number of members at the end of June, 1909, amounted to less than 100 in 77 constituencies of the Reichstag. There are members: from 100 to 200 in 42, from 200 to 300 in 22, from 300 to 400 in 28, from 400 to 500 in 14, from 500 to 600 in 13, from 600 to 700 in 12, from 700 to 800 in 12, from 800 to 900 in 16, from 900 to 1,000 in 8, from 1,000 to 1,500 in 27, from 1,500 to 2,000 in 25, from 2,000 to 3,000 in 23, from 3,000 to 4,000 in 22, from 4,000 to 5,000 in 6, from 5,000 to 6,000 in 9, from 6,000 to 7,000 in 3, from 7,000 to 8,000 in 2, from 8,000 to 9,000 in 2, from 9,000 to 10,000 in 2, from 10,000 to 11,000 in 2, from 11,000 to 12,000 in 3 constituencies.

In 7 constituencies there were 14,000 to 15,000, 15,000 to 16,000, 19,000 to 20,000, 22,000 to 23,000, 23,000 to 24,000, 24,000 to 25,000, 26,000 to 27,000 members respectively.

Our larger associations have been forced to appoint permanent secretaries to deal with their increasing work. Sixty-two constituencies have their own permanent secretaries at the present time.

Development and numerical strength of the Party.

Business year	Total number of constituencies of the Reichstag	Number of constituencies with Party organizations	Number of localities with organizations of the Party	Membership of the Party			Number of members of our Party in proportion to the number of socialist votes cast for the Reichstag
				Total	Male	Female	
1907	397	325	2704	530,466	519,523	10,943	16.4
1908	397	366	3120	587,336	557,878	29,458	18.0
1909	397	378	3281	633,309	571,050	62,259	19.1

Income and Expenditure of the Party.

Business Year	Income Mk.	Expenditure Mk.
1907	1,191,819.42	1,358,122.39
1908	852,976.10	783,958.13
1909	1,105,249.77	621,202.45

The last general election took place during the business year 1907. This explains the comparatively high income and expenditure of that year.

4. Parliamentary Representation of the Party

Our Party is represented in the German *Reichstag*, which numbers 397 members, by 47 deputies. The by-elections, which have taken place since the last general election, have shown splendid results to our Party. We have won in these by-elections four seats, namely Landau, Coburg, Halle, and Eisenach.

Our Party has furthermore 185 representatives in the *Parliaments of the Federated States*.

State	Number of Deputies	Number of Social-Democratic Deputies
Anhalt	36	1
Baden..........................	73	20
Bavaria.........................	163	21
Bremen.........................	150	16
Hamburg........................	160	20
Hessen	50	5
Lippe	21	1
Lübeck..........................	120	12
Oldenburg......................	44	4
Prussia	443	6
Reuss	16	3
Saxony..........................	91	25
Saxe-Altenburg	32	7
Saxe-Coburg	30	8
Saxe-Meiningen	24	9
Saxe-Weimar.....................	33	4
Schaumburg-Lippe.................	15	1
Schwarzburg-Rudolstadt............	16	7
Württemberg.....................	92	15

We have no representation yet in the Parliaments of six federated states.

We dealt fully with the activity of the *Social-Democratic party in City and Borough Councils* in our last report. The number of social-democratic councillors increases from year to year. Our Party has now 1,368 representatives on 300 city councils and 4,789 representatives on 1,779 rural district councils. We have furthermore 115 aldermen in 38 cities and 159 in 93 rural districts.

5. Feminist Movement

The Party keeps a "social democratic woman's bureau" which is to carry on a special propaganda among the proletarian women. The address of this Bureau is the following: Ottilie Baader, Berlin SW. 68, Lindenstr. 3. The Women's Bureau circulates weekly articles on the feminist movement to all papers of the Party. Special leaflets and pamphlets, with the objects of social democracy and with criticisms on the political events of the day, are published for the women and girls of the working classes. Female speakers for special propaganda tours are provided for the various organizations of the party. As a result of this activity the number of female members in our political organization has increased in 1909 by 32,801. They number now 62,259. Special women's reading clubs have been organized in a great number of cities with the aim of providing for a better training of our female comrades. The organ of the socialist women is "Die Gleichheit" (Equality) which had in 1909, 77,000 regular subscribers. The women's bureau gives great attention to the establishment of *Committees for the Protection of Children.* They are composed of women and men of the working classes, organized at the instance of our bureau and the trade unions. These committees provide for the enforcement of legal regulations relating to the protection of children.

6. Juvenile Movement

Up till 1908 we had two central organizations of young people, one for Northern Germany and one for Southern Germany. Our new association law has a very reactionary clause on this matter, this clause providing for penalties for young people under eighteen years of age, if they joined a political society or take part in a political meeting. Our central juvenile organizations therefore have dissolved, whilst in many places unpolitical local societies of young people are still in existence.

The Party, as well as the trade unionists, have bestowed great attention on the juvenile movement during the last few years. Their congresses thoroughly and exhaustively dealt with this question. Our Party's national congress at Nuremburg (1908) voted the following motion with regard to the juvenile movement.

The encouragement of the culture of young male and female workers is a most important task in the struggle for emancipation of the working classes.

The national congress pledges the affiliated organizations to do all in their power that the youth of the working classes be educated in the spirit of proletarian ideas.

With this end in view regular lectures should be arranged, which are suitable to the intelligence of youth. Arrangements for serious and amusing occupations, also sports, recreations, and comradeship should also be provided for.

Special committees should be appointed in every locality. They should consist of representatives of the local Party organization, of the trade union councils, and of the young male and female workers. Every delegation must include at least one female comrade.

No fee shall be charged for lectures, nor, as far as this is possible, for all other arrangements.

These committees should engage the trade union councils to do everything for the legal protection of the apprentices.

This congress charges the Party's executive with the publication of a special organ for the education of the youth of the working classes.

The defence of interests on the economic field and the decision in political matters remains solely the task of the trade union and political organizations.

Declaration.

It is to be understood from this resolution that nothing should stand in the way of local unpolitical organizations of the youth who manage their own affairs with the cooperation of adults.

The trade unions passed a similar resolution at their congress at Hamburg which had taken place a little earlier. The juvenile movement in the Germany of today has become an important part of our political and trade union movement. Both the party and trade unions work in unison on this field.

A center for the working youth of Germany, Berlin SW. 68, Lindenstrasse 69, has been established to ensure the execution of the above decisions. The Party's executive, the general commission of the trade unions, and the juveniles are represented each by four delegates on this central body. Every group must delegate at least one female member for this purpose.

Committees for the juveniles are in existence in 330 localities consisting equally of representatives of the Party, the trade unions, and the juveniles. Their activity circulates within the limits of the decisions of the Nuremburg congress. Special guides for the various branches of activity for these committees have been issued by the Berlin center, which also furnishes all sorts of propaganda material, chiefly leaflets. The local committees of the center are in constant relation to each other. A conference of these local committees for the juveniles has recently taken place, where 129 delegates from all parts of the Empire were present. This conference has outlined the program for future work.

The *Arbeiter-Jugend* (the working youth), the special organ published by the Berlin center every fortnight has sixteen pages. This new paper has met with a good reception among the juveniles. The number of its readers increases continually. It numbers more than 40,000 regular subscribers at the present time.

The costs of this juvenile movement are borne by both the Party and the trade unions together. The total expenses of the Berlin center amount to about 20,000 marks up till now.

7. Press and Literature

The number of social democratic dailies has increased in Germany from sixty-five to seventy-four, since the International Socialist Congress at Stuttgart. They are printed in fifty-six printing offices owned by the Party. The number of regular subscribers of these social-democratic papers has from 1906 to 1909 risen from 837,790 to 1,041,498. This does not include our monthlies and the *Neue Zeit*. The income from subscriptions amounted to 6,706,151 marks in 1909 and the income through advertisements was 4,363,761 marks. It must be mentioned, however, that the economic depression resulted in a decline of the amount of subscriptions. Our illustrated paper *Die Neue Welt* is added to the Sunday editions of some of our dailies. Its weekly circulation is 475,000. The two humorous papers of the Party, the *Wahre Jacob* and the *Postillon* have a combined circulation of 250,000. The party's scientific organ, the *Neue Zeit* is now published in its twenty-eighth year. Its circulation is 8500 copies weekly. A special propaganda paper for women *Die Gleichheit* is published fortnightly, by the Party. *Die Gleichheit* had in 1909 a circulation of 37,000. The *Kommunale Praxis* has been published since the last ten years as a review for municipal socialism and politics, in order to adequately equip the socialist councillors for their many-sided activities. The circulation of this paper is 2,700 copies. The speakers of our Party, members of Parliament, and editors of our papers, receive free of charge the *Social-Demo-cratische Partei-Correspondenz* (Correspondence Circular of the Social-Democratic Party) which collects all documents that may be important for propaganda purposes and which furthermore refutes briefly the attacks of dissenting organizations and papers. This fortnightly paper has a circulation of 3,000 copies.

Leaflets and pamphlets are issued annually in large numbers by the Party's executive and the district and local organizations. Favorite means of propaganda in many districts are also agricultural almanacs. They are distributed broadcast free of charge. The turnover of the bookselling department of the *Vorwärts* has been 522,082 marks in 1906–7; 563,737 marks in 1907–8 and 511,727 marks in 1908–9. The publishing office of J. H. W. Dietz, successor at Stuttgart, which is also owned by the Party and which bestows special care on the publication of theoretical socialist books, has in the year of report published the fiftieth volume of the *International Library*.

The Social Democratic Press Agency has been established since July 15th, 1908. This agency furnishes our press with political and trade union news and prepares also extracts of new bills and parliamentary documents. A newsletter is circulated daily to our press, and a special news service by telephone and telegraph is established. The annual budget of this press agency amounts to 46,000 marks. The sum of 32,000 marks is contributed by such of our papers as are in sound financial position, whilst the deficiency is met by the central funds. The proposed organization of a foreign news service could not yet be organized on account of the probable high cost.

8. The Party's School

The social democratic party has in autumn, 1906, established in Berlin a permanent Party school.

The first four terms, which last six months each, were attended by twenty-six to thirty-one students. The candidates for this school are proposed by the district or national federations from their number of male and female comrades who are actively working for our cause. Their applications are laid before the board of teachers whereupon those to be admitted to the school are selected by the executive. The trade unions have also sent several students to the last few courses of lectures, in accordance with an agreement that has been arrived at between the Party and the trade unions. The rooms have been specially adapted for the purpose of this school. The number of lectures in every six months is about 780 to 800. The school curriculum is limited. The student is not to be filled with a mass of unsystematized knowledge, but he shall be able, free from all everyday cares, and also from all propaganda work for the party or trade union, to devote six months purely to the study of social problems. The student is to get in the first instance a thoroughly theoretical schooling. The educational subjects treated are as follows: Political Economy, Sociology, German History (Modern), History of Socialism, Workers' Rights, Penal Code, Civil Law, Natural Science, Municipal Politics, Art of Composition, Oratory, Technics of Journalism.

The material cost of this school, the salaries of lecturers, and the cost of keeping the students during their stay at Berlin are paid from the central funds of our Party. The families of the students receive special grants during the absence of their wage earner from their district organization. This can easily be borne also by poorer districts, because they get regular subsidies from the central fund. These courses or lectures have afforded for the first terms a total outlay from our central funds to the amount of 203,900 marks.

9. Education

The national congress of the Party at Mannheim nominated an educational committee, consisting of several members. This committee gives advice and help to all organizations of our party and provides suitable instructors for scientific lectures and courses, as well as artists for good entertainments. Local educational committees have been formed in all larger cities of the Empire. They are composed of representatives of the local Party organizations and of the trade union councils. In some parts of the country they have formed special district federations. The central educational committee provides traveling speakers for lectures and courses of lectures dealing with scientific questions, especially the "stages of development of the economic history" and also "Marx's Economic Teachings." One of the new traveling lecturers deals especially with questions of natural science and the history of culture. These courses generally extend to four weeks. They are usually held in three neighboring cities at the same time, there being eight lectures in each city. The lectures are usually attended by 250 to 300 male and female comrades, whilst from 30 to 40 are usually enrolled for the courses of lectures. In 1908–9, for instance, 57 larger cities and 144 smaller towns have profited from these courses of lectures. Nineteen instruction and 38 lecture courses have been organized in the same year. They were attended by 8,969 comrades including 666 women. The educational committee published furthermore guides for artistic entertainment in the form of regular winter programs, also introductions to dramatic, operatic, and musical works. It is proposed hereby to facilitate the appreciation of performances that are especially organized for the working classes. The same committee has also issued a model catalog for libaries giving as the basis of a library a set of books to the value of ten marks. The catalog gives supplementary lists of books, the value of the suggested libraries increasing from 10 to 25, 50, 100 up to 500 marks. Another publication of the educational committee is an illustrated catalog of artistic wall-decorations, in which special attention is drawn to comparatively cheap but first-class lithographic designs of wel-known artists. Regularly and shortly before Christmas a catalog of recommended *juvenile literature* is forwarded to all organizations. The last year's catalog included 184 selected books for presents to the children of the proletariat. This list of books has then been reprinted or reproduced by nearly all our political and trade union papers. In larger towns it has become the custom to organize shortly before Christmas an exhibition of recommendable juvenile literature. The educational work has thus in a short period of time become a comprehensive branch of the activities of the social democratic party.

10. The Social Democratic Party and the Trade Unions

A separate report of the German trade unions has been submitted to congress. The negotiations with locally organized trade unionists on the questions of their amalgamation with the central federations, of which we made mention in our last report, have resulted in about 5,000 locally organized comrades joining the central federations. The others remained in the localist societies, adopting entirely the principles of an anarcho-socialist syndicalism. This group is small, however, and of no importance at all in the political and economic movement.

The national congress of our Party at Nuremburg (1908) passed the following resolution in connection with this matter:

> This congress welcomes the amalgamations of local societies with the central federations of trade unions that have been brought about by negotiations.
>
> Those societies, who, in spite of these negotiations, have remained in the field of the free association of unions, have thereby manifested that they do not want the absolutely necessary unity of economic organization of the working classes, in spite of the decisions of our national congresses and of the international social congress at Stuttgart. The free association of unions has thereby put itself into open opposition to the Party by purposely fighting and traducing social democracy, in connection with their anarcho-syndicalist endeavors.
>
> The negotiations with the amalgamated German metal-workers' union which has been formed contrary to the decision of the Lübeck congress and which has been called a serious injury to the interests of the working-class by our national congress at Mannheim have not led to any practical results. This congress therefore declares:
>
> Every cooperation of members of the Party within the societies affiliated to the Free Association of Unions or within the ranks of the amalgamated German metal-workers' union, is incompatible with the principles and interests of the Social-democracy.

In important questions where the interests of the Party and the trade unions are concerned the central executives arrange for a combined action. This cooperation of the Party and trade unions has proved a great success.

On the Mayday question the following agreement has been entered into by the Party and trade unions.

> A Mayday committee should be appointed in every locality, if possible, at the beginning of the year, consisting of an equal number of representatives of the trade unions and of the Party organization. This committee selects its own chairman.

It is incumbent on these committees under consideration of the local and trade conditions, of the decisions of the trade unions and of the national congresses of the social democratic party, to provide for an appropriate festival. This festival should not take place on any other day but the first of May.

Special relief can be given to those workers who are locked out on the ground of a Mayday demonstration. Entitled to this support are all workers belonging to the Party or the trade unions.

District funds shall be established for those locked-out, these districts to be ascertained with the consent of the interested towns. The necessary means for such support should be provided by the organization of the party and of the trade unions of the district engaged in a lock-out by voluntary subscriptions and collections.

Those towns that cannot be properly included in one of these district funds should establish their own local fund to support those locked-out in their respective localities.

11. Our Relations to other Socialist Parties and Our International Activity

The social democratic party of Germany gives the utmost attention to the struggles of the socialist parties abroad. Our press has done its best to ensure full success to the collections made on behalf of the Swedish mass strike. We have in Germany, collected for our Swedish comrades the sum of 1,283,161 marks. Our Party gives an annual subsidy of 2,500 francs to the International Socialist Bureau at Brussels, apart from a number of subsidies given to various Socialist papers abroad.

12. The Cooperative Movement

Cooperative societies cannot affiliate to a political party on account of legal restrictions. The German proletariat, however, has given its attention to the politically neutral workers' Cooperative societies. The workers have taken a keen interest in the work of these cooperative societies which are politically neutral. The enormous rise in the cost of living and of all articles of daily use has been caused by our protective policy. New indirect taxes indeed compelled the working classes to try and obtain the benefits of cooperation. It is about ten years that the workers, for this very reason, organized special propaganda on a large and general scale in order to induce their fellow-workers to join the cooperative societies en masse. The middle class and liberal leaders of the "General Federation of German cooperative associations" thereupon committed a veritable coup d'état at their congress at Kreuznach (1902); they expelled ninety-nine societies from the federation. The expelled societies organized a new movement, and at their meeting at Dresden on May 17th and 18th, 1903, established a central federation of German cooperative societies. The members of our Party are on friendly terms with the last-named central federation.

The Year Book of the Central Federation of German cooperative societies (7th edition, 1909) gives the following statistical details of the actual state of the cooperative movement:

Number of affiliated societies	1,068
Number of societies reporting	1,060
Membership	949,744
Number of shops	2,829
Number of persons employed	14,910

Annual turnover	Mk.	349,728,334
Amount of articles produced by the affiliated societies	"	44,482,900
Benefits	"	21,102,782
Stock	"	36,457,971
Inventory and Machines	"	8,308,435
Book value of land and house property	"	48,500,087
Capital of the societies	"	32,467,578
Borrowed capital	"	51,315,909

The question of tariff agreements between cooperative societies and trade unions has been discussed in 1908, at the Cooperative Congress at Eisenach, as well as at the National Trade Union Congress at Hamburg. Tariff agreements have been concluded with the federation of bakers and with the transport workers' federation. A permanent tariff board, consisting of representatives of trade unions and cooperative societies, has been established for the purpose of settling any differences that might arise.

13. Other Forms of Organization

The various cooperative societies of the workers, so-called free subsidiary insurance funds of the workers and so forth, have in Germany no relations with political parties, on account of legal restrictions.

Translator Unknown

SOCIALISM AND MAJOR ISSUES OF THE DAY

WOMEN

August Bebel

Woman and Socialism

By the enactment of the German factory laws of 1891 the work day of adult women workers in factories was limited to eleven hours, but a number of exceptions were permitted. Night work for women was also prohibited, but here too exceptions were made for factories that run day and night, and for manufacturers limited to certain seasons. Only after the international convention at Bern on September 26, 1906, determined on a night's rest of eleven hours for factory workers, and after socialists for many years energetically demanded the prohibition of night work for women and the establishment of an eight-hour day, the government and the bourgeois parties are yielding at last. The law of December 28, 1908, limits the hours of work for women to ten hours daily in all factories where no less than ten workers are employed. On Saturdays and on days preceding holidays the limit is eight hours. Women may not be employed for eight weeks prior to and after their confinement. Their readmission depends upon a medical certificate stating that at least six weeks have elapsed since their confinement. Women may not be employed in the manufacture of coke, nor for the carrying of building materials. In spite of the energetic opposition of socialists, an amendment was accepted that the controlling officials may permit overtime work for fifty days annually. Especially noteworthy is the clause which constitutes a first interference with the exploitation by domestic industry. This clause determines that women and minors may not be given work to take home on days when their hours of work in the factory have been as long as the law permits. Regardless of its imperfections the new law certainly means progress compared to the present state of affairs.

But women are not only employed in growing numbers in those occupations that are suited to their inferior physical strength, they are employed wherever the exploiters can obtain higher profits by their labor. Among such occupations are difficult and disagreeable as well as dangerous ones. These facts glaringly contradict that fantastic conception of woman as a weak and tender creature, as described by poets and writers of novels. Facts are stubborn things, and we are dealing with facts only, since they prevent us from drawing false conclusions and indulging in sentimental talk. But these facts teach us, as has been previously stated, that women are employed in the following industries: The textile trades, chemical trades, metallurgy, paper industry, machine manufacture, wood work, manufacture of articles of food and luxury, and mining above the ground. In Belgium women over twenty-one are employed in mining underground also. They are furthermore employed in the wide field of agriculture, horticulture, cattle-breeding, and the numerous trades connected with these occupations, and in those various trades which have long since been their specific realm—dressmaking, millinery, manufacture of underwear, and as salesladies, clerks, teachers, kindergarten teachers, writers, artists of all kinds, etc. Tens of thousands of women of the poorer middle class are employed in stores and in other commercial positions and are thereby almost entirely withdrawn from housekeeping and from the care of their children. Lastly, young, and especially pretty women, find more and more employment as waitresses, in restaurants and cafes, as chorus girls, dancers, etc., to the greatest detriment of their morals. They are used as bait to attract pleasure-seeking men. Horrible conditions exist in these occupations from which the white slave traders draw many of their victims.

Among the above-named occupations there are many dangerous ones. Thus danger from the effects of alkaline and sulphuric fumes exist to a great degree in the manufacture and cleaning of straw hats. Bleaching is dangerous owing to the inhalation of chloral fumes. There is danger of poisoning in the manufacture of colored paper, the coloring of artificial flowers; the manufacture of metachromatypes, chemicals, and poisons; the coloring of tin soldiers and other tin toys, etc. Silvering of mirrors means death to the unborn children of pregnant workers. In Prussia about 22 percent of all infants die during their first year of life; but among the babies of working women employed in certain dangerous occupations we find, as stated by Dr. Hirt, the following appalling death-rate; mirror makers, 65 percent; glass cutters, 55 percent; workers in lead, 40 percent. In 1890 it was reported that among seventy-eight pregnant women who had been employed in the type founderies of the government district of Wiesbaden, only thirty-seven had normal confinements. Dr. Hirt asserts that the following trades become especially dangerous to women during the second half of their pregnancy: the manufacture of colored paper and flowers, the finishing of Brussels laces with white lead, the making of metachromatypes (transfer pictures), the silvering of mirrors, the rubber industry, and all manufactures in which the workers inhale poisonous gases, such as carbonic acid, carbonic oxide, sulphide of hydrogen, etc. The manufacture of shoddy, and phosphoric matches are also dangerous occupations. The report of the factory inspector for Baden shows that the average annual number of premature births among working women increased from 1,039 during the years 1882 to 1886 to 1,244 during the years 1887 to 1891. The number of births that had to be preceeded by an operation were on an average 1,118 from 1882 to 1886, and 1,385 from 1887 to 1891. More serious facts of this sort would be revealed if similar investigations were made throughout Germany. But generally the factory inspectors in framing their reports content themselves with the remark: "Particular injuries to women by their employment in factories have not been observed." How could they observe them during their short visits and without consulting medical opinion? That furthermore, there is great danger to life and limb, especially in the textile trades, the manufacture of explosives and work at agricultural machinery, has been shown. Moreover a number of enumerated trades are among the most difficult and strenuous, even for men; that can be seen by a glance at the very incomplete list. It is very easy to say that this or that occupation is unsuited to a woman. But what can she do if no other more suitable occupation is open to her? Dr. Hirt* gives the following list of occupations in which young girls ought not to

---

*Industrial activity of women.

be employed at all on account of the danger to their health: Manufacture of bronze colors, manufacture of emery paper, making of straw hats, glass cutting, lithographing, combing flax, picking horse hair, plucking fustian, manufacture of tin plate, manufacture of shoddy, and work at flax mills.

In the following trades young girls should be employed only if proper protection (sufficient ventilation, etc.) has been provided: Manufacture of wall paper, porcelain, lead pencils, lead shot, volatile oils, alum, prussiate of potash, bromide, quinine, soda, paraffin and ultramarine (poisonous), colored paper (poisonous), colored wafers, metachromatypes, phosphoric matches,* Paris green, and artificial flowers. Further occupations on the list are the cutting and assorting of rags, the assorting and cutting of tobacco leaves, assorting of hair for brushes, cleaning (with sulphur) of straw hats, sulphurizing of India-rubber, reeling wool and silk, cleaning bed-feathers, coloring and printing of goods, coloring of tin soldiers, packing of tobacco leaves, silvering mirrors, and cutting steel pins and pens. It is certainly no pleasant sight to behold women, even pregnant women, working at the construction of railways, together with men and drawing heavily loaded carts, or helping with the building of a house, mixing lime, and serving as hod-carriers. Such occupations strip a woman of all womanliness, just, as on the other hand, many modern occupations deprive men of their manliness. Such are the results of social exploitation and social warfare. Our corrupted social conditions turn the natural order upside down.

It is not surprising that workingmen do not relish this tremendous increase of female labor in all branches of industry. It is certain that the extension of the employment of women in industry disrupts the family life of the working class, that the breaking up of marriage and the home are a natural result, and that it leads to a terrible increase of immorality, degeneration, all kinds of disease, and infant mortality. According to the statistics of the German Empire, infant mortality has greatly increased in those cities that have become centers of industry. As a result infant mortality is also heightened in the rural districts owing to the greater scarcity and increased cost of

---

*By an international agreement between Denmark, Germany, France, Italy, the Netherlands and Switzerland on Sept. 26, 1906, the use of white phosphorus in the manufacture of matches will be forbidden as of Jan. 1, 1911. In Germany the manufacture of these goods has been prohibited since Jan. 1, 1907, and since Jan. 1, 1908, they may neither be sold nor otherwise distributed. In England a similar law was enacted in 1909.

milk. In Germany, infant mortality is greatest in Upper Palatine, Upper Bavaria and Lower Bavaria, in some localities of the government districts of Liegnitz and Breslau, and in Chemnitz. In 1907 of every 100 infants the following percentage died during the first year of life: Stadtamhof (Upper Palatinate) 40.14 percent; Parsberg (Upper Palatinate) 40.06; Friedberg (Upper Bavaria) 39.28; Kelheim (Lower Bavaria) 37.71; Munich 37.63; Glauchau (Saxony) 33.48; Waldenburg (Silesia) 32.49; Chemnitz, 32.49; Reichenbach (Silesia), 32.18; Annaberg, 31.41, etc. In the majority of large manufacturing villages conditions were still worse, some of which had an infant mortality of from 40 to 50 percent.

And yet this social development which is accompanied by such deplorable results means progress. It means progress just as freedom of trade, liberty of choosing one's domicile, freedom of marriage, etc., meant progress, whereby capitalism was favored, but the middle class was doomed. The workingmen are not inclined to support small trades people and mechanics in their attempts again to limit freedom of trade and the liberty of choosing one's domicile and to reinstate the limitations of the guild system in order to maintain industry on a small scale. Past conditions cannot be revived; that is equally true of the altered methods of manufacture and the altered position of women. But that does not preclude the necessity of protective legislation to prevent an unlimited exploitation of female labor and the employment in industry of children of school age. In this respect the interests of the working class coincide with the interests of the state and the general humane interests of an advanced stage of civilization. That all parties are interested in such protective measures has frequently been shown during the last decades, for instance, in Germany in 1893, when an increase of the army made it necessary to reduce the required standard, because our industrial system had greatly increased the number of young men who were unfit for military service.* Our final aim must be to remove the disadvantages that have been caused by the introduction of machinery, the improvement in the means of production and the modern methods of production, and so organize human labor that

---

*The following percentage of men examined were found fit for military service: 1902, 58.5; 1993, 57.1; 1994, 56.4; 1905, 56.3; 1906, 55.9; and 1907, 54.9. The following percentage had to be discharged owing to disability after they had been enrolled: from 1881 to 1895; 2.07 percent; from 1891 to 1895, 2.30 percent; from 1901 to 1905, 2.47 percent. W. Classen—*The Decrease in Military Efficiency of the German Empire.*

the tremendous advantage machinery gave to humanity and will continue to give may be enjoyed by all members of society. It is preposterous and a crying evil that human achievements which are the product of social labor, should only benefit those who can acquire them by means of their power of wealth, while thousands of industrious workingmen and women are stricken by terror and grief when they learn of a new labor saving device, which may mean to them that they have become superfluous and will be cast out.* What should be joyfully welcomed by all thereby becomes an object of hatred to some, that in former decades frequently led workingmen to storm factories and demolish the machinery. A similar hostile sentiment prevails to some extent at present between workingmen and working women. This sentiment is unnatural. We must therefore seek to bring about a state of society in which all will enjoy equal rights regardless of sex. That will be possible when the means of production become the property of society, when labor has attained its highest degree of fruitfulness by employing all scientific and technical improvements and advantages, and when all who are able to work shall be obliged to perform a certain amount of socially necessary labor, for which society in return will provide all with the necessary means for the development of their abilities and the enjoyment of life.

Woman shall become a useful member of human society enjoying full equality with man. She shall be given the same opportunity to develop her physical and mental abilities, and by performing duties she shall be entitled to rights. Being man's free and equal companion no unworthy demands will be made upon her. The present development of society is tending in this direction, and the numerous and grave evils incidental to this development necessitate the introduction of a new social order.

*In December 1871, factory inspector A. Redgrave delivered a lecture at Bradford in which he said among other things: "My attention has recently been called to the changed appearance in the wool mills. Formerly they were full of women and children; now the machines seem to do all the work. Upon my inquiry a manufacturer gave me the following information: 'Under the old system I employed sixty-three persons; after the introduction of improved machinery I reduced my hands to thirty-three; and recently, as a result of further great improvements, I was able to reduce them from thirty-three to thirteen'." Within a few years then the number of workers was reduced by almost 80 percent while the same amount of goods were produced. Further interesting information on this subject may be found in *Capital* by Karl Marx.

* * *

At present matters have an entirely different aspect. The development of our social conditions and all social relations have undergone a tremendous transformation and have at the same time transformed the position of women. In all civilized states we find hundreds of thousands and millions of women employed in the most varied professions, just like men, and every year the number of women increases, who must rely on their own strength and ability in the struggle for existence. The nature of our social and political conditions, therefore, can no longer remain a matter of indifference to women. They must be interested in questions like the following: Whether or not the control of domestic and foreign affairs favor war; whether or not the state should annually keep hundreds of thousands of healthy men in the army and drive tens of thousands from the country; whether or not the necessities of life should be raised in price by taxes and duties at a time when the means of subsistence are very scarce to a great majority, etc. Women also pay direct and indirect taxes from their property and their earnings. The educational system is of the greatest interest to women, for the manner of education is a determining factor in the position of their sex; it is of special importance to mothers.

The hundreds of thousands and millions of women employed in hundreds of trades and professions are personally and vitally concerned in the nature of our social legislation. Laws relating to the length of the workday, night-work, child labor, wages, safety appliances in factories and workshops, in one word, all labor laws, as also insurance laws, etc., are of the greatest interest to working women. Workingmen are only very insufficiently informed about the conditions existing in many branches of industry in which women are chiefly or exclusively employed. It is to the interest of the employers to conceal existing evils that they have caused; and in many instances factory inspection does not include trades in which women are exclusively employed; yet in these very branches of industry protection is most needful. We need but point to the workshops in our large cities, where seamstresses, dressmakers, milliners, etc., are crowded together. We hardly ever hear a complaint from their midst, and there is no investigation of their condition. Women as bread-winners are also interested in the commerce and custom laws and in all civil laws. There can no longer be any doubt, that it is as important to women as it is to men, to influence the nature of our conditions by means of legislation.

The participation of women in public life would give it a new impetus and open new vistas.

Demands of this sort are briefly set aside, with the reply: "Women don't understand politics; most of them do not wish to have a vote and would not know how to use it." That is both true and false. It is true that until now, in Germany, at least, not very many women have demanded political equality. The first German woman to proclaim the rights of women, as early as the sixties of the last century, was Hedwig Dohm. Recently the Socialist working women have been the chief supporters of woman's suffrage and have undertaken an active agitation for the winning of the ballot.

The argument that women have until now shown only a very moderate interest in politics, does not prove anything at all. If women have failed to care about politics formerly, that does not signify that they ought not to care about them now. The same arguments that are advanced against woman suffrage were, during the first half of the sixties, advanced against universal manhood suffrage. In 1863 the writer of this book himself was among those who opposed it. Four years later it made possible his election to the diet. Tens of thousands experienced a similar development. Nevertheless there still are many men who either fail to make use of their political right, or do not know how to use it. Yet that would be no reason to deprive them of it. During the parliamentary elections usually from 25 to 30 percent of the voters fail to vote, and among these are members of all classes. While among the 70 to 75 percent who do vote, the majority, in our opinion, vote as they ought not to vote if they understood their own advantage. That they do not understand is due to a lack of political education. But political education is not obtained by withholding political rights from the masses. It is obtained only by the practice of political rights. Practice alone makes perfect. The ruling classes have always known it to be in their own interest to keep the great majority of the people in political dependence. Therefore it has been the task of a determined, class conscious minority to struggle for the common good with energy and enthusiasm, and to arouse the masses from their indifference and inertia. It has been thus in all the great movements of history, and therefore it need not surprise or discourage us that it is the same with the woman's movement. The success that has been obtained so far shows that work and sacrifice are not in vain and that the future will bring victory.

As soon as women shall have obtained equal rights with men, the consciousness of their duties will be awakened in them. When asked to vote they will begin to question "why" and "for whom."

Thereby a new source of interest will be established between man and woman that, far from harming their mutual relation, will considerably improve it. The inexperienced woman will naturally turn to the more experienced man. There from an exchange of ideas and mutual instruction will result, a relation that until now has been very rare between man and woman. This will give their life a new charm. The unfortunate differences in education and conception between the sexes that frequently lead to disputes, breed discord in regard to the various duties of the man, and injure the public welfare, will be adjusted more and more. A congenial and like-minded wife will support a man in his endeavors, instead of hindering him. If other tasks should prevent her from being active herself, she will encourage the man to do his duty. She will also be willing to sacrifice a fraction of the income for a newspaper and for purposes of agitation, because the newspaper will mean instruction and entertainment to her, and because she will understand that by the sacrifices for purposes of agitation, a more worthy human existence can be won for herself, her husband, and her children.

Thus the common service of the public welfare, that is closely linked with the individual welfare, will elevate both man and woman. The opposite of that will be attained which is claimed by short-sighted persons or by the enemies of equal rights, and this relation between the sexes will develop and become more beautiful as improved social conditions will liberate both man and woman from material care and excessive burdens of toil. Here, as in other cases, practice and education will help along. If I do not go into the water I will never learn to swim; if I do not study and practice a foreign language, I will never learn to speak it. That is readily understood by everyone; but many fail to understand that the same holds true of the affairs of the state and society. Are our women less capable than the inferior Negro race that was given political equality in North America? Or shall a highly cultured, educated woman be entitled to fewer rights than the most coarse and ignorant man, only because blind chance brought the latter into the world as a male being? Has the son a greater right than the mother from whom he has perhaps inherited his best qualities and who made him what he is? Such "justice" is strange, indeed.

Moreover, we are no longer risking a leap into the dark and unknown. North America, New Zealand, and Finland have paved the way. On the effects of woman suffrage in Wyoming, Justice Kingman, from Laramie, wrote to "The Woman's Journal," on November 12, 1872, as follows: "It is three years today that women were enfranchised in our territory and were also given the right to be elected to office, as all other voters. During this time they have taken part in the elections and have been elected to various offices; they have acted as jurors and as justices of the peace. Although there probably still are some among us who oppose the participation of women, on principle, I do not believe any one can deny that the participation of women in our elections has exerted an educational influence. The elections became more quiet and orderly, and at the same time our courts were enabled to punish various kinds of criminals who had been allowed to go unpunished until then. When the territory was organized, for instance, there was hardly a person who did not carry a revolver and make use of same upon the slightest provocation. I do not remember a single case where a person had been convicted of shooting by a jury composed entirely of men; but, with two or three women among the jurors, they always followed the instructions of the judge."

The prevailing sentiment in regard to woman suffrage in Wyoming, twenty-five years after its introduction, was expressed in a proclamation by the legislature of that state to all the legislatures of the country. It read:

> **Whereas,** Wyoming was the first state to adopt woman suffrage, which has been in operation since 1869, and was adopted in the constitution of the state in 1890; during which time women have exercised the privilege as generally as men, with the result that better candidates have been elected for office, methods of election purified, the character of legislation improved, civic intelligence increased, and womanhood developed to a greater usefulness by political responsibility; therefore,
>
> **Resolved,** by the House of Representatives, the Senate concurring, that, in view of these results, the enfranchisement of women in every state and territory of the American Union is hereby recommended as a measure tending to the advancement of a higher and better social order.

It is certain that the enfranchisement of women has shown many advantageous results for Wyoming, and not one single disadvantage.

That is the most splendid vindication of its introduction. The example set by Wyoming was followed by other states. Women were given full parliamentary suffrage in Colorado in 1894, in Utah in 1895, in Idaho in 1896. Women have municipal suffrage in Kansas, and school suffrage, tax-paying suffrage, etc., in a number of other states in the Union. In 1899, after the innovation had been in force in Colorado for five years, the legislature decided upon the following resolution, by forty-five against three votes:

> **Whereas,** equal suffrage has been in operation in Colorado for five years, during which time women have exercised the privilege as generally as men, with the result that better candidates have been selected for office, methods of election have been purified, the character of legislation improved, civic intelligence increased and womanhood developed to greater usefulness by political responsibility; therefore,
> **Resolved,** by the House of Representatives, the Senate concurring, that, in view of these results, the enfranchisement of women in every state and territory of the American Union is hereby recommended as a measure tending to the advancement of a higher and better social order.

In a number of states the legislatures have passed woman suffrage bills, but these decisions were annulled by the vote of the people. This was the case in Kansas, Oregon, Nebraska, Indiana, and Oklahoma. In Kansas and Oklahoma this proceeding has been twice repeated, and in Oregon even three times. The noteworthy fact is that each time the majorities against the political emancipation of women became smaller.*

"The municipal rights obtained by women are very varied, but, taken all in all, do not amount to much. As a matter of course, women enjoy the full municipal rights of citizenship in those four states in which they have been given national suffrage. But only one other state, Kansas, has given women municipal suffrage, which also includes school and tax-paying suffrage and makes them eligible to school boards. A limited municipal suffrage, founded upon an educational qualification, has been exercised by the women of Michigan since 1893. Louisiana, Montana, Iowa, and New York give women the right to vote on municipal questions of taxation. The women have not obtained as much influence in the general admin-

---

*At present, suffrage amendments are pending in Washington and Oklahoma. (Tr.)

istration of municipal affairs as they have in regard to the administration of schools. They have school suffrage and are eligible to school boards in the following states: Connecticut, Massachusetts, New Hampshire, Vermont, New York, New Jersey, Delaware, Ohio, Illinois, Wisconsin, Minnesota, North and South Dakota, Nebraska, Montana, Arizona, Oregon, and Washington. In Kentucky and Oklahoma they have school suffrage, but are not eligible to office; in Kentucky the school suffrage is limited by certain restrictions. In Maine, Rhode Island, Pennsylvania, Louisiana, Iowa, and California, women are eligible to school boards, but only to certain offices."*

In New Zealand, women have had full parliamentary suffrage since 1893. They have actively participated in the parliamentary elections, more actively than the men, but they are not eligible to office. Only men may be elected. In 1893, of 139,915 women of voting age no less than 109,461 registered; 785 for each 1,000; 90,290—645 for each 1,000—took part in the elections. In 1896, 108,783 (68 percent) of the women voted; in 1902, 138,565; in 1905, 175,046.

In Tasmania, women were given municipal suffrage in 1884 and national suffrage in 1903. In South Australia, women have had national suffrage since 1895, in West Australia since 1900, in New South Wales since 1902, in Queensland since 1905, in Victoria since 1908. Federated Australia introduced parliamentary woman's suffrage in 1902. The parliamentary suffrage implies the eligibility of women to parliament, but until now no woman has been elected. Women who are of age may vote for members of parliament and be voted for on the same terms as men. The municipal administration is less democratic. The right of participation in the administration of municipal affairs is connected with military service. Since 1889, tax-paying women are eligible to the charity-boards of town and rural communities. They may also be elected as directors of charitable institutions and members of school boards.

The grand general strike of October, 1905, and the victory of the Russian revolution made possible the restoration of the constitution in Finland. The working class, by bringing pressure to bear upon the National diet, succeeded in obtaining the passage of a law that provided for the introducction of universal suffrage, including the

*Clara Zetkin—*Woman Suffrage.* Berlin, 1907.

women. Only such persons were excluded who received aid from public funds, or who owed their personal tax to the state, 50 cents for men and 25 cents for women. In 1907, nineteen women, and in 1908 twenty-five women were elected to the parliament of Finland.

In Norway, women have participated in the administration of schools since 1889. In cities, the city councils may appoint them to school boards, and women having children of school age take part in the election of school inspectors. In the rural districts all who pay school taxes, regardless of sex, are entitled to take part in the school meetings of the communities. Women may hold the office of school inspector. Gradually women were given a voice in other municipal matters also. In 1901, municipal suffrage was extended to all Norwegian women who had attained their twenty-fifth year, who were Norwegian citizens, having been in the country at least five years, and who paid taxes on an income of at least 300 crowns, in the rural districts, and 400 crowns in the cities, or whose husbands paid the required amount of taxes. Women answering these requirements were also made eligible to municipal offices. By this law 200,000 women were enfranchised, 30,000 of them in Christiania alone. During the first election in which the women participated, 90 women were elected as members of town and city councils, and 160 as alternates. In Christiania, 6 women councillors and one alternate were elected. On July 1, 1907, the Norwegian women were given parliamentary suffrage, but not upon the same terms as men. Parliamentary suffrage was extended to women on the same terms on which they had been given municipal suffrage; 250,000 proletarian women still remain excluded from political rights.

In Sweden, unmarried women take part in municipal elections since 1862, on the same terms as men; that is, they must be of age and must pay taxes on an income of at least 140 dollars. In 1887 only 4,000 women among 62,000 voted. At first, women were not eligible to any municipal office, but in 1889 a law was enacted which declared them eligible to school boards and boards of charity. In February, 1909, Swedish women were declared eligible to all town and city councils. In 1902 parliamentary woman suffrage was rejected by the lower house by 114 against 64 votes; in 1905 by 109 against 88 votes.

In Denmark, after many years of agitation, women were given municipal suffrage in April, 1908, and were also made eligible to. municipal offices. All those women are enfranchised who have attained their twenty-fifth year and who have an annual income of at least 225 dollars in the cities (less in rural districts), or whose husbands pay the required amount of taxes. Moreover, servant girls are enfranchised, in whose case board and lodging are added to the wages they receive. During the first election in which women participated, which took place in 1909, seven women were elected to the city council of Copenhagen. In Iceland, women have had municipal suffrage and are eligible to municipal offices since 1907.

The struggle for woman suffrage in England has a considerable history. According to an old law, in the medieval ages, ladies of the manors had the right of suffrage and also exercised judicial power. In the course of time they were deprived of these rights. In the election reform acts of 1832, the word "person" had been employed, which includes members of both sexes. Yet the law was construed not to refer to women, and they were barred from voting wherever they made an attempt to do so. In the election reform bill of 1867, the word "person" had been replaced by the word "man." John Stuart Mill moved to reintroduce the word "person" instead of "man," explicitly stating as the object of his motion that thereby women would be given the suffrage on the same terms as men. The motion was voted down by 194 against 73 votes. Sixteen years later, in 1883, another attempt was made in the house of commons to introduce woman suffrage. The bill was rejected by a majority of only 16 votes. Another attempt failed in 1884, when a much larger membership of the house voted down a suffrage bill by a majority of 136 votes. But the minority were not discouraged. In 1886 they succeeded in having a bill providing for the introduction of parliamentary woman suffrage passed in two readings. The dissolving of parliament prevented a final decision.

On November 29, 1888, Lord Salisbury deliverd an address in Edinburgh, in which he said, among other things: "I sincerely hope that the day may not be distant when women will participate in parliamentary elections and will help to determine the course of the government." Alfred Russell Wallace, the well-known scientist and follower of Darwin, expressed himself upon the same question in the following manner: "When men and women shall be free to follow their best impulses, when no human being shall be hampered by unnatural restrictions owing to the chance of sex, when public opinion will be controlled by the wisest and best and will be systematically impressed upon the young, then we will find that a system of human selection will manifest itself that will result in a transformed humanity. As long as women are compelled to regard marriage as a means whereby they may escape poverty and neglect, they are and remain at a disadvantage compared to men. Therefore, the first step in the emancipation of women is to remove all the restrictions which prevent them from competing with men in all branches of industry and in all occupations. But we must advance beyond this point and permit women to exercise their political rights. Many of the restrictions from which women have hitherto suffered would have been spared them if they had had a direct representation in parliament."

On April 27, 1892, the second reading of a bill by Sir A. Rollit was again rejected by 175 against 152 votes. On February 3, 1897, the house of commons passed a suffrage bill, but, owing to various maneuvers of the opponents, the bill did not come up for the third reading. In 1904 the same scene was reenacted. Of the members of parliament elected to the house of commons in 1906, a large majority had declared themselves in favor of woman suffrage prior to their election. On June 21, 1908, a grand demonstration was held in Hyde Park. On February 28, a bill providing that women should be given parliamentary suffrage on the same terms as men, had been passed by 271 against 92 votes.*

In regard to municipal administration, woman suffrage in Great Britain is constantly expanding. In the parish councils tax-paying women have a voice and vote as well as men. Since 1899, women in England have the right to vote for town, district, and county councils. In the rural districts all proprietors and lodgers—including the female ones—who reside in the parish or district are entitled to vote. All inhabitants who are of age may be elected to the above-named bodies, regardless of sex. Women vote for members of school boards, and, since 1870, are eligible to same on the same terms as men. But in 1903 the reactionary English school law deprived women of the right of being elected to the school board in the county of London. Since 1869 independent and unmarried women have the right to vote for the privy councils. Two laws enacted in 1907 made unmarried women in England and Scotland eligible to district and county councils. But a woman who may be elected as

---

*A similar bill, known as the "conciliation bill," drawn up by a committee consisting of members of all parties, passed its second reading in July 1910 by 299 against 189 votes. Prime Minister Asquith prevented the third reading and final vote upon the bill during that session of Parliament. *(Tr.)*

chairman of such a council, shall thereby not hold the office of justice of peace that is connected with it. Women are also eligible to parish councils and as overseers of the poor. The first woman mayor was elected in Aldeburgh on November 9, 1908. In 1908 there were 1,162 women on English boards of charity and 615 women on school boards. In Ireland, tax-paying women have had municipal suffrage since 1887, and since 1896 they may vote for members of boards of charity and be elected to same. In the British colony of North America [Canada—*eds.*], most of the provinces have introduced municipal woman suffrage on similar terms as in England. In the African colonies of England, municipal woman suffrage has likewise been introduced.

In France the first slight progress was brought about by a law enacted on February 27, 1880. By this law a school board was created consisting of women school principals, school inspectors, and inspectors of asylums. Another law of January 23, 1898, gave women engaged in commerce the right to vote for members of courts of trade, and, since November 25, 1908, women may be elected as members of courts of trade themselves.

In Italy women may vote for members of courts of trade and be elected as such since 1893. They are also eligible to boards of supervisors of hospitals, orphan asylums, foundling asylums, and to school boards.

In Austria women belonging to the class of great landowners may vote for members of the diet and the imperial council, either personally or by proxy. Taxpaying women, over twenty-four, may vote for town and city councillors; married women exercise the suffrage indirectly through their husbands, others through some other authorized agent. All the women belonging to the class of great landowners have the right to vote for members of the diet, but, with the exception of Lower Austria, they do not exercise it personally. Only in the one domain referred to, the law of 1896 provides that the great landowners, regardless of sex, must cast their vote in person. Women may also vote for members of courts of trade, but may not be elected to same.

In Germany women are explicitly excluded from voting for any law-making bodies. In some parts of the country women may vote for town councillors. In no city or rural community are women eligible to municipal offices. In the cities they are also excluded from the right to vote for any office. The exceptions to this rule are some cities in the Grand-duchy of Saxony-Weimar-Eisenach, in the principalities of Schwarzburg-Rudolstadt, and Schwarzburg-Sondershausen, in Bavaria, and the little town of Travemünde, in Lübeck.

In the Bavarian cities all women who are house owners, and in the cities of Saxony-Weimar and Schwarzburg, all women citizens are given the suffrage, but only in Travemünde are they permitted to exercise it in person.* In most of the rural communities where the right of suffrage depends upon a property or tax-paying qualification, women are included in this right. But they must vote by proxy and are not eligible to any office themselves. This is the case in Prussia, Brunswick, Schleswig-Holstein, Saxony-Weimar, Hamburg, and Lubeck. In the Kingdom of Saxony a woman may exercise the suffrage if she be a landowner and unmarried. When she becomes married, her suffrage devolves upon her husband. In those states in which municipal suffrage depends upon citizenship, women are generally excluded. This is the case in Württemberg, in the Bavarian Palatinate, in Baden, Hessia, Oldenburg, Anhalt, Gotha, and Reuss. In Saxony-Weimar-Eisenach, Coburg, Schwarzburg-Rudolstadt, and Schwarzburg-Sondershausen, women can become citizens on the same terms as men, and they have the suffrage, not limited by any property qualification. But here, too, they are prohibited from exercising this right in person.

In those Prussian districts where a limited form of woman suffrage exists, the enfranchised women participate directly or indirectly in the elections for members of the dietines. In the electoral groups of great landowners and the representatives of mining and manufacturing establishments, the women vote for members of the dietines directly; but in the rural communities they vote indirectly, since here the town council does not elect the representatives themselves, but only their electors. As the local dietines elect representatives to the provincial diets, the small number of enfranchised women are enabled to exert a very modest influence on the administration of the provinces.

During recent years women have been admitted to boards of charity, and have been made overseers of the poor and of orphan asylums in growing numbers and with marked success. (Bavaria constitutes the only exception.) In some cities (in Prussia, Baden, Württemberg, Bavaria, and Saxony), they have also been admitted to

*Political Manual for Women. Berlin, 1909.

school boards, and in one city (Mannheim), they have been made members of a commission for the inspection of dwellings. Insurance against sickness is the only public institution in connection with which women may vote and be voted for. They remain excluded from voting for members of courts of trade.

The above-quoted instances show that suffrage in Germany and Austria is determined, almost without exception, not by the person, but by property. Politically, human beings are mere ciphers if they have no money and no possessions. Neither intellect nor ability, but property is the determining factor. It is very instructive to note this fact in regard to the morality and justice of the present state.

We see that a number of exceptions have already been made to the theory that women are in the same class with minors and that the franchise must accordingly be withheld from them. And yet people vehemently oppose the endeavor to give women full political equality. Even progressive people argue that it would be dangerous to enfranchise women because they are conservative by nature and are susceptible to religious prejudices. But these arguments are true to some extent only, so long as women are maintained in ignorance. Our object must therefore be to educate them and to teach them where their true interest lies. Incidentally it may be stated that the religious influence on elections has been overestimated. The ultramontane agitation was so successful in Germany only because it wisely combined the religious interests with social interests. For a long time the ultramontane chaplains vied with the socialists in revealing social deterioration. It was this that caused them to become so influential with the masses. But with the end of the struggle between church and state this influence gradually declines. The clergy are obliged to abandon their struggle against the power of the state; at the same time the increasing class differences compel them to show greater consideration for the Catholic bourgeoisie and the Catholic nobility and to be more reticent in regard to social questions. Thereby they lose their influence upon workingmen, especially if consideration for the ruling classes compels them to favor or to tolerate actions and laws that are directed against the interests of the working class. The same reasons will eventually also destroy the influence of the clergy upon women. When women learn in meetings, or from newspapers, or by personal experience, where their true interests lie, they will emancipate themselves from clerical influence just as men.*

In Belgium, where ultramontanism still predominates among large circles of the population, a number of the Catholic clergy favor woman suffrage because they deem it an effective weapon against socialism. In Germany, too, a number of conservative members of the diet have declared themselves in favor of the woman suffrage bills introduced by socialist members and have explained their position by asserting that they consider woman suffrage a weapon against socialism. Undoubtedly there is some truth in these opinions, taking into consideration the present political ignorance of women and the strong influence exerted over them by the clergy. But still this is no reason to disfranchise them. There are millions of workingmen, too, who vote for candidates of bourgeois and religious parties against their own class interest and thereby prove their political ignorance, yet no one would propose to disfranchise them for this reason. The withholding or the rape of the franchise is not practiced because the ignorance of the masses—including the ignorance of women—is feared; for what these masses are, the ruling classes have made them. It is practiced because the ruling classes fear that the masses will gradually become wise and pursue their own course.

Until recently the various German states were so reactionary that they even withheld from women the right of political organization. In Prussia, Bavaria, Brunswick, and a number of other German states, they were not permitted to form political clubs. In Prussia they were not even permitted to participate in entertainments arranged by political clubs, as was distinctly set down by the supreme court in 1901. The rector of the Berlin University even went so far as to forbid a woman to lecture before a social science club of students. In the same year the police authorities of Brunswick forbade women

---

*That this danger exists the clergy themselves have soon recognized. Since the woman movement has grown and developed even in bourgeois circles, the leaders of the Catholic party recognized that they could no longer oppose it, and they accordingly completely reversed their attitude. With that sublety which has always characterized the servants of the church, they favor at present what they opposed until quite recently. They not only favor higher education for women, they also declare themselves in favor of unrestricted right of assembly and organization for women. Some of the more farsighted even support woman suffrage, hoping that the church may derive the greatest gain from the introduction of same. In the same way the industrial organization of women is supported by the Catholic clergy, even the organization of servant girls. But all these social endeavors are fostered, not from an innate sense of justice, but to prevent the women from flocking to the camp of religious and political opponents.

to take part in the proceedings of the social congress of Evangelists. In 1902 the Prussian secretary of state condescended to give women the permission to attend the meetings of political clubs, but under the condition that they had to take their seats in a part of the hall specially set aside for them, like the Jewish women in their synagogues. Nothing could have better characterized the pettiness of our conditions. As late as Feburary, 1904, Pasadowsky solemnly declared in the diet: "Women shall keep their hands off politics." But eventually this state of affairs became unbearable even to the bourgeois parties. The new national law on assembly and organization of April 19, 1908, brought the only marked improvement by establishing equal rights of women in regard to political organization and public assembly.

The right to vote must of course be combined with the right to be elected to office. We hear the cry: "How ridiculous it would be to behold a woman on the platform of the diet!" Yet there are other states where women have ascended to the platforms of parliaments, and we, too, have long since become accustomed to see women on platforms in their meetings and conventions. In North America women appear on the pulpit and in the jury box; why not on the platform of the diet? The first woman to be elected to the diet will know how to impress the other members. When the first workingmen were elected to the diet they, too, were the objects of cheap wit, and it was asserted that workingmen would soon recognize the folly of electing men of their type. But the working-class representatives quickly succeeded in winnning respect, and at present their opponents fear that there may be too many of them. Frivolous jesters exclaim: "But picture a pregnant woman on the platform of the diet; how shocking!" Yet the same gentlemen consider it quite proper that pregnant women should be employed at occupations which shockingly degrade their womanly dignity and decency and undermine their health. That man is a wretch, indeed, who dares to ridicule a pregnant woman. The very thought that his mother was in the same condition before she gave him birth must drive the blood to his cheeks in shame, and the other thought, that his wife's being in the same condition may mean the fulfillment of his fondest hopes, must silence him.*

*"Half of the women members of Parliament in Finland are wives and mothers. Three of the socialist married women members became mothers during their parliamentary activity without any other disturbing results except that they remained away

The woman who gives birth to children is serving the community at least as well as the man who risks his life in defense of the country. For she gives birth to and educates the future soldiers, far too many of whom must sacrifice their lives on the battlefield. Moreover, every woman risks her life in becoming a mother. All our mothers have faced death in giving us life, and many of them have perished. In Prussia, for instance, the number of deaths in childbirth—including the victims of puerperal fever—by far exceeds the number of deaths from typhoid. During 1905 and 1906 0.73 and 0.62 percent of typhoid patients died. But among 10,000 women 2.13 and 1.97 percent died in childbirth. "How would conditions have developed," Professor Herff rightly remarks, "if men were subjected to these sufferings to the same extent? Would not the utmost measures be resorted to?"* The number of women who die in childbirth or are left sickly as a result of same, is far greater than the number of men who die or are wounded on the battlefield. From 1816 to 1876, in Prussia alone, no less than 321,791 women fell victims of puerperal fever; that is an annual average of 5,363. In England, from 1847 to 1901, 213,533 women died in childbirth, and still, notwithstanding all hygienic measures, no less than 4,000 die annually.†

That is a far greater number than the number of men killed in the various wars during the same time. To this tremendous number of women who die in childbirth must furthermore be added the still greater number of those who become sickly as a result of childbirth and die young.‡ This is another reason why woman is entitled to

---

from the sessions for a few weeks. Their pregnant condition was regarded as something natural that was neither wonderful nor noteworthy. It may rather be said that this factor was of educational value to the assembly. In regard to the parliamentary activity of these women members it should be noted that their parties elected them to the special committees also, which proves that they were convinced of their ability. The committee on labor where the laws for workingmen's protection, workingmen's insurance, and the new trade laws were drawn up, consisted of twelve men and four women, and three women had been chosen as alternates. The legislative and constitutional committees each had two women members, and for each there was one woman alternate, and the women have ably maintained their place in these committees." Miss Hilda Paerssinen, member of the diet of Finland, "Woman Suffrage and the Participation of Women in the Parliamentary Work of Finland." *Documents of Progress*, July, 1909.

*Professor Dr. Otto V. Herff, *The Struggle Against Puerperal Fever*, Leipzig, 1908.
†W. Williams, *Deaths in Child-bed*. London, 1904.
‡"For every woman who dies in childbirth we must assume from fifteen to twenty who are more or less seriously infected with resulting diseases of the abdominal organs and general debility from which they frequently suffer for the remainder of their lives." Dr. Mrs. H. B. Adams, *The Book of Woman*. Stuttgart, 1894.

full equality with man. Let these facts be especially noted by those persons who advance the military service of men as an argument against the equal rights of women. Moreover, our military institutions enable a great many men to escape the performance of this duty.

All these superficial objections to the public activity of women would be impossible if the relation of the sexes was natural, instead of there being an artificially stimulated antagonism between them. From their early childhood on the sexes are separated in their education and their social intercourse. It is especially the antagonism we owe to Christianity that keeps the sexes apart and maintains one in ignorance about the other, whereby free social intercourse, mutual confidence, and the ability to supplement each other's traits of character are prevented.

One of the first and most important tasks of a rationally organized society must be to remove this detrimental discord and to restore the rights of nature. We begin by making even the little children in school unnatural, firstly, by separating the sexes, and secondly, by failing to instruct our children as to the sex nature of human beings. In every fairly good school natural history is being taught at present. The child learns that birds lay eggs and hatch them. He learns when birds mate and that both the male and female bird build the nest, hatch the eggs, and feed the young. He also learns that mammals bring forth their young alive. He hears of the mating season and that the male animals fight one another for possession of the females. Perhaps he even learns how many young one or another species of animal usually brings forth and how long the female is pregnant. But profoundest secrecy is maintained in regard to the origin and development of the human being. When the child seeks to satisfy its natural curiosity by questioning his parents, especially his mother—he rarely ventures to question the teacher—he is told the most ridiculous fairy tales that cannot satisfy his thirst for knowledge and that must exert an all the more harmful influence when, some day, he nevertheless learns the true nature of his origin. There are few children who have not learned of it by the time they are twelve years old. In every small town, and especially in the country, even very young children have occasion to observe the pairing of poultry and domestic animals at close range in the yards, in the streets, and on pasture. They hear that the pairing of domestic animals and the birth of the young is discussed without a sense of shame by their parents, their elder brothers and sisters, and the servants. All this causes the child to doubt the truth of what his parents told him in regard to his own coming into the world. Finally the child learns the truth, but not in the manner in which he ought to learn it if his education were a natural and rational one. The fact that the child keeps his knowledge a secret leads to an estrangement between him and his parents, especially between him and his mother. The parents have accomplished the opposite of what they sought to accomplish in their ignorance and shortsightedness. Those who recall their own childhood and the childhood of their playmates know to what this may lead.

An American woman* tells us that in order to satisfactorily answer the constant questions of her eight-year-old son as to his origin, and because she did not wish to tell him fairy tales, she revealed to him the truth about his birth. The child, she says, listened to her with utmost attention, and from the day upon which he had learned how much suffering he caused his mother, he had treated her with unwonted tenderness and respect and had also transferred these feelings to other women. The writer upholds the correct view that only by means of a natural education men can be led to treat women with more respect and self-control. Every unprejudiced person is bound to agree with her.

Whatever starting point one may choose in the criticism of present-day conditions, one is bound always to reiterate the following: A thorough reorganization of our social conditions, and thereby a thorough transformation in the relation of the sexes, is needful. Woman, in order to attain her aim more quickly, must look about for allies, and she naturally finds such allies in the proletarian movement. The class-conscious proletariat has long since commenced to storm the fortress of the state that is founded on class rule, which includes the rule of one sex over the other. The fortress must be surrounded on all sides, and, by arms of all calibers, it must be forced to surrender. The beleaguering army finds its officers and suitable arms on all sides. The social sciences, the natural sciences, historical research, pedagogics, hygiene, and statistics furnish the movement with arms and munition. Philosophy comes forward, too, and, in Mainlaender's *Philosophy of Deliverance*, proclaims the early realization of the "ideal state."

*Isabella Beecher Hooker, *Womanhood, Its Sanctities and Fidelities*. New York, 1874. Lee, Shepard & Dillingham.

The conquest of the class state and its transformation is made easier by dissension in the ranks of its defenders, who, notwithstanding their community of interests against the common enemy, fight one another in the struggle for the spoils. The interest of one group is opposed to the interest of another. Another point in our favor is the growing mutiny in the ranks of the enemy. To a great extent their soldiers are blood of our blood and flesh of our flesh, but, owing to ignorance, they, until now, fought against us and against themselves. More and more of these join our ranks. We are, furthermore, helped by the desertion of honest men of intellect, who were hostile to us at first, but whose superior knowledge and profound insight impels them to rise above their narrow class interest, to follow their ideal desire for justice, and to espouse the cause of the masses that are longing for liberation.

Many still fail to recognize that state and society are already in a state of decay. Therefore an exposition of this subject also becomes necessary.

Translated by Meta L. Stern (Hebe)

Clara Zetkin

What the Women Owe to Karl Marx

On March 14th is the twentieth anniversary of Karl Marx's death in London. Engels, whose life for forty years in both struggle and work was intimately linked to Marx's life, wrote at that time to their mutual friend Comrade Sorge in New York:

> Humankind has been shortened by one head, which also happens to be the most significant head of our times.

His evaluation hit the bull's eye.

It cannot be our task within the framework of this article to discuss what Karl Marx has bestowed upon the proletariat in his role as a man of science, as a revolutionary fighter, and what he means today to the proletariat. If we would do this, we would only repeat what is written during these days in the socialist press of Marx's immensely fertile and profoundly scholarly and practical life's work as well as his gigantic, homogeneous personality which stood so totally devoted in the service of the proletariat. Instead we prefer to indicate what the proletarian, or better yet, the entire women's movement owes to him.

To be sure, Marx never dealt with the women's question "per se" or "as such." Yet he created the most irreplaceable and important weapons for the women's fight to obtain all of their rights. His materialist concept of history has not supplied us with any ready-made formulas concerning the women's question, yet it has done something much more important: It has given us the correct, unerring method to explore and comprehend that question. It was only the materialist concept of history which enabled us to understand the women's question within the flux of universal historical development and the light of universally applicable social relationships and their historical necessity and justification. Only thus did we perceive its driving forces and the aims pursued by them as well as the conditions which are essential to a solution of these problems.

The old superstition that the position of women in the family and in society was forever unchangeable because it was created on moral precepts or by divine revelation was smashed. Marx revealed that the family, like all other institutions and forms of existence, is subjected to a constant process of ebb and flow which changes with the economic conditions and the property relationships which result from them. It is the development of the productive forces of the economy which push this transformation by changing the mode of production and by coming into conflict with the prevailing economic and property system. On the basis of the revolutionized economic conditions, human thought is revolutionized and it becomes the endeavor of people to adjust their societal superstructure to the changes that have taken place in the economic substructure. Petrified forms of property and personal relationships must then be removed. These changes are wrought by means of the class struggle.

We know from Engels' foreword to his illuminating study, *The Origin of the Family, Private Property and the State,* that the theories and viewpoints developed in this book are derived in good measure from Marx's unpublished work, which his incomparably loyal and brilliant friend watched over as testamentary executor.

Whatever parts of it can be (and ought to be) dismissed as hypotheses, one thing is for sure: Taken as a whole, this work contains a dazzling number of clear theoretical insights into the complex conditions which gave rise to the present forms of the family and marriage and the influence of economic and property relationships which are connected with it. It teaches us not merely to judge correctly the position of women in the past, but it enables us to comprehend the social, legal, and constitutional positions of the female sex today.

Das Kapital shows most convincingly that there are incessant and irresistible historical forces at work in today's society which are revolutionizing this situation from the bottom up and will bring about the equality of women. By masterfully examining the development and nature of capitalist production down to the most refined details, and by discovering its law of motion, i.e., the theory of surplus value, he has conclusively proven in his discussions of women and child labor that capitalism has destroyed the basis for the ancient domestic activity of women, thereby dissolving the anachronistic form of the family. This has made women economically independent outside of the family and created a firm ground for their equality as wives, mothers, and citizens. But something else is clearly illustrated by Marx's works: The proletariat is the only revolutionary class which by establishing socialism, is able to and must create the indispensable prerequisites for the complete solution of the women's question. Besides the fact that the bourgeois suffragettes neither want nor are able to achieve the social liberation of women proletarians, they are incapable of solving the serious new conflicts which will be fought over the social and legal equality of the sexes within the capitalist order. These conflicts will not vanish until the exploitation of man by man and the contradictions arising therefrom are abolished.

Marx and Engels' common work *The Communist Manifesto* concisely summarizes what *Das Kapital* teaches us in scholarly fashion about the disintegration of the family and its causes:

> The less the skill and exertion of strength implied in manual labor, in other words, the more modern industry becomes developed, the more is the labor of men superseded by that of women. Differences of age and sex have no longer any distinctive social validity for the working class. All are instruments of labor, more or less expensive to use according to their age and sex. . . .
>
> The bourgeoisie has torn away from the family its sentimental veil and has reduced the family relation to a mere money relation. . . .
>
> In the conditions of the proletariat, those of old society at large are already virtually swamped. The proletarian is without property; his relation to his wife and children has no longer anything in common with the bourgeois family relations. . . .
>
> On what foundation is the present family, the bourgeois family, based? On capital, on private gain. In its completely developed form this family exists only among the bourgeoisie. But this state of things finds its complement in the practical absence of the family among the proletarians, and in public prostitution. . . .
>
> The bourgeois claptrap about the family and education, about the hallowed co-relation of parent and child, becomes all the more disgusting as by the action of modern industry all family ties among the proletarians are torn asunder, and their children transformed into simple articles of commerce and instruments of labor. . . .

Marx, however, does not only show us that historical development demolishes, but he also fills us with the victorious conviction that it constructs a newer, better, and more perfect world.

Das Kapital states:
> As horrendous and disgusting as the disintegration of the old family system within capitalism appears to be, modern industry, by involving women and young people of both sexes in the socially organized production processes outside of the domestic sphere, has, nevertheless, created the economic basis for a higher form of the family and the relationship between the two sexes.

Proud and with superior scorn, Marx and Engels in *The Communist Manifesto* counter the dirty suspicions cast upon this future ideal by this merciless characterization of present conditions:

> The bourgeois sees in his wife a mere instrument of production. He hears that the instruments of production are to be exploited in common and, naturally, can come to no other conclusion than that the lot of being common to all will likewise fall to the women.
>
> He has not even a suspicion that the real point aimed at is to do away with the status of women as mere instruments of production.
>
> For the rest, nothing is more ridiculous than the virtuous indignation of our bourgeois at the community of women which, they pretend, is to be openly and officially established by the communists. The communists have no need to introduce community of women; it has existed almost from time immemorial.
>
> Our bourgeois, not content with having the wives and daughters of their proletarians at their disposal, not to speak of common prostitutes, take the greatest pleasure in seducing each other's wives.
>
> Bourgeois marriage is in reality a system of wives in common and thus, at the most, what the communists might possibly be reproached with is that they desire to introduce, in substitution for what is hypocritically concealed, an openly legalized community of women. For the rest, it is self-evident that the abolition of the present system of production must bring with it the abolition of women springing from that system, i.e., of prostitution both public and private.

The women's movement, however, owes much more to Marx than just the fact that he, as no other person before him, shed bright light upon the painful path of the development that leads the female sex from social servitude to freedom and from atrophy to a strong, harmonious existence. By his profound, penetrating analysis of the class contradictions in today's society and its roots, he opened up our eyes to the differences of interest that separate the women of the different classes. In the atmosphere of the materialist concept of history, the "love drivel" about a "sisterhood" which supposedly wraps a unifying ribbon around bourgeois ladies and female proletarians, burst like so many scintillating soap bubbles. Marx has forged and taught us to use the sword which has severed the connection between the proletarian and the bourgeois women's movement. But he has also forged the chain of discernment by which the former is inextricably tied to the socialist labor movement and the revolutionary class struggle of the proletariat. Thus he has given our struggle the clarity, grandeur, and sublimity of its final goal.

Das Kapital is filled with an immeasurable wealth of facts, perceptions, and stimuli concerning women's work, the situation of the female workers and the legal protection of women. It is an inexhaustible spiritual armory for the struggle of our immediate demands as well as the exalted future socialist goal. Marx teaches us to recognize the small, everyday tasks which are so necessary in raising the fighting ability of the female proletarians. At the same time, he lifts us up to the firm, farseeing recognition of the great revolutionary struggle by the proletariat to conquer political power without the attainment of which, a socialist society and the liberation of the female sex will remain empty dreams. Above all, he fills us with the conviction that it is this exalted aim that lends value and significance to our daily work. Thus he saves us from losing sight of the great fundamental meaning of our movement when we are beset by a plethora of individual phenomena, tasks, and successes, and stand in danger of losing our ability, during the enervating daily toil, to view the wide historical horizon which reflects the dawn of a new age. Just as he is the master of revolutionary thought, so he remains the leader of the revolutionary struggle in whose battles it is the duty and the glory of the proletarian women's movement to fight.

Die Gleichheit Stuttgart, March 25, 1903

Translated by Kai Schoenhals

MILITARISM

Karl Liebknecht

Military Pedagogy

That proper "military spirit," also called "patriotic spirit" and, in Prussia-Germany, "loyalty to the king," signifies in short a constant readiness to pitch into the exterior or the interior enemy whenever commanded to do so. Taken by itself the most suitable condition for its production is a state of complete stupidity, or at least as low an intelligence as possible which enables one to drive the mass as a herd of cattle in whatever direction is demanded by the interest of the "existing order." The avowal of the Prussian war minister, von Einem, who said that he liked a soldier loyal to his king, even he were a bad shot, better than a less loyal one however good a shot he might be, certainly came from the depth of the soul of this representative of German militarism. But here militarism finds itself in a bad quandary. The handling of arms, strategy, and tactics demand of the modern soldier not a small measure of intelligence and cause the more intelligent soldier also to be the more efficient, *cæteris paribus*. For that reason alone militarism would no longer be able to do anything with a merely stupid mass of men. Moreover, capitalism could not use such a stupid mass, as the great mass of the people, especially the great mass of the proletariat, have to perform economic functions requiring intelligence. To be able to exploit, to secure the highest possible rate of profit—the task of its life which it cannot escape—capitalism is compelled by a tragical fate to foster systematically and to a large extent among its slaves the same intelligence which, as it knows quite well, must bring death and annihilation to capitalism. All the attempts to guide the ship of capitalism by skillful tacking, by a cunning cooperation of church and school, safely between the Scylla of too low an intelligence which would be too great an impediment to exploitation and would make the proletarian even unfit as a beast of burden, and the Charybdis of an education which revolutionizes the minds of the exploited, enabling them to grasp their class interests in their entirety and necessarily bringing destruction to capitalism, must end in dreary and hopeless failure. It is only the East Elbian farmhands (who still may be, as was once said, the most stupid workers indeed and the best workers—for the junkers, be it noted) who largely furnish militarism with human material that can be commanded in herds without trouble, purely like slaves, but can be used to advantage in the army only with care and within certain limits, on account of an intelligence which is even too low for militarism.

Our best soldiers are social democrats, is a much quoted expression. It shows the difficulty of the task of imbuing the conscript army with the proper military spirit. As the mere unquestioning and slavish obedience does no longer suffice and is also no longer possible, militarism must seek to dominate the will of its human material by a roundabout way in order to create its shooting automata. It must bend the will by working upon the men's mind and soul or by force, it must decoy its pupils or coerce them. The proper "spirit" needed by militarism for its purpose against the foreign enemy consists of a crazy jingoism, narrow-mindedness, and arrogance; the spirit it needs for its purposes against the enemy at home is that of a lack of understanding or even hatred of every kind of progress, every enterprise and movement even distantly endangering the rule of the actually dominating class. It is in that direction that militarism, when molding the character of its charges by its milder means, must turn the mind and sentiments of those soldiers whose class interest removes them entirely from the sphere of jingoism and makes them see in every step in advance, including the overthrow of the existing order of society itself, the only reasonable goal to be aimed at. We do not deny that with the proletarian of military age class consciousness is usually not yet firmly rooted, though he generally greatly surpasses the bourgeois youth of the same age in independence of character and political understanding.

It is an extremely bold and cunning system, this system of molding a soldier's intellect and feeling, which attempts to supplant the class-division according to social status by a class-division according to ages, to create a special class of proletarians of the ages from twenty to twenty-two, whose thinking and feeling are directly opposed to the thinking and feeling of the proletarians of a different age.

In the first place the proletarian in uniform must be separated locally, sharply, and without any consideration, from members of his class and his own family. That purpose is attained by removing him from his home district, which has been accomplished systematically especially in Germany, and above all by shutting him up in barracks. One might almost describe the system as a copy of the jesuitical method of education, a counterpart of the monastic institutions.

In the next place that segregation must be kept up as long a time as possible, a tendency which, as the military necessity of the long period of training has long since disappeared, is thwarted by untoward financial consequences. It was substantially that circumstance to which we owe the introduction of the two year military service in 1892.

Finally, the time thus gained must be utilized as skillfully as possible to capture the souls of the young men. Various means are employed for that purpose.

All human weaknesses and senses must be appealed to to serve the system of military education, exactly as is done in the church. Ambition and vanity are stimulated, the soldier's coat is represented as the most distinguished of all coats, the soldier's honor is lauded as being of special excellence, and the soldier's status is trumpeted forth as the most important and distinguished and is indeed endowed with many privileges. The love of finery is appealed to by turning the uniform, contrary to its purely military purpose, into a gay masquerade dress, to comply with the coarse tastes of those lower classes who are to be fascinated. All kinds of little glittering marks of distinction, marks of honor, cords for proficiency in shooting, etc., serve to satisfy the same low instinct, the love for finery and swagger. Many a soldier has had his woes soothed by the regimental band to which, next to the glittering gew-gaw of the uniforms and the pompous military ostentation, is due the greatest part of that unreserved popularity which our "magnificent war army" can amply boast of among children, fools, servant girls, and the riff-raff. Whoever has but once seen the notorious public attending the parades and the crowds following the mounting of the Berlin palace guard must be clear on that point. It is sufficiently known that the popularity of the military uniform thus actually created among certain portions of the civilian population, is a factor of considerable importance to allure the uneducated elements of the army.

The lower the mentality of the soldiers, the lower their social condition, the better is the effect of all these means; for such elements are not only more easily deceived by tinsel and finery on account of their weak faculty of discernment, but to them the difference between the level of their former civilian existence and their military position also appears to be particularly great and striking. (One need only think of an American negro or an East Prussian agricultural slave suddenly invested with the "most distinguished" coat.) There is thus a tragic conflict going on, in as much as those means have less effect with the intelligent industrial proletarian for whom they are intended in the first line, than with those elements that need hardly be influenced in that direction, for the present at least, since they furnish without them a sufficiently docile military raw material. However those means may in their case, too, contribute to the *preservation* of the "spirit" approved of by militarism. The same purpose is served by regimental festivals, the celebration of the Emperor's birthday, and other contrivances.

When everything has been done to get the soldier into the mood of drunkenness, as it were, to narcotize his soul, to inflame his feelings and imagination, his *reason* must be worked upon systematically. The daily military school lesson begins in which it is sought to drum into the soldier a childish, distorted view of the world, properly trimmed up for the purposes of militarism. This instruction, too, which is mostly given by entirely incapable and uneducated people, has no effect whatever on the more intelligent industrial proletarians, who are quite often much more intelligent than their instructors. It is an experiment on an unsuitable material, an arrow rebounding on him that shot it. That has only lately been proved, in a controversy with General Liebert about the anti-socialist instruction of soldiers, by *The Post* and Max Lorenz, with the acumen generated by the capitalist competition for profits.

To produce the necessary pliability and tractableness of *will* pipe-clay service, the discipline of the barracks, the canonization of the officer's and non-commissioned officer's coat, which in many respects appears to be truly sacrosanct and *legibus solutus,* have to do service, in short, discipline and control which bind the soldier as in fetters of steel in regard to all he does and thinks, on duty and off duty. Each and every one is ruthlessly bent, pulled, and stretched in all directions in such a manner that the strongest back runs danger of being broken in bits and either bends or breaks.

The zealous fostering of the "church" spirit, which was explicitly demanded as a special aim of military education in a resolution submitted to the budget commission of the Reichstag in the month of February, 1892, and then voted down (without prejudice, by the way), is another method of the kind to complete the work of military oppression and enslavement.

Military instruction and ecclesiastical influence are at one and the same time methods of kind persuasion and compulsion, but the latter mostly only in a carefully veiled form of application.

The most attractive bait that is employed to make up and fill the important standing formations of the army is the system of re-engagement of men whose time has expired, who are given a chance to earn premiums as noncommissioned officers and are promised employment in the civil service after they leave the army. It is a most cunningly devised and dangerous institution which also infects our whole public life with the militaristic virus, as will be shown further on.

The whip of militarism, the method by which it forces men to obey, reveals itself above all in the disciplinary system, in the military penal law with its ferocious threats for the slightest resistance against the so-called military spirit; in the military judiciary with its semi-medieval procedure, with its habit of meting out the most inhuman and barbaric punishments for the slightest insubordination and its mild treatment of the transgressions committed by superiors against their subordinates, with its habit of juggling away, almost on principle, the soldier's right of self-defense against his superiors. Nothing can arouse more bitter feeling against militarism and nothing can at the same time be more instructive than a simple perusal of the articles of war and the records of the military penal cases.

This chapter also includes the maltreatment of soldiers, which will be specially dealt with on a later occasion. It forms, it is true, not a legal, but in practice perhaps the most effective, of all violent disciplinary methods of militarism.

Thus they attempt to tame men as they tame animals. Thus the recruits are drugged, confused, flattered, bribed, oppressed, imprisoned, polished, and beaten; thus one grain is added to the other and mixed and kneaded to furnish the mortar for the immense edifice of the army; thus one stone is laid upon the other in a well calculated fashion to form a bulwark against the forces of subversion.

That all those methods of alluring, disciplining, and coercing the soldier partake of the nature of a weapon in the class struggle is made evident by the institution of the one-year volunteer. [Young men with a high school education, which in Germany can hardly be attained by youths belonging to the working class, have the privilege of serving but one year instead of two, paying for their food, lodgings, uniform, etc.] The bourgeois offspring, destined to become an officer of the reserves, is generally above the suspicion of harboring anti-capitalist, anti-militarist, or subversive ideas of any description. Consequently he is not sent out of his home district, he need not live in the barracks, nor is he obliged to attend the military school or the church, and he is even spared a large part of the pipe-clay drill. Of course, if he falls into the clutches of discipline and the military penal law, it is exceptional and usually with harmless results, and the habitual oppressors of the soldiers, though they frequently nourish a hatred against all "educated people," only rarely venture to lay hands on him. The education of officers furnishes a second striking proof for this thesis.

Of exceptional importance for the discipline of an army is *the cooperation of masses of men* which does away with the initiative of the individual to a large extent. In the army each individual is chained to all the rest like a galley slave, and is almost incapable of acting with freedom. The combined force of the hundreds of thousands forming the army prevents him with an overwhelming power from making the slightest movement of his own volition. All the parts of this tremendous organism, or rather of this tremendous machinery are not only subject to the suggestive influence of the word of command, but also to a separate hypnotism, a mass suggestion whose influence, however, would be *impotent* on an army composed of enlightened and resolute opponents of militarism.

The two tasks of militarism, as will be seen, do not at all harmonize always in the department of military education, but are often at cross-purposes. That is not only true of training, but also in regard to equipment. War training demands ever more imperatively a continuously growing measure of initiative on the part of the soldier. As a "watchdog of capital" the soldier does not require any initiative, he is not even allowed to possess it, if his qualification as a suicide is not to be destroyed. In short, war against the foreign foe requires men; war against the foe at home, slaves, machines. And as regards equipment and clothes, the gaudy uniforms, the glittering buttons and helmets, the flags, the parades, the cavalry charges, and all the rest of the nonsense cannot be dispensed with for producing the spirit necessary for the battle against the interior enemy, though in a war against the exterior enemy all these things would positively bring about a calamity; they are simply impossible. That tragic conflict, the numerous aspects of which cannot be dealt with exhaustively in this book, has not been comprehended by the well-intentioned critics of our militarism, who in their simplicity only use the standard applicable to a system of training for war.

That antagonism of interests within militarism itself, that self-contradiction from which it suffers, has the tendency of becoming more and more acute. Which of the two opposing sets of interest gets the upper hand depends at a given time on the relation existing between the tension in home and foreign politics. Here we see clearly a potential self-destruction of militarism.

When the war against the interior enemy, in case of an armed revolution, puts such great demands on military art that dressed-up slaves and machines no longer suffice to fight him down the last hour of the violent domination of the minority, of capitalistic oligarchy will also have struck.

It is of sufficient importance for us to note that the described military spirit as such confuses and leads astray the proletarian class-consciousness and that militarism, by infecting our whole public life, serves capitalism with that spirit in all other directions, apart from the purely military, for instance, by creating and promoting proletarian docility in face of economic, social, and political exploitation and by thwarting as much as possible the struggle for the liberation of the working class. We shall have to deal with this later on.

Translated by Sidney Zimand

Rosa Luxemburg

Working Class and Militarism

In order to diminish the supply on the labor market and to reduce competition, the worker first of all gives away a part of his wages in the form of taxes, to support his competitor as a soldier; secondly he turns this competitor into a tool, whereby the capitalist state can keep down all of his efforts to improve his condition (strikes, coalitions etc.), if necessary even suppress them in blood, to thwart this improvement of the worker's condition, because of which militarism was necessary, according to Schippel.* Thirdly the worker turns this competitor into the most solid pillar of reaction per se, thus causing his own social enslavement.

In other words: through militarism the worker prevents an immediate reduction of his wages by a certain amount, but as a result by and large loses the possibility to fight for a raise of his wages and for the improvement of his condition. He wins as the seller of his manpower, but at the same time loses his freedom of action as a citizen, to find himself losing his manpower in the end as well. He eliminates a competitor from the labor market in order to see a guardian of wage slavery rise, and he prevents a wage reduction, thus diminishing both the chance of a lasting improvement as well as the chance of final economic, political, and social liberation. This is the actual meaning of the economic "relief" of the working class through militarism. Here as in all other speculations of opportunistic politics we see the major goals of socialist class liberation sacrificed to petty interests of the moment; interests which, in addition, prove essentially imagined at closer examination.

Translated by Renate Steinchen

*Max Schippel: In the beginning at the left wing of the SPD; since the end of the eighties a leading representative of the right wing, as of 1890 Reichstag deputy; vacated his seat in 1905.

ANTI-SEMITISM

Friedrich Engels

On Anti-Semitism

. . . However, I would want you to consider whether you don't cause
more harm than good with anti-Semitism. Anti-Semitism is the
characteristic of a backward culture and is, therefore, only to be
found in Prussia and Austria, or Russia. Whoever tried to advocate
anti-Semitism here in England or in America would be the target of
ridicule, and in Paris Mr. Drumont's writings—which are intellectually infinitely superior to those by German anti-Semites—cause
ultimately nothing but some momentary sensation. Besides, now
that he figures as a candidate for the municipal council, he has to
maintain that he is as much against the Christian capital as against
the Jewish! And Mr. Drumont would be read even if he were to
advocate a diametrically opposed view. Today in Prussia it is the
petty gentry, the Junkers who earn ten thousand marks and spend
twenty thousand marks and therefore fall prey to usurers, who
dabble in anti-Semitism, and in Prussia and Austria it is the petit
bourgeois doomed to ruin by big-capitalist competition, the guild
artisan, and the petty trader, who make up the choir to all this and
shout along. But if the capital is to destroy *these* classes of society, it
does what it is supposed to do in the execution of its duty and it
performs a good deed, no matter whether it is Semitic or Aryan,
circumcised or baptized; it helps the backward Prussians and Austrians to get ahead, to arrive finally at a modern position, where all
social differences merge into one great antagonism between capitalists and wageworkers. Only where this is not yet the case, where

no strong class of capitalists yet exists, where capital is still too weak to take over the entire national production and therefore has the stock exchange as the main forum of its activities, in other words, where production is still in the hands of farmers, landowners, artisans, and similar backward classes from the Middle Ages—only there, anti-Semitism is to be found.

In all of North America, where there are millionaires whose wealth can hardly be translated into our paltry marks, guilders or francs, among these millionaires there is *not one single Jew,* and the Rothschilds are veritable beggars compared to these Americans. And even here in England, Rothschild is a man of modest means compared, for instance, to the duke of Westminster. Even with us at home on the Rhine, where, ninety-five years ago, with the help of the French we chased the aristocracy out of the country and built our own industry, where are the Jews there?

Hence, anti-Semitism is nothing but a reaction of declining medieval social strata against modern society—a society that mainly consists of capitalists and wageworkers—and therefore serves only reactionary ends under a seemingly socialist guise; it is a variety of feudal socialism, and we cannot have any dealings with that. If anti-Semitism is possible in a country, then it is proof that there is still not enough capital. Capital and labor are inseparable today. The stronger capital will be, the stronger the working class will be as well, and consequently, the nearer the end of the capitalists' rule. Therefore, I would wish us Germans—and I also count the Viennese in here—a speedy development of the capitalist economy and by no means its deterioration into stagnation.

In addition, anti-Semitism distorts the whole picture. It does not even know the Jews that it condemns. Otherwise it would know that here in England and in America, there are tens of thousands of *Jewish proletarians,* thanks to the East European anti-Semites, and also in Turkey, thanks to the Spanish Inquisition; and as a matter of fact, it is precisely these Jewish workers who are the most badly exploited and the most miserable. In the past twelve months we had *three* strikes here in England by Jewish workers and taking that into account are we to advocate anti-Semitism as a means of struggle against capital?

Besides, we owe far too much to the Jews. Not to mention Heine and Börne, Marx was as Jewish as can be; Lassalle was a Jew. Many of our best men are Jews. My friend Victor Adler, who at the moment pays for his dedication to the proletariat's cause in a Vienna prison, Eduard Bernstein, editor of the London *Social Democrat*, Paul Singer, one of our best men in the Reichstag—people whose friendship I am proud of and all of them Jews! Haven't I myself been made into a Jew by the *Gartenlaube* and, admittedly, if I were to choose, I would rather be a Jew than "Herr *von*"!

London, April 19, 1890

Translated by Renate Steinchen

August Bebel

Anti-Semitism and Social Democracy

Anti-Semitism springs from the dissatisfaction of certain sections within the middle class that find themselves burdened by the development of capitalism and who are doomed to ruin partly due to this development. Misunderstanding, however, the true causes of their situation, they do not aim their fight against the capitalist economic system, but against a common phenomenon within the same system, which becomes a nuisance to them in the trade competition: against the Jewish exploiter.

With this origin, anti-Semitism is forced to make demands that are contradictory to both the economic as well as the political laws governing bourgeois society, hence they are antiprogressive. This is also the reason why anti-Semitism is predominantly supported by the Junkers and the clergy.

Anti-Semitism's one-sided fight against the Jewish exploiters must necessarily be a failure therefore, since the exploitation of men by men is not a specifically Jewish way of making a livelihood, but an intrinsic element pertaining to bourgeois society, which will not come to an end until bourgeois society declines.

As social democracy is the most determined enemy of capitalism, no matter whether its exponents are Jews or Christians, and as it aims at eliminating bourgeois society by bringing about its transformation into a socialist society, which will put an end to all oppression of men by men and all exploitation of men by men, social democracy is opposed to wasting its energies fighting against the existing political and social order by initiating an illegitimate and hence ineffectual fight against a phenomenon that is totally interrelated with bourgeois society.

Social democracy fights against anti-Semitism as a movement opposed to the natural evolution of society, which, however, ultimately will have a revolutionary effect despite its reactionary nature and against its own will, because the petite bourgeoisie and the small farmers, incited by anti-Semitism, are to realize that not only the Jewish capitalist, but the capitalist class at large is their enemy and that only the establishment of socialism will end their misery.

When the executive committee of the party put the issue of "Anti-Semitism and Social Democracy" on the agenda of the party convention in Berlin last year, it was particularly the anti-Semitic press that took note of this with satisfaction; pointing out that officially debating this question at our party convention proved how much significance anti-Semitism had attained in Germany. Certainly the anti-Semitic movement in Germany had to gain a certain weight first, before we would decide to take a position on it; but they are wrong in believing—and today's discussion will hopefully prove it—that this happens because we attribute any particular importance to these gentlemen. Concerning this question we only did what we have to do as a party vis-à-vis newly arising phenomena, which gained a certain significance in the sociopolitical and economic sectors. Our party in particular, more than any other, has always been trying not to close its eyes to such phenomena, but rather made a point of closely examining them as to their value and their impact.

Speaking of anti-Semitism as a new phenomenon is both correct and incorrect. Anti-Semitism, in terms of hostility against the Jews aiming at their extermination or at least their expulsion, is more than one and a half thousand years old. However, what we mean by anti-Semitism and an anti-Semitic party today is a new phenomenon insofar as the hostile endeavors aimed against Jewry have been united in a single political party that participates in public life. In addition, there is still some uncertainty as to this movement's significance among our own ranks. A few days before the party convention, I gave a lecture in Berlin concerning this present party convention and I also dealt briefly with this issue. Then a comrade said that far too much importance was attributed to this matter and anti-Semitism was nothing but the product of slogans. The applause from parts of this very well attended meeting that ensued from this statement showed me that a not unconsiderable segment of our comrades does not see clearly what this question is about. If anti-Semitism were only the result of empty phrases, we would not have to deal with it here now. Discarding anti-Semitism in such a way is tantamount to the ways our opponents have been trying to discard us for the longest time. There, too, it was said that social democracy was merely the outcome of some people's agitation, whose disappearance or silencing would make social democracy disappear from the scene. Through the enormous growth of our movement and on account of other experiences, all of our fiercest enemies realized that this point of view was totally wrong. It is impossible to ignore phenomena that gain popularity with the masses; instead, one has to examine their causes and once the causes of the phenomena have been found, means will have to be sought how to cure the evil that created the phenomena.

Concerning the latter issue, we take a stand against the anti-Semitic movement different from other phenomena. We are in a position to declare that the evils that created anti-Semitism will disappear, but not through anti-Semitism's victory, rather through making the evils, and together with the evils making anti-Semitism itself obsolete, and causing both to disappear.

Anti-Semitism, understood in terms of hatred against the Jews, is a very old phenomenon. From the moment the old Jewish empire was destroyed, Jerusalem demolished and the Jewish population dispersed and scattered all over the countries of the ancient civilized world, certain anti-Semitic tendencies developed. Already Tacitus in his *Annals* speaks of the Jews in a hostile way. Until their expulsion, the Jews used to be a mostly agrarian and trading nation in their home country; unlike their ethnic kin, the Phoenicians, Tyrians, and Carthaginians, the Jews did not play a prominent role as traders in the ancient civilized world, primarily because their country was not located near the sea. It is characteristic, however, that immediately after their dispersion and scattering, most of them turned to trading. On the other hand, they could not assimilate as workers into a social order based on slave labor—as was characteristic of most countries of the ancient civilized world—as they were outside these societies. Consequently, trade was the only possible occupation, for which, in addition, the Semitic race undoubtedly always had a great natural inclination. For this reason Jews have been engaging in trade to this very day in places where they live as a small minority; in places, however, where they live together in masses, as in Hungary, Poland, Galicia, in parts of Russia, the majority of them turned to crafts or even to agriculture, mainly, because they were forced to, since not everybody can engage in trading, which is why only a small number of them are involved in trade. There, the masses of working Jews get exploited by Jewish capitalists and entrepreneurs in an equally shameless way as the Christian workers in Christian Europe get exploited by Christian and Jewish exploiters. Only where Jews live rather in isolation, as it is the case in Germany, where there are 50 million inhabitants to roughly 500,000 Jews, their main occupation is trade. This development has been highly favored by circumstance for almost the past two thousand years. With the exception of the golden age in the Islamic-Arabic Empire, the Jews have been deliberately excluded from any other occupation by legislation, until most recent times. As we all know, Judaea was the cradle of Christianity; very early, however, Christianity adopted a hostile attitude against Judaism. On the other hand, Jews were bitterly opposed to the Christians, as some of the first Christians had been Jews and the Jews regarded them as black sheep, as apostates of their faith, and persecuted them. In addition, taking into account the representation by the Christian church of Christ's tribulations and his death on the cross, caused by the Jews, it becomes clear that this religious element prevailing among the masses from the Middle Ages until today, necessarily increased, at least to a considerable degree, if not generated, anti-Semitism. Furthermore, a general dislike against one another is to be found among people of different races, particularly with people of a lower cultural level. There is definitely a difference of race between the Jews and the rest of the population. After all, we realize how deeply ingrained national chauvinism—which the bourgeoisie keeps stirring up—is even today, and being milder than racial hatred, it becomes all the more clearly understood why racial hatred exists. We are, in fact, dealing with two races, who are completely different in terms of character and their entire nature, whose basic differences have been maintained throughout a period of two thousand years until today. Should a Jew living in a foreign nation be unlucky enough to be conspicuous by his appearance, so that one can already tell by his nose that he is a Jew, being, in the negative sense of the word, a marked one, racial antagonism will be fostered even more.

With seeming rightfulness the anti-Semites rebuke the Jews for being a race particularly hostile to the Germans, with specially unpleasant racial characteristics, because they would otherwise not have been able to maintain their separation from Christian Germanic society for more than two thousand years. In this connection they ignore, however, that Jews have been forced until most recent times to live in separation from the rest of the population, unless they gave up their faith. Throughout the Middle Ages legislation, however changing in detail, was in its entirety thoroughly hostile against Jews, oppressing them and almost forcing them into isolation. And this persisting pressure for more than a thousand years was extremely conducive to the close ties among them. From the very beginning it was the legislation of the Middle Ages that greatly sinned against the Jews, thus promoting phenomena against the will of the legislators, which, in my opinion, looking at it objectively, the Jews are often wrongly accused of. In addition, the most rigorous and brutal pogroms against the Jews occurred, in the period between 1198 and 1331, no fewer than fifty-two of vast dimension. All major cities of Germany without exception were involved in these pogroms in those times, such as Cologne, Mayence, Nuremburg, Augsburg, Frankfurt am Main and so on and so forth. And they were not the kind of persecutions we came to know under the state of emergency against us. The Jews were chased from their house and home, robbed, cruelly mistreated and more often than not murdered, because of their faith, their race, and mainly because of their wealth. In some of these pogroms the number of victims totaled ten thousand. I confess that I cannot refrain from a certain admiration for a race that, despite all of these terrible persecutions has been developing in its own way and maintained its autonomy; a phenomenon that only manifested itself in one other people in history, the gypsies.

While this demagogy and these acts of violence often took place with the approval and the support of the religious and secular authorities, the secular authorities, on the other hand, were inclined to grant the Jews certain privileges. As they did not belong to any German tribe, the Jews were under the protection of the emperor and ranked as the "Holy Roman Empire's chamberlains" and as such they were obliged to pay a certain annual "protection tax" known as the Jewish protection tax. Several emperors permitted the Jews to take twice the interest rate on the money they had lent out, as was normally permissible according to the existing laws, in order to be able to increase the protection tax. Usury, that is, the taking of interest, was originally looked down upon by the Catholic church in general and was considered un-Christian. As soon as capital started accumulating, however, the prohibition of taking interest was unfeasible. And when the church itself started acquiring capital and real estate and begin leasing the latter, that is, when it started practicing usury itself, its own vested interest was turned against the prohibition of taking interest. From then on maximum tariffs for the taking of interest were introduced—in other words, restrictions on interest rates as they existed until most recent times and in ways that the anti-Semites would like to see reestablished. With the increase of the interest rates the Jews were allowed to take, the amount of protection tax payable to the emperors increased. Thus the latter favored the Jews' usury for their own benefit. Throughout the Middle Ages the position of Jews in Germany was circumscribed by the following main restrictions: they were prohibited from acquiring or owning real estate; they were not allowed to be craftsmen; they were declared uncapable of exercising political rights; they were burdened with special taxes; they were forced to live in certain quarters of the cities or special villages—like the famous ghetto, which existed in Rome until some decades ago; they were forced to wear distinctive visible signs, the typical nose as a characteristic feature was not enough; they were not allowed to marry Christians, and were thus forced to reproduce themselves, at least officially, within their own race; Christians were prohibited under penalty from using a Jewish physician; Christian midwives were not allowed to lend assistance to Jewish women in childbed. For reasons of state the Jews were stigmatized in such ways as outcasts and haunted ones from all sides. These restrictions basically existed, for instance in Prussia, until 1812. Then, in the wake of the defeats of 1806 and the new era following these events, a new decree was passed, admitting the Jews to middle-class occupations, to teaching positions, to the military services with eligibility for promotion, to farming, and permitting them to purchase land. Despite the fact that this decree was law, the actual situation remained the same for the Jews during the following decades. As late as 1833, the provincial diets of the former Prussian provinces unanimously agreed, on the basis of their expertise, that, regarding the effects of the 1812 decree, a basic change in the relationship between Jews and the rest of the population had not occurred; and at the same time they advocated for an abolishment of these new liberties and the reintroduction of the old restrictions, particularly the prohibition of peddling, of keeping Christian domestic servants, of acquiring real estate, and of holding honorary offices. In addition the profession of pharmacist was to be prohibited and the keeping of restaurants and saloons was to be allowed only in relation to their own coreligionists. From 1812 to 1833 no Jew acted as representative of the municipal council of the capital, Berlin, a situation that—as we all know—today's anti-Semites consider their professed ideal. Not until 1848 were there major improvements for the Jews concerning their social and political situation. The fact that Jews were prominently engaged in all new reforms and in the Revolution, can easily be explained through their position in state and society as a subjugated and oppressed race. Shortly after the victory of the reaction, again steps were taken against the Jews, namely in 1851, in the Prussian Upper Chamber. A motion was made to eliminate article 12 of the constitution, guaranteeing religious freedom and the privilege of civic rights to the Jews and all non-Christians. They were not to be allowed to become members of the Representative Assemblies and were to be excluded from judicial and all other offices invested with executive power. These were to be reserved for members of the officially accepted Christian churches. This motion was made and dealt with at a time when the official leader of the upper chamber, Stahl, was a Jew himself; he had himself baptized! The motion failed, however, and by the new legislation, according to the formulation of the North German Confederation concerning the German Empire, the last civic restrictions on the Jews were repealed. Legislation of a thousand years against the Jews and their constant restriction not having achieved what they were intended to achieve, should be proof for the enemies of the Jews that their aspirations are not feasible, even if they should come to power some day, which is not at all likely.

During the first years of the German Empire, no anti-Semitic tendencies of significance were noticeable. This movement made its first public appearance only in 1877, when Stöcker in Berlin set himself up as their spokesman and was the first to organize them, which he still is particularly proud of today. This phenomenon, however, was the natural effect and the consequence of the economic situation in Germany as a result of the great collapse of 1873. The latter had brought about a general depression. The newly founded industrial mammoth enterprises and their production were in fierce competition with the craftsmen; now for the first time, the feeling of decline befell the members of the petit bourgeois and middle-class trades- and craftsmen. The golden era of prosperity of the early seventies, the greatest we ever had, will never come back, because all of its preconditions have irrevocably disappeared. After the middle classes had run into such a critical economic situation and had become aware of it, they naturally started exploring the reason for it. Now it is clearly undisputable that the Jews—and I keep referring here merely to the majority of them—after receiving full emancipation and as a result of the new economic and social legislation of the North German Confederation and the German Empire, opening new, hitherto unimagined avenues of capitalist development—ranked first among those engaging in trade and being financially powerful during this development. In addition, the Jew is in many cases superior to the Christian in his ways of trading. Undoubtedly, what has become known as haggling is particularly typical for some of the Jews. The Jew knows how to calculate and, if need be, he contents himself even with the smallest of profits; besides, he trades in a host of items, which to others seem worthless or plain, maybe even disdainful. By engaging in this kind of haggling themselves or through the earlier efforts of their immediate ancestors, many Jewish capital magnates created the foundation of their present position. As a result of all of these circumstances in combination with the tribal particularities of the Jews mentioned above, it was foremost among tradesmen that anti-Semitism first fell on fertile ground; their hatred was directed against the Jew as competitor.

Indeed, Jewry has become the decisive factor in a large number of business branches. It leads in the retailing of manufactured goods in the most general sense; it completely dominates the trading of all kinds of agrarian products in large parts of Germany, such as in Hesse-Nassau, Baden, Württemberg, North Bavaria, Alsace-Lorraine, Thuringia, etc. Recently a comrade in the *Vorwärts* remarked very correctly in an article on the origins of anti-Semitism that, for the farmer, capitalist and Jew were identical terms. Now that the overall economic development was forced the farmers into recession and brought them to the insight that despite all great promises made by the political parties throughout the decades, their material circumstances keep deteriorating, that they are irretrievably lost if help does not come soon, they readily embrace those telling them, "Get rid of the Jew and a period of well-being will start anew!" The anti-Semitic demagogues operate by this simple recipe. Naturally, the small farmer, petty craftsman, or trader does not feel like perishing in this struggle, and he sees his savior in the one who holds out a straw in his misery. What makes agitation in these circles so difficult for us is the fact that as honest people we have to tell them: Within the framework of present society, we have no remedy to save you for good. Therefore, we will draw only a few sympathizers from these strata in the beginning, even though comrade Katzenstein's assertion is wrong, claiming that we have no single real farmer in our party. But we cannot entice them with promises that we know are unfeasible. This is, however, what the anti-Semites are doing. If we were to follow their example, we would degrade ourselves to demagogues of the basest kind. These are the main reasons why anti-Semitism took root with the farmers.

A farmer selling his products today—potatoes, grain, hops, tobacco, wine—who are the buyers? Jews. Who lends him the capital, who buys and sells his cattle? Jews. Anti-Semitic tendencies consequently have to surface as a result. Like the farmer, the small business likewise suffers from the tremendous capitalistic development sweeping over Germany since 1871, comparable only to the development in North America. This development has long reached a point where capital competes with itself, with the big capitalist putting to death and devouring the medium-sized and small ones. The protective duty specifically intended to protect the crafts and the farmers extraordinarily promoted big industry during these past fifteen years. Our class of capitalists, comprising of a few tens of thousands of people, certainly retain about 2000 millions of extra marks each year, which are invested in new enterprises. And now the Jew also starts competing in the industrial sector. Industrial shoemaking, tailoring, the trade in clothing, old and new, cloth mills, etc., are all more or less in the hands of Jews. The Jew, who as a wholesaler employs a great number of artisans, who as a wholesale capitalist, as an exploiter, appears in this sector as well, must necessarily provoke anti-Semitism among his competitors. And whenever an anti-Semitic agitator approaches the circles of artisans and farmers, shouting, "Get rid of the Jew and your situation will be different!" they will believe him. Our small businessmen, our rural folks, whose ideals are directed towards the ways of the past, fall for such promises. In their desire to be saved at any rate they blindly follow the anti-Semites' call, saying: Just be on our side, vote for us, then you will certainly be helped. Indeed, if there is anybody who impertinently and impudently makes promises to the voters, it is the anti-Semitic agitators. A social democrat could not dare do such a thing: his own party comrades would make a clean sweep and out he goes off the assembly.

Furthermore, we can see that the state and the communities award large contracts for all kinds of orders. Who alone can supply cheaply, fast, and in large quantities, who is able to buy raw materials cheaply because he has loads of capital at hand? Often enough it is only Jews! Naturally the orders are entrusted to them. Now, if they start bringing down the artisans, as is only natural, the latters' feelings of hatred and enmity will not boil over against the capitalist, but against the Jew.

Anti-Semitism found sympathizers in the circles of the trading classes basically for the same reasons as with the farmers and small businesses. But anti-Semitism is more far-reaching. Large segments of our civil servants are anti-Semites. A considerable part of them are forced into debt, due to their bad salaries and because of the demand made on them to act in so-called keeping with their social standing, and they are forced to go into debt with the usurer, the cutthroat; he cannot furnish secure guarantees, because as a rule he does not own any property. According to the economic principle that a greater risk ought to be parallel with a greater profit—a theory that not a Jew, but a middle-class economist postulated, and which was taught with enthusiasm in Germany by Schulze-Delitzsch—the interest rates are high; they are usurious interests. But the majority of usurers are Jews again. The Jews are falsely accused of being cowards. No one risks more than the Jew; hoping for a higher profit, he persistently engages in such business deals. Among the ranks of the indebted civil servants anti-Semitism naturally takes root as well. Besides, sailing under the flag of anti-Semitism, the civil servants may eventually oppose something actively. It is a kind of opposition allowed by the state, which otherwise is not possible for civil servants. They are allowed to show up at conservative or anti-Semitic meetings only, and nowhere else. And since the first are terribly boring as a rule, while the anti-Semites kick up a racket and cause excitement, he [the civil servant] prefers the latter; besides, there they do not have to strain themselves displaying loyalty and royalism. Due to similar causes, anti-Semitism is to be found in the circle of officers and the feudal aristocracy. Our Junkers have fallen prey to the usurers partly because of their prodigality, partly because of their social standing, forcing them to meet expenses beyond their means. First of all the Jew lends money, then he acts as the buyer of the manors, often he becomes the owner himself and in doing so multiplies the reasons why the feudal aristocracy is in the anti-Semitic camp. This does not prevent the aristocrat of exquisitely noble birth, however, from catching a Jewish goldfish to save his shaky existence and regild his coat of arms.

Another element is anti-Semitic and even influential in the movement: these are the students. The great majority of them is anti-Semitic today. They, too, are anti-Semites for material reasons, even though this may seem improbable at first sight. It is they who are annoyed with the Jews most. Today competition also plays a great role among the circles of scholars, those circles with higher education. Already in the first edition of my book *The Woman* I pointed out that today we are suffering from a surplus of goods, similarly from one of intellectuals. Our small businessmen, our midsize farmers often don't even consider letting their sons become artisans or farmers anymore. They know that this leads nowhere, feeling that they have problems maintaining their own livelihood. With all of their remaining resources, they see to it that their sons may study, in order to obtain a position with the state, to make a career as a civil servant, or to make a livelihood as physicians or jurists, or to find a permanent position for life as architects, chemists, engineers, etc., with a state-owned or industrial company. But a surplus of employees prevails in all of these fields, due to an enormous influx, causing a dramatic disproportion with the demand. While the middle-class sons felt a dislike for the clerical profession during the time of the *Kulturkampf**—causing a noticeable shortage of clergymen— a new interest in studying theology has arisen again, characteristically, "obeying the laws of necessity, rather than one's own inclinations," now that all other fields of study are crammed and as a result all clerical positions have been filled again. With the Jews' affluence and prosperity and with their undeniable aspirations for higher education, they send their sons to the universities in great numbers and they study law, medicine, etc. Our "Germanic" students consider them very undesirable, unpleasant competition. The generally known fact that Jews distinguish themselves by extraordinary resilience, toughness, and often by sobriety, too, turns their opponents against them even more. As a rule the Christian artisan or retailer feels that he did not have a good day unless he spent at

---

*Conflict between the State and the Roman Catholic church under Bismarck.

least a couple of hours over his morning pint. A Jew will not even dream of such a thing. The Jew stays home at his business. Concerning the consumption of alcohol, he can even be considered the ideal of our teetotalers. The Jewish student spends most of his time studying diligently while he is at the university; the "Germanic" student loafs around the bars, the fencing loft, and in other places I would rather not name. The Jews are diligent, they study and often they outdo their Germanic fellow students during exams. If only the latter would work and study as diligently as the Jews do on average, the current secretary of cultural affairs, Bosse, would not have had a reason to give a lecture on the study of law and the ignorance prevailing among a larger number of the young jurists, in which he made it rather clear that many of the young jurists were opportunistic thrusters trying to compensate for a lack of knowledge and character with servile behavior.

Thus I have sketched in as short a form as possible the phenomena that—in my opinion—contributed to turn anti-Semitism into the phenomenon the way it presents itself. It is striking how anti-Semitism could gain popularity in Saxonia, of all places, where there are relatively few Jews. Well, it does not really matter whether a Jew lives in close proximity, but whether he makes himself felt as an uncomfortable competitor. But this is the case in Saxonia as well as anywhere else. Moreover, the majority of the Saxonian conservatives are noted for their unusual degree of lack of principles and servility toward their superiors, thus greatly inciting the voters' discontent with their behavior and causing them to join the anti-Semites who set themselves up as helpers and braggarts. Besides, they make seemingly radical demands, which are bound to find approval with any petit bourgeois who has democratic convictions deep down inside. Why, for instance, is it not possible any longer to have a genuine democratic party in Germany? Because artisans and farmers who constituted the main foundation of such a party keep losing power. It was substituted for liberalism, the representative of the bourgeoisie, captivating the majority of the above-mentioned strata. The more difficult the struggle of survival will be for the middle classes of our society in the coming years, the more rapidly they see themselves drifting toward their ruin—and this is going to happen—the more readily they will, let's not deceive ourselves about that, turn to the anti-Semitic movement. With these classes our time will not come, until anti-Semitism has lost its attraction to them and they have realized through the anti-Semitic representative in the Reichstag and elsewhere that they have been deceived. Then the hour of our harvest will arrive, not earlier. In its struggle for power anti-Semitism will be forced to overshoot its own marks against its own will, as has already been demonstrated in the case of Mr. Ahlwardt, who entered into the battle arm in arm with the Junkers and in the course of time was then forced by the voters' mood to issue the slogan: Against the Jews and the Junkers! For the anti-Semitic movement in Hesse it is not sufficient anymore, either, to agitate against the Jews alone, it has to agitate against capital per se; once this moment has arrived, the time has come also for our views to fall on fertile ground and we will find the followers that we look for in vain right now.

The contradictory nature of anti-Semitism finds expression in its contradictory program, which is partly ultrareactionary and conservative and partly democratic, and concerns some aspects congruent with the demands of our own program.

For instance, the anti-Semites demand a representation of the people based on professional categories, a totally reactionary demand going back to the Middle Ages; but as long as this has not been achieved, they agree to universal suffrage and, naturally, they desire diets, too. At the present point they would vehemently support us in our struggle against the abolition of universal suffrage because this alone renders their presence in the Reichstag possible. Furthermore they would like to introduce censorship against the immoral excesses in the press, in literature and the arts, which would leave the door open to reaction of the worst kind; to maintain the Christian and national character of the school system, obviously a conservative demand. On the other hand, however, they demand educational opportunities at the state's expense for highly talented students without means, which is similar to what we included in our program. Strong military forces for the preservation of peace in the exterior and in the interior. I guess I don't have to tell you against whom the one in the interior is deemed necessary. In addition they demand sliding income and inheritance taxes, which is, by all means, democratic, but then they also demand a defense tax and the retention of the grain duties, by which they hope to win the farmers. Furthermore, demands for a social reorganization of the professional and industrial groups are made—again, a purely medieval demand! Restrictions concerning the freedom of trade, chambers of handicraft with disciplinary powers, nationalization of the mortgages.

The last-mentioned demand is also made in the *Communist Manifesto* and has been made similarly by our comrades in some German state assembly. Isn't it wonderful that anti-Semites, farmer unionists, and we come forth with seemingly the same demand! But these demands have basically nothing in common with one another. The *Communist Manifesto* demands the nationalization of mortgages with the assumption that a socialist government is already in power. As is generally known, we demand the nationalization of all real estate, and the demand of nationalization of mortgages is made by the *Communist Manifesto* only for a transitional stage. This means, if we cannot expropriate the class of capitalists at once, we are willing to cut off the dog's tail piecemeal *(Laughter)*, by ruining capital gradually through the reduction of the interest rate. The men who wrote the *Communist Manifesto* knew very well that this demand had basically little significance, but might find the approval of many and it may be necessary during a transitional period. But when the nationalization of mortgages is suggested to a bourgeois government, to a powerful class of big landowners and agrarians, so the gentlemen agrarians will have to pay lower interest rates, then it is a through-and-through conservative measure even if social democrats make this demand; it means favoring one class at the expense of the majority, at the expense of the working class. If the state were to provide a cheaper interest rate on mortgages, not only the small farmer would benefit from that, but the big landowners as well. If the state's interest rates were as high as 3 percent, while the state would have to pay 3½ percent just to borrow money, then the ½ percent of interest for billions in mortgage payments would have to be raised from tax sources; the burden would have to be carried by the great masses and not the capitalists. It is, therefore, dubious to suggest such a wrong remedy, out of sheer zeal for practical actions. I can only warn those comrades who will become members of the Assemblies to agitate in their zeal among circles who at present are not to be won anyway and in part cannot be won at all, thus cooperating in the artificial upkeep of social conditions, on whose upkeep we least of all are supposed to cooperate. I do not consider the Independents' verdict, speaking of our party's decay, justified, but we have to keep our eyes open.

Further demands in the anti-Semitic program—restriction of peddling, prohibiting bazaars, and advertising, etc.—are nothing but an interesting proof of the anti-Semites' demagogy. During the elections for the Representative Assembly in Saxony, for instance, one of theirs thunders against the Jewish exploiters, yelling that no Christian must buy from a Jew; but when he takes off his coat in the assembly, one of our comrades recognizes the label of a Jewish company on it! I was told that the person in question was so much in debt that none of his fellow Christians was any longer willing to lend him money. Furthermore, the program includes the demands of restricting consumers' cooperatives, the establishment of penal colonies overseas, the promotion of internal colonialization. I guess I don't have to elaborate on who are supposed to be the first for shipment to these penal colonies. Finally, demands are made to abolish Jewish emancipation and to put them under laws, treating them as resident aliens. According to experience made during the Middle Ages, nobody will get very far with that; because, in relation to the admonition, Be fertile and multiply like the sand on the sea! the Jews have always strictly adhered to their fathers' commandments and are still doing so today.

In short, this hodgepodge of a program totally corresponds with the contradictory nature of anti-Semitism. What I told you concerning the probability, even the necessity of its spreading, will lead to its becoming revolutionary against its own will, which is when we have to employ social democracy.

Translated by Renate Steinchen

PHILOSOPHY AND RELIGION FOR THE MASSES

Joseph Dietzgen

Scientific Socialism

A considerable number of readers of the *Volksstaat* are opposed to elaborate and searching essays in these columns. I doubted therefore whether the following would be suitable for publication. Let the editor decide. Yet I beg to consider whether it is not as valuable to engage the more advanced minds and to gain qualified thorough-going comrades as to strive for great numbers by publishing popular articles. Both these aims, I think, should be kept in view. If the party is really of opinion that the emancipation from misery cannot be accomplished by mending particular evils but by a fundamental revolution of society; it necessarily follows that an agitation on the surface is inadequate and that it is moreover our duty to undertake an enquiry into the very basis of social life. Let us now proceed:

Contemporary socialism is communistic. Socialism and communism are now so near each other that there is hardly any difference between them. In the past they differed from each other as does liberalism from democracy, the latter being in both cases the consistent and radical application of the former. From all other political theories communistic socialism is distinguished by its principle that the people can only be free when they free themselves from poverty, when their struggle for freedom is fought out on the social, i.e., on the economic field. There is this difference between the modern and the older socialistic and communistic theories: in the past it was the feeling, the unconscious rebellion, against the unjust distribution of wealth, which constituted the basis of socialism; today it is based on knowledge, on the clear recognition of our historic development. In the past socialists and communists were able only to find out the deficiencies and evils of existing society. Their schemes for social reconstruction were fantastic. Their views were evolved not from the world of realities, not from the concrete conditions surrounding them, but from their mental speculations, and were therefore whimsical and sentimental. Modern socialism, on the other hand, is scientific. Just as scientists arrive at their generalizations not by mere speculation, but by observing the phenomena of the material world, so are the socialistic and communistic theories not idle schemes, but generalizations drawn from economic facts. We see for instance that the communistic mode of work is being more and more organized by the bourgeoisie itself. Only the distribution still proceeds on the old lines and the product is withheld from the people. The small production is disappearing while production on a large scale takes its place.

Those are facts resulting from the economic development of history and not from any conspiracy of communistic socialists. If we define *work* as an industrial undertaking whose products the worker uses for his own consumption, and an *industrial undertaking* as the work whose products go to the market, then it is not difficult to perceive how the development of industry must finally result in an organization of productive work. On the material organization of society scientific socialism is based.

Scientific socialists apply the inductive method. They stick to facts. They live in the real world and not in the spiritualist regions of scholasticism. The society we are striving for differs from the present but by formal modifications. Indeed, the society of the future is contained in the present society as the young bird is in the egg. Modern socialism is as yet more of a scientific doctrine than of a political party creed, though we are also rapidly approaching this stage. And strange to say, the *international* is of purely national descent: it proceeds from the German philosophy. If there be a grain of truth in the prating of "German" science, then the scientific German can only be found in his philosophic speculation. This speculation is on the whole an adventurous journey, yet at the same time a voyage of discovery. As the clumsy musket of our forefathers represents a necessary stage to the Prussian needle gun of the present time, so the metaphysical speculations of a Leibnitz, Kant, Fichte, Hegel are the inevitable paths leading up to the scientific proposition, that the idea, the conception, the logic, or the thinking are not the premise, but the result of material phenomena. The interminable discussions between idealism and materialism, between nominalists and spiritualists on the one hand, and the realists or sensualists on the other hand, as to whether the idea was produced by the world or the world by the idea, and which of the two was the cause or the effect—this discussion, I say, forms the essence of philosophy. Its mission was to solve the antithesis between thought and being, between the ideal and the material. A proof of this view I find in the fortnightly review *Unsere Zeit* for the second half of January, 1873, in an essay on intoxicating articles of consumption, as wine, tobacco, coffee, brandy, opium, etc. The author, after having stated that the use of intoxicants was to be found among all nations, at all times and under all conditions of human society, proceeds to declare the cause of that fact must be looked for there, "where the cause of all religion and philosophy lies, in the antithesis of our being, in the partly divine, partly animal nature of man." This antagonism between divinity and animality in human nature is in other words the antithesis between the ideal and the material. Religion and philosophy work towards a reconciliation of those conflicting principles. Philosophy proceeded from religion and began to rebel against its conception of life. In religion the idea is the primary element which creates and regulates matter. Philosophy, the daughter of religion, naturally inherited a good deal of her mother's blood. She needed ages of growth to generate the antireligious, scientific result, the apodictically safe proposition, that the world is not the attribute of spirit, but, on the contrary, that spirit, thought, idea is only one of the attributes of matter. Hegel, it is true, did not carry science to that height, yet so near was he to it that two of his followers, Feuerbach and Marx, scaled the summit. The clearing up of speculation helped Feuerbach to give us his wonderful analysis of religion, and enabled Marx to penetrate the deepest recesses of law, politics, and history. When we see, however, Herbart, Schopenhauer, Hartmann, etc., still going on speculating and philosophizing, we cannot regard them as more than stragglers, lost in the fantastic depth of their own thoughts, lagging behind in the backwoods and not knowing that the speculative fire has been overcome in the front. On the other hand, Marx, the leader of scientific socialism, is achieving splendid success by applying inductive logic to branches of knowledge which have hitherto been maltreated by speculation. As far back as the year 1620 Francis Bacon declared in his *Novum Organum* the inductive method as the savior from unfruitful scholasticism and as the rock on which modern science was to be built.

Indeed, where we have to deal with concrete phenomena, or, as it were, with palpable things, the method of materialism has long since reigned supremely. Yet, it needed more than practical success: it needed the theoretical working out in all its details in order to completely rout its enemy, the scholastic speculation or deduction. In his famous *History of Civilization in England* Thomas Buckle speaks at great length of the difference between the deductive and inductive mind, without, as it seems, having grasped the essence of the matter; he but proves what he admits himself in the introduction to his work that, though having made German philosophy a serious study, he did not *fully* penetrate it. If this happens to ripe and ingenious scholarship, what shall become of immature and superficial general knowledge which deals not with specialties but with the general results of science? In order to indicate clearly the scientific basis of socialism, I venture to enter more fully into the general result of philosophy, into the solution of the antithesis between the deductive and inductive method. But I fear lest the result of metaphysics, so ostentatiously announced, may appear to the reader as somewhat insignificant and commonplace. I beg, therefore, to remind you of Columbus who by means of an egg once for all furnished the proof that great discoveries resolve themselves into an ingenious, yet simple, idea.

When we retire to the solitude of our cell to search there in deep contemplation, or, as it were, in the innermost of our brains, for the right way we want to follow the next morning, we must remember that our mental effort can be successful only because of our previous, if involuntary, experiences and adventures which we, by help of our memory, have taken along into our cell.

That tells the whole story of philosophic speculation or deduction. These philosophers imagine they have drawn their theories, not from concrete material, but from the innermost of their brains, while, as a matter of fact, they have but performed an unconscious induction, a process of thought, of argument not without material, but with indefinite and therefore, confused material. Conversely, the inductive method is distinguished only by this that its deduction is done consciously. Scientific "laws" are deductions drawn by human thinking from empiric material. The spiritist needs material just as the materialist needs spirit. This thesis, when brought out with mathematical precision, is the result of philosophic speculation.

That may appear simple enough, yet even a cursory examination of any of our reviews will teach us how little familiar that truth is not only to our journalists and writers but also to our historians and statesmen who are untiring in their attempts to evolve views and theses not from the existing conditions but from their heads, hearts, consciences, categorical imperatives, or from some other unreal, mystical, and spiritual corner. The concrete questions of the day are, as a rule, solved by, or with the help of, given material. But in the discussion with Bismarck whether might goes before right or conversely; in the squabbles of theology whether the gods are made by the world or the world by the gods; whether catechisms or natural sciences enlighten the mind; whether history moves upward to a higher stage or goes down to its Day of Judgment; in political and economic questions: whether capital or labor creates value, whether aristocracy or democracy is the right form of government, whether we have to work on conservative, liberal, or revolutionary lines; in short, in abstract categories, in matters of philosophy, religion, politics, and social life, our leaders of science find themselves in the most unscientific confusion. They test human institutions by such principles or ideas as the idea of justice, of liberty, of truth, etc. "We," says Frederick Engels, "describe things as they are. Proudhon, on the other hand, wants our present society to arrange itself, not according to the laws of its economic development, but in conformity with the precepts of justice." Proudhon is in this respect the prototype of all unscientific doctrinairism.

A far superior guide in all such questions is modern socialism. Owing to its philosophical foundation it stands out prominently as a unanimous, firm and compact, method amidst the endless and shifting dissensions of its political opponents of every shade and opinion. What the dogma is to the religious belief, material facts are to the science of inductive socialism, while the views of liberalism are as whimsical and elusive as the ideal conceptions, as the ideas of eternal justice or liberty on which the liberals believe to be safely based.

The fundamental proposition of inductive socialism may be thus formulated: there is no eternal principle or an *a priori* idea of the divine, just and free; there is no revelation or a chosen people, but there are material factors which govern human society.

Far from bewailing that fact, we acknowledge it as absolutely necessary and reasonable, as something which may be denied by power of imagination, but which cannot be altered, nor, indeed, ought it to be altered. By granting that society is dominated by material interests we do not deny the power of the ideals of the heart, mind, science, and art. For we have no more to deal with the absolute antithesis between idealism and materialism, but with their higher synthesis which has been found in the knowledge that the ideal depends on the material, that divine justice and liberty depend on the production and distribution of earthly goods. In the wide range of human needs the bodily ones are the most indispensable; our physical needs must first be satisfied before we are able even to think of our mental ones and those of our heart, eye, and ear. The same holds good in the life of nations and parties. Their abstract conceptions depend on the way they make their living. Tribes living by warfare and booty have not the same heaven, the same sense of justice or of liberty as our patriarchs are supposed to have had who, as is well known, were living on cattle-breeding. Knights and monks had notions of righteousness, of virtue and honor which were decidedly illiberal and *anti-bourgeois,* because their means of life were not supplied by factory labor and financial transactions.

Of course, the defenders of Christianity strongly object to those views. In order to prove the independence of spirit from matter and of philosophy from economics they make the assertion that the same Christian truth is invariably taught to all sorts and conditions of men, and under all climes. They forget, however, how they trimmed the sails to the wind. They forget likewise that the love preached by the apostles and church fathers—the love which gave away the second coat is no more the many-coated love under the overcoat which strips the poor to the skin—of course, rightfully. To the diverse modes of property and trade correspond diverse Christianities. The institution of slavery in the United States was Christian, and Christianity was slave-holding there. The religious reformation of the sixteenth century was not the cause, but the effect, of the social reformation that followed upon the shifting of the economic center from the manor to the city. And that was preceded by the rise of navigation and the discovery of the New World and new trade routes, which indicate the rise of manufacture. Industrial life having no use for ascetic bodies introduced the protestant doctrine of grace that abolished religious exercises in favor of stern industrial work.

That the materialist conception of history is scientific induction and not idle speculation manifests itself even more clearly when we apply it to political party problems. With its help the tangled mass of party struggles can be easily unravelled into a clear, running thread. The squire is enthusiastic over the absolute monarchy because the absolute monarchy cared for the squirearchy. Manufacturers, merchants, bankers, in short, capitalists are liberal or constitutional, for constitutionalism is the political expression of capitalism; which liberalizes trade and commerce, supplies the factories with free labor, promotes banking and financial transactions, and, in general, takes care of the interests of industrial life. Philistines, shopkeepers, small tradesmen, and peasants join alternately one party or the other according to the promises made with regard to the promotion of their wellbeing and to the relief from the effects of competition with big capital.

The familiar accusation of political hypocrisy which the Parliamentary parties throw at each other was suggested to Bismarck by one of the renegades of our camp whom he likes to employ. That accusation is based on the recognition that the aristocratic and middle-class consciousness was formed by the material requirements of the landed and manufacturing and trading classes, and that behind their idealistic watchwords of religion, patriotism, freedom, and progress lurks the concrete interest as the motor power. I cannot deny that many of their followers are not conscious of their real motives, and that they sincerely believe their political work to be purely idealistic. But I should like to remark that it is with recognitions as with epidemics, they are in the air and people feel them somehow. Indeed, the political hypocrisy of our time is half conscious, half unconscious. There are many people who take the ideological phrases as gospel truth, but also the artful are by no means rare who want them to be taken as such. The matter can be easily explained. Different classes, distinguished by their different material conditions, succeed each other to political power. The interests of the ruling class are always for a certain time in harmony with the interests of the community, that is with the progressive forces of civilization. And it is that harmony which justifies the ruling class in regarding itself as the spring of social welfare. However, the onward march of history changes everything, also the justification for ruling power. When the economic interests of the ruling class cease to be in harmony with the general welfare, when the ruling class loses its functions and falls into decay, then its leaders can only save their predominant position by hypocrisy; their phraseology has been emptied of all reality. It is no doubt true that some individuals rise above class interests and join the new social power which represents the interest of the community. So did Abbé Sieyès and Count de Mirabeau in the French Revolution, who, though belonging to the ruling classes, became the advocates of the third Estate. Still, these are exceptions proving only the inductive rule that, in social as in natural science, the material precedes the ideal.

It may appear rather contradictory to make the Hegelian system of philosophy with its pronounced idealism the starting point of the materialist conception of history. Yet, the Hegelian "Idea" is striving for realization; it is indeed a materialism in disguise. Conversely, the Hegelian reality appears in the mask of the "Idea," or of the logical conception. In one of the latest issues of *Blätter für Unterhaltung,* Herr J. Volkelt makes the following remark: "Our modern thinkers have to submit to the crucial test of empiricism. The Hegelian principle has no reason to be afraid of such a test. Consistently followed up it means that the spirit of history can only be conceived through the existing material." Gleams of truth like these we can find now here and there in the periodical literature, but for a consistent and systematic application of the theory we must go to scientific socialism. The inductive method draws its mental conclusion from concrete facts. Scientific socialism considers our views dependent upon our material needs, and our political standpoint dependent upon the economic position of the class we belong to. Moreover, this conception corresponds with the aspirations of the masses whose needs are in the first place material, while the ruling class must necessarily base itself on the deductive principle, on the preconceived unscientific notion that the spiritual salvation and the mental training of the masses are to precede the solution of the social question.

Translated by M. Beer and Thomas Rothstein

Franz Mehring

On the Philosophy of Capitalism

Nietzsche is not, as Mr. Lindau's "North and South" wants to make us believe, the "social philosopher of the aristocracy," but the social philosopher of capitalism. It is among the most significant phenomena of German history that, while the working classes have been able to maintain their connections with the classical era of German culture, the bourgeois classes, unfortunately, have not. If this culture found its highest, most condensed expression in Hegel's philosophy, then its revolutionary elements were developed even further by Lassalle and carried on even much sharper to its clearest pronunciation by Engels and Marx. Whereas the conservative elements of the same philosophy perhaps could not find, or at any rate did not find expression of equal rank. The year 1848 was the fall of man that opened the eyes of the ruling classes about the fly in the ointment of "Prussian state religion," which Hegel's philosophy had been turned into during the thirties and forties. This resulted from a misunderstanding of the sentence, "Everything that is real is reasonable and everything that is reasonable is real." The bourgeoisie discarded it without concern as to whether its revolutionary potential would not eventually become all the stronger and the bourgeoisie threw itself into Schopenhauer's arms, the philosopher of the Philistines who received their pension and wanted to be left alone. For thirty years Schopenhauer had poured out a torrent of abuse against Hegel and finally found the long awaited recognition of his servile and pathetic, if at times quite amusing philosophy from the bourgeois classes, who had been overcome by a servile and pathetic mood after 1848. It was, in fact, Schopenhauer on whom Nietzsche oriented himself, a faithful student both in terms of abusing Hegel as well as in his bourgeois class consciousness and in that he—as a result of the progress of time—no longer crowned the Philistine's pension with his laurels but exploitative big capital.*

One thing is, indeed, true: In his essay "Beyond Good and Evil" Nietzsche somehow made a certain turn back to Hegel. He not only talks of Schopenhauer's "unintelligent anger of Hegel" that "led the entire last generation of Germans to break out of the relation with German culture," but also both the title and contents of this essay reflect Hegel's words in many ways. One believes it is a great thing to say, man is good by nature, but one forgets that something much greater is said by the words: man is evil by nature. And Nietzsche then promptly dwells on Hegel's thoughts at great and tiring length, without, however, quoting Hegel—particularly that man's bad impulses, such as greed and thirst for power, become a driving force of historical development. Nietzsche makes this out as if he had come across a discovery hitherto never made in "this immense almost new empire of dangerous insights," and it is difficult to retain the appropriate philosophical seriousness when he attached an apostrophe to a solemn statement that had long since Hegel's times become a commonplace: "Once your ship has been driven off here, well! Here we go! Now clench your teeth! Open your eyes! Keep the helm firmly in your hand!—We are about to run straight *over* morality; maybe we weigh down, we crush the rest of our own morality by taking and venturing to take our journey there—but who are *we!*" Not much, indeed, if "we" frolic about things that "we" are either incapable of understanding or do not want to understand.

Because the very "evil" that Hegel saw as the driving force of historical development has, according to his dialectic method with both its conservative and revolutionary sides, yet a second meaning. By "evil" he also means that every new progress appears as desecra-

*Karl Hillebrand, a bourgeois writer and as such an admirer of Schopenhauer's and patron of Nietzsche's, but whose intellectual formation dated back to the first, decisive impressions of 1848, despite all other praise, wrote about one of Nietzsche's first publications in his book, *Times, Nations, and People,* II, 354, that "Mr. Nietzsche overshoots the mark by far and makes himself guilty of doing shameful injustice to German thinking, namely against its most eminent exponent, Hegel. His intentions are obviously the best, however, there is no need for rebelling against authority successfully by subduing oneself to the infallible authority of the master as is the case with him towards Schopenhauer. Not wanting to realize that Hegel basically ordered the basic idea of German culture into a system—and consequently also showed its absurdity at times—means to either ignore Germany's intellectual development from Herder to Feuerbach or to present Germany's contribution to European civilization as worthless!"

tion against something holy, as a rebellion against the old declining conditions made sacred by their habituality. As Nietzsche was incapable or not willing to think Hegel's thought through to the end, he calls the French Revolution, of which Hegel had always spoken with great enthusiasm, a "horrifying, and judged from close by, a superfluous clownery." And he calls the revolutionary thinkers—who just made Hegel's method fertile by diverting it from the region of the unfindable "Absolute Idea" to the area of economic conditions— "some kinds of small-minded, imprisoned spirits tied to a chain who somehow want the opposite of what is in our intentions and instincts"—presumably! And he goes on: "The wrongly termed 'free spirits,' eloquent and crazy writing slaves of democratic taste," "unfree and ridiculously superficial, most of all in their basic tendency to view the structures of the old society as the cause for nearly *all* human misery and failure, which is how truth comes finally to stand on its head." This belongs to the same series of somersaults that make up Nietzsche's philosophy when he is at feud with Christianity, a feud based not so much on the abuse of ecclesiastical structures for profane ends, such as greed and thirst for power—this he rather views as the sole and true purpose of religion—but because of the "herdlike mentality" that prompted Christianity to present charity as the highest human virtue.

Hegel's dialectic method destroyed all solid concepts; its conservative character lay in accepting the rightfulness of certain hierarchies of insight and of society depending on time and circumstances, but its revolutionary character saw the historical development as a continuous process of decaying and becoming. In its course—despite all seeming coincidences and temporary setbacks— a progressive development from a lower to a higher level comes about. According to Hegel's method, therefore, there was neither final and perfect morality, nor a final and perfect state. Consequently, morality was merely the result of the historical spirit and terms such as *good* and *evil* were not considered absolute but relative. *One* "absolute" Hegel recognized, however, namely, the "Absolute Idea" of his system, the secret and invisible ruler of his universal process of becoming and decaying, thus limiting the consequences of his method of thinking. These consequences were not made until Engels and Marx did away with the "Absolute Idea," stating that real things are not reflections of our ideas; but rather that our ideas are merely the reflection of real things—in other words, that man has to eat, drink, and have a home before he can think and write poetry. In the same way as "absolute truths" thus disappear from philosophy, politics, etc., likewise all moral rules considered valid for all people and all times will disappear; there are no absolutely valid ethics any longer, but only relative moral systems that take different shapes according to the economic living conditions of individual nations and individual classes. In class struggles as fierce as the present ones, these differences of moral systems become palpable in the strangest tests of "class ethics" every day.

Unlike Engels and Marx, Nietzsche does not deduce from the relativity of morality, already present in embryo in Hegel, that morality is historically determined but that any morality is invalid per se. He arrives at the conclusion through a one-sided interpretation of "evil," which, according to Hegel, is the driving force of historical development. Only in envy, hatred, greed, and striving for power does he see life-generating emotive impulses, the "basic and quintessential" in the total process of history. Calling these impulses "evil" is as much indebted to "the plebeian enmity against everything privileged and arbitrary" as is the impertinent presumptuousness of "those following the crowd" to term "good" those characteristics convenient for them, such as compassion, the ability for sacrifice, devotion, etc. However, Nietzsche recognizes the existence of class struggle, too, and the "morality of master and of slave" associated with it, but he does not understand it as a dialectic process of world history bringing forth a development from lower to higher level, but as an unswerving and unalterable law of nature. In this struggle, the rulers and oppressors, the "free spirits," will always possess power and be right as a consequence, while the submitted and oppressed ones, "those following the crowd," will always be condemned to be without power and, therefore, be wrong. The only and real morality for Nietzsche is the "law for the conditions of domination" that historical life originates from; it is nothing but a roguish prank that the "moral" notions of "good" and "evil" were smuggled into this morality through which "those following the crowd" try to take revenge on the "free spirits," thus having, indeed, caused terrible mischief in history—see, for instance, Christianity!—but these times of delusion are fading away and the "philosophers of the future" emerge, the "free," the "very free," the "refined," and "noble spirits." They are beyond good and evil.

Needless to say, the thought content of this graceful and edifying philosophy is a very meager one, and it takes a host of ideological ornaments to expand it into some kind of Weltanschauung at all. After doing away with the decoration, approximately the following propositions may be established that I take from the publication *Beyond Good and Evil:*

> Where the people eats and drinks, even where it worships, there is usually a stink. One should not go into churches if one wants to breathe *pure* air.

> There is nothing for it: the feelings of devotion, self-sacrifice for one's neighbor, the entire morality of self-renunciation must be taken mercilessly to task and brought to court. . . .
> There is much too much sugar and sorcery in those feelings of "for others," of "*not* for me," for one not to have to become doubly distrustful here and to ask: "are they not perhaps—*seductions?*" That they *give pleasure*—to him who has them and to him who enjoys their fruits, also to the mere spectator—does not yet furnish an argument in their *favor,* but urges us rather to caution. So let us be cautious!

> The philosopher as *we* understand him, we free spirits . . . will make use of the religions for his work of education and breeding, just as he will make use of existing political and economic conditions. The influence on selection and breeding, that is to say the destructive as well as the creative and formative influence which can be exercised with the aid of the religions, is manifold and various depending on the kind of men placed under their spell and protection. For the strong and independent prepared and predestined for command, in whom the art and reason of a ruling race is incarnated, religion is one more means of overcoming resistance so as to be able to rule: as a bond that unites together ruler and ruled and betrays and hands over to the former the consciences of the latter, all that is hidden and most intimate in them which would like to exclude itself from obedience. . . .
> In the end, to be sure, to present the debit side of the account to these religions and to bring into the light of day their uncanny perilousness—it costs dear and terribly when religions hold sway, *not* as means of education and breeding in the hands of the philosopher, but in their own right and as *sovereign,* when they themselves want to be final ends and not means beside other means.

> The strange narrowness of human evolution . . . [is] due to the fact that the herd instinct of obedience has been inherited best and at the

expense of the art of commanding. If we think of this instinct taken to its ultimate extravagance there would be no commanders or independent men at all; or if they existed, they would suffer from a bad conscience and in order to be able to command would have to practice a deceit upon themselves: the deceit, that is, that they too were only obeying. This state of things actually exists in Europe today: I call it the moral hypocrisy of the commanders. They know no way of defending themselves against their bad conscience other than to pose as executors of more ancient or higher commands (commands of ancestors, of the constitution, of justice, of the law or even of God), or even to borrow herd maxims from the herd's way of thinking and appear as "the first servant of the people" for example, or as "instruments of the common good." On the other hand, the herd-man in Europe today makes himself out to be the only permissible kind of man and glorifies the qualities through which he is tame, peaceable and useful to the herd as the real human virtues: namely public spirit, benevolence, consideration, industriousness, moderation, modesty, forbearance, pity.

Morality is in Europe today herd-animal morality . . . indeed, with the aid of a religion which has gratified and flattered the sublimest herd-animal desires, it has got to the point where we discover even in political and social institutions an increasingly evident expression of this morality: the *democratic* movement inherits the Christian. But that the tempo of this movement is much too slow and somnolent for the more impatient, for the sick and suffering of the said instinct, is attested by the ever more frantic baying, the ever more undisguised fang baring of the anarchist dogs which now rove the streets of European culture: apparently the reverse of the placidly industrious democrats and revolutionary ideologists, and even more so of the stupid philosophasters and brotherhood fanatics who call themselves socialists and want a "free society," they are in fact as one with them all in their total and instinctive hostility towards every form of society other than that of the *autonomous* herd (to the point of repudiating even the concepts "master" and "servant"—*ni dieu ni maître* says a socialist formula—).

. . . corruption is something fundamentally different according to which life-form it appears in. When, for example, an aristocracy such as that of France at the start of the Revolution throws away its privileges with a sublime disgust and sacrifices itself to an excess of moral feeling, then that is corruption. . . . The essential thing in a good and healthy aristocracy is, however, that it does *not* feel itself to be a function (of the monarchy or of the commonwealth) but as their *meaning* and supreme justification—that it therefore accepts with a good conscience the sacrifice of innumerable men who *for its sake* have to be suppressed and reduced to imperfect men, to slaves and instruments.

One has to think this matter thoroughly through to the bottom and resist all sentimental weakness: life itself is *essentially* appropriation, injury, overpowering of the strange and weaker, suppression, severity, imposition of one's own forms, incorporation and, at the least and mildest, exploitation—but why should one always have to employ precisely those words which have from of old been stamped with a slanderous intention? . . .

On no point, however, is the common European consciousness more reluctant to learn than it is here; everywhere one enthuses, even under scientific disguises, about coming states of society in which there will be "no more exploitation"—that sounds to my ears like promising a life in which there will be no organic functions.

At the risk of annoying innocent ears I set it down that egoism pertains to the essence of the noble soul, I mean the immovable faith that to a being such as "we are" other beings have to be subordinate by their nature, and sacrifice themselves to us. The noble soul accepts this fact of its egoism without any question mark, also without feeling any severity, constraint, caprice in it, but rather as something that may be grounded in the primal law of things:—if it sought a name for it, it would say "it is justice itself."

In such lapidary phrases Nietzsche writes the history of capitalism. Seen as a purely intellectual product, his historical view has a brutal and flat crudeness, which becomes all the more disgustingly evident through his "witty," sparkling language, while it is, at the same time, full of vagueness and contradictions—just note how Nietzsche approaches the terms *good* and *bad* with a "good" or "bad" conscience!. And even with the most moderate pretensions this historical view can possibly make, it is not even original. In his *Capital* Karl Marx brought to light a whole series of strange characters in England half a century ago or even earlier who wrote the philosophy of capitalism in exactly the same way as Nietzsche writes his in *Beyond Good and Evil*. If Nietzsche considers the Christian religion "dreadful"—as long as it is not a tool of secular purposes of domination, but wants to be "sovereign"—because it attempts to keep alive the "surplus of failures, sick ones, degenerates, invalids, those fated to suffer," he is merely paraphrasing "parson Towns-end"—see *Capital* I, 634—who reproached the English Poor Laws for striving to destroy "the harmony and beauty, the symmetry of this *system*, which *God and Nature* established in this world." There is no use arguing that Nietzsche has always been a stranger to the capitalist stratagem, that, in his own way, he struggled for truth, that he wanted to climb the highest heights of the most intellectual idea, so to speak, that he only felt at ease in the solitude of the high mountains and that any kind of human communion was "vulgar" to him. All of this only proves how profoundly capitalism has under-mined our intellectual life already and Engels's and Marx's mate-rialistic historical view achieves great triumphs once again compared to a philosophy that can only breathe in the boundless ethereal heights, and ignoring the conditions of real life, relapses into matter exactly where it is most disgusting and unclean. And exactly for this reason *Beyond Good and Evil*—which from a philosophical and scholarly viewpoint is not worth the ink it took to write it with—is of eminent systematic and sociopolitical signifi-cance. This struggle against morality is, in effect, the formulation of a new morality. The red thread running through all of Nietzsche's contradictions is the attempt to discover capitalism's class morality at the contemporary level of its development and to throw off the chains that still bind class morality, dating back from earlier levels of development like petit bourgeois integrity and grand bourgeois respectability.

Translated by Renate Steinchen

Christianity and Social Democracy

In the past two big social democratic conventions have taken place here that will have reminded older party comrades of old times; of the debate that the court preacher Stoecker led with Most about Christianity and socialism. We have absolutely no wish to compare comrade Göhre with Stoecker or with the comrades who argued with him during those meetings. The decisive point of comparison is that once again the position of the party toward Christianity is being hotly discussed in heavily attended workers' meetings—a situation that has not occurred, at least not with such intense and fruitless passion for decades—in fact, not since the days of Most and Stoecker.

Whatever the cause for all this was can now be forgotten; but for the sake of justice let it be said that, in the second of those meetings, Göhre showed himself to be the challenged one rather than the challenger. We have little doubt about this, since an undoubtedly lively interest in religious matters exists among German workers, a result of the unhappy fact that in our marvelous primary schools the workers are stuffed with religious matters throughout their fourteenth year of age. The more energetically this spiritual force-feeding is carried out, the more vehement the intellectual reaction against it, which explains how a book, such as Corvin's *Mirror of Priests* has gained such widespread popularity, often exceeding that of their economic and political classics. From this standpoint the propaganda, willingly or unwillingly started by Göhre, finds some general interest that deserves some explanatory remarks.

The social democratic program defines religion as a private matter and, as a result, it self-evidently sets itself against every form of religious organization. Both these demands of Göhre have long since been realized, and it is not easy to understand why he still demands their "reinforcement." Here and there one might hear of circumstances in which social democratic speakers or writers touch too closely on the principle that religion should be a private matter, but such cases will always occur in opposing the churches. Göhre does not want to know about them either. As long as churches remain the tools of political or social repression, and hold the shield of religion above them, it will be unavoidable for workers who are not philosophical hairsplitters to fight against religion when they mean church. It can be a nuisance, and whether or not Göhre has enough strength to be able to gather people together for large meetings remains questionable. Anyway, it would be more practical to gather everything together at the opposite end, with the learned and pious church fathers, who never stop using religion as the hypocritical cover of very worldly ruling powers.

On the other hand, Göhre then puts the emphasis of his arguments on the third demand, which he makes "in the interest of the Social Democratic Party." He asks that "on the basis of most recent theological research, the socialist literature of the past forty years should be revised and everything be discarded that cannot be upheld any longer"; he does not want to make propaganda for his Christian ideas within the party, but as a modern scholar of theology he does not want the party to lag behind on this issue. For in Göhre's opinion, Strauß and Bauer were completely on the wrong track in their critique on the book of Gospels; he thinks that modern theological scholars like Harnack and Holzmann proved that Jesus had, indeed, been a historical figure and that the four books of the gospel were authentic representations of his life. According to this view, Christianity was actually based on a powerful, harmonically rounded personality, the only superhuman known in history; Christianity turned into a mass movement through Jesus and not as a result of the circumstances. Göhre acknowledges that he denies historical materialism by such a view, but he thinks not to impair its validity in any way. The materialist view of history had the merit—so he argues—of giving the science of history new perspectives for looking at history, but not *all* conditions could be explained by it, particularly not the origin of religion.

In this evaluation of historical materialism Göhre joins the circle of bourgeois historians, most of whom say these days that historical materialism was an inspiring perspective, but not a scientific method. We mention this only in passing not so much as to denounce it as Göhre's violation of the party program. Accepting the party program does not oblige anybody to accept historical materialism. However, the old error of believing that a scientific method may be undermined arbitrarily as if it were a rule to be validated particularly by its exceptions cannot be rejected strongly enough. The exception Göhre makes with the "only superhuman," Jesus, everybody else may naturally and rightfully make with such "superhumans" as Alexander or Caesar or Kant or Nietzsche; in that case, what is right with one ought to be right with the other. If historical materialism is a scientific method then it does, indeed, explain all historical conditions and particularly also the origin of religion; since, to some extent, it developed around this problem in the first place. On the other hand, if this method fails in only one single case, if only with the "only superhuman," Jesus, then it is a broken sword, of which it would be justified to claim that its broken pieces are very useful for the working classes despite it all.

Judging from his lectures, or at least the newspaper reports on his lectures, it has not become quite clear how Göhre himself wants us to interpret his plan for revision. If he only wants to improve on possibly untenable statements on Christianity, as could certainly be found in the older party literature, his demand would be totally irrelevant and even somewhat comical. A party will survive its errors, but it does not correct its students like a teacher. If everything in the older party literature that is scientifically untenable would have to be "revised" on issues such as the iron law of wages or the theory of value, where would it lead to? One can hardly read any party literature or a party paper from the sixties or seventies without finding, let's say, one statement on every page that has become obsolete in the meantime. But who would deny respect to these documents, which are the historical milestones of the labor movement?

On the other hand, if Göhre does not intend his plan of revision in such a formal sense—and it can hardly be assumed that he does—he truly makes a very serious, important and, if he should be right, a very necessary demand on the party. The critique of the Gospels made by Strauß and Bauer was the first battle in the great liberation struggle, which the working class is fighting today. Marx and Engels elaborated on these critiques of the Gospels and it is impossible to say how deeply and how far the consequences of this ridiculous error, which Harnack and Holzmann allegedly discovered now, will extend to the scholarly party literature. We say "of this ridiculous error," for, if the Gospels are authentic historical sources, Strauß and Bauer have, indeed, been genuine Don Quixotes, defending this fact with an immense expenditure of erudition and astuteness. And having pointed out this error, they performed a miracle surpassing any biblical miracle by far; by doing what they did they started an intellectual revolution that culminates in the modern proletariat's struggle for emancipation, which has the guarantee of unstoppable victory in this struggle. If "modern-scientific theology" should actually prove Strauß's and Bauer's critique of the Gospels and their historical consequences erroneous, a revision of the scholarly party literature cannot—it has to be truly admitted—be denied.

As far as public statements exist at all on the subject matter, Göhre is the only one in the party right now to hold such views. At this point it is up to him to justify the necessity of his demand for a revision in such a way as to be plausible to the party. However incontestable his conviction may be on a subjective level, it still is no proof. If Göhre considers the revisions he demanded to be the party's obligation, it will be *his* obligation first to make his demands in such a way so they may be discussed for the use and benefit of the party. This is least possible in general assemblies, which can never be tribunals for contesting scientific questions and can never decide as to whether Strauß and Bauer, or Harnack and Holzmann, hit the score with their critiques of the Gospels. Particularly, if one esteems general assemblies as powerful weapons of the labor movement, one should be careful not to make demands on them that they cannot accomplish. They don't exist for the sake of scholarly explorations, but for political, social, and—if you want—for religious propaganda. Göhre defends himself against the suspicion of making religious propaganda. He only wants to clean the party's intellectual weapons of rust and we do not doubt his words by any means. But it stands to reason that he will then become the victim of one of those confusions to which "modern-scientific theology" incessantly falls prey.

Let's assume that any party comrade had gained the conviction that everything that the party literature contains about Alexander or Caesar or Kant or Nietzsche was entirely wrong and ought to be thoroughly revised. Do you really believe this comrade would call a general assembly to justify his demands? Certainly he would not even dream of such a thing, but rather turn to the scientific literature and press. In Kant's case, by the way, the issue has actually become practical reality already; not one of the Neo-Kantians in the party even thought once of advocating a revision of Kant's works on a general assembly. Göhre's choice of treating this unseemly path is very simply explained by the fact that to him Jesus is not just another human being like Kant, but a superhuman, the only superhuman in history, who transcended the generally accepted and valid laws of historical development; or, to put it briefly and clearly, because Jesus is God to him. However, this is not a scientific fact, but religion. His demand to revise the party literature according to the allegedly proven findings of "modern-scientific theology" is religious propaganda. On the other hand, if a Neo-Kantian would call a general assembly with an agenda like, "Kant and Social Democracy," do you really believe that it would draw such large audiences as Göhre's lectures? Not even a hundred workers would show up and not even ten would be able to sit through a discussion on Kant for several hours. Like the lecturer, the audience was likewise, consciously or unconsciously, attracted by the negative or positive interest in religious propaganda. These general assemblies, which were to underline the principle that religion was a private matter, have put him to the hardest test he has ever had to face in past decades.

The actual course of these general assemblies confirmed entirely what was to be expected, taking into account their logical origin. They were conducted in a spirit of a religious dispute, which the above-mentioned regulation of the party program wants to suppress as a hindering encumbrance in the proletarian struggle for emancipation. Göhre said himself, however, that the assemblies had not been "unfruitful" and we are afraid that he may be right in a certain sense, although certainly not in the sense that he thinks of. Harnack's lectures on the essence of Christianity will never make it into a library of a workers' association, not to speak of a working class library, but Corvin's *Pfaffenspiegel* (Mirror of priests) might even gain greater popularity in workers' circles than it unfortunately already has. If, in fact the propaganda started by Göhre with its so far unproven assertions—that cannot be possibly decided upon by general assemblies—representing a slap in the face of the party's historical tradition, should prove "fruitful," it can only be so in stirring up again the kind of flat, phrasy, and fanatical hatred of religion—one would wish along with Göhre—which has long ago been overcome as a point of view by the German working class.

On the other hand, great harm is not really to be expected from this; it is not likely that these general assemblies will go on for long, no matter how much enthusiasm they have been started with. One may think, therefore, it would be advisable to accelerate religion's decay by hushing it up. However, hushing something up is generally a matter of bad style and, besides, some of the phenomena occurring during these assemblies suggest that there is a necessity of discussing as to what the phrase in the party program, "religion is a private matter," is really all about.

Translated by Renate Steinchen

Proletariat and Religion

In the Christian church Pentecost is the festival of the Holy Spirit that, during the church congress in Constantinople in A.D. 381, was vested with the attributes of divine glory next to God the Father and God the Son, so that all three should be one, a holy mystery and venerable miracle, and as such it is a mockery of profane arithmetic that secular humanity had long since managed to learn.

For fifteen hundred years much has been preached, spoken, and written about this Holy Spirit without any single individual having succeeded in getting to the bottom of this wonderful secret, which stood in such hopeless contradiction to the simple fact that three times one is three and not just one. The one who best understood how to represent the warp and woof of the Holy Spirit was Heinrich Heine when he sang:

> He has worked the greatest wonders,
> And he works them still; he broke,
> Once for all, the tyrant's power,
> And he burst the bondman's yoke.
>
> All the ancient scars have vanished,
> Justice takes its rightful place;
> Now all men are free and equal
> In a pure and noble race.*

This Holy Spirit we don't object to, and He offers an excellent text for a Pentecost sermon and a far more excellent one than the muddled story of the Apostles, which is preached from every pulpit all during Pentecost. But we don't want to preach a Pentecost sermon, not even a secular one that may eventually be even more

*Translation from Heinrich Heine, *Poetry and Prose,* volume 32 of The German Library.

unbearable than a religious one. Our special message to our readers is a short one about the proletariat and religion.

One of the essays written by the young Marx contains the sentence that the existence of any religion is the existence of a deficiency. This sentence is truer in a higher and broader sense than its author meant it to be when writing it. All religions come into being through a lack in either the natural or social sciences. Thus distinctions are made between natural religions that try to come to terms with the forces of nature not understood by men, and social religions that try to reconcile themselves with the effects of a not yet understood social process of production in relation to higher forces; this is done for instance in such a way that, given the undisputable fact that three equals three and one equals one, higher beings are conjured up in whom three equals as much as one as one equals three.

This is, put in the shortest and at the same time most trivial form, the origin and essence of all religions. They always originate from and consist of a delusion. But they are no random chimera made up by each and every individual. The delusions they originate from are related to the historically given cultural development. The further the knowledge of nature proceeds, the more the natural religions are in decline; wherever the natural cause of fire is known the fire worshiper will be laughed at. Social religions fare the same way. The more man learns to control and master the social process of production, the less he feels the need to communicate with supernatural forces through prayer and sacrifice, and the more social religions die.

Hence it is clear that there is a profound, a totally irreconcilable contradiction between the proletariat and religion. All of the working class's hopes for redemption are based on the knowledge, control, and mastering of the capitalist process of production. The more the modern working class will grow into its world historical task and the more mature it will become to solve it, the more it will be liberated from religion. When, on the other hand, the working class includes a sentence in its program declaring religion a personal matter, then this means, firstly, that the state shall not nourish religious chimeras, and secondly, that individuals should not be prevented from nourishing such chimeras. From this we can neither derive that religion and its supporters shall be spared in cases where they are promoted by the state and out of gratefulness and let themselves be used for the furthering of political and social means of oppression, nor that the proletarian struggle for emancipation shall be some kind of playground for religious games.

Precisely because the class-conscious proletariat is aware of the origin and nature of religion, because it realizes that the shadow within religion prevails wherever the light of economic knowledge has not yet gone on, they abstain from eliminating the shadow that will never be removed as long as the light does not yet shine. However, the shadow will disappear by itself once the light is turned on. The more enlightened the working class, still caught up in religion, will be economically and politically, the more its religious chimeras will disappear, while fighting against this chimera will remain completely ineffective as long as those seized by it will not understand the inner nature of the capitalist process of production; as long as it, therefore, believes to be the toy of uncontrollable forces with whom one had better be on friendly terms. If religion were not to possess this social root, it would have already been destroyed completely by the Enlightenment and it is, indeed, a step back of fifty or even a hundred years that lately remakes of yesteryear's enlightening pamphlets keep creeping into the party literature.

It is equally abominable if the statement that religion was a private matter is being misused again for smuggling religious aspirations into the proletarian struggle for emancipation, to talk in terms of a "religious element" in socialism and what else there may be. No, socialism does not have a "religious element"; the modern working class's struggle for liberation is the antidote to all religion, and, therefore, shall not be decorated with religious beauty spots, which, like all religions testify to nothing but a deficit, namely a lack of understanding of the uncomparable greatness and nobility of a struggle that surpasses all religions in its healing, strengthening, and comforting power that history keeps recounting us.

All aspirations trying to embellish socialism religiously will always remind us of Ludwig Feuerbach's coarse, yet true words: "What is most incurable is the venereal disease, the modern poets' and esthetes' syphilis, who, judging the value of things merely by their esthetic attraction, are so dishonorable and shameless that they will even defend the recognized illusion because of its claimed beauty and charity; they are so devoid of character and truth that they do no longer feel that an illusion is only *beautiful* as long as it is not considered an illusion, but *truth*." Feuerbach wrote this already sixty years ago.

Only those who place a higher value on the simple spirit of truth than on the glamorous aesthetics of the lie, only those who find truth beautiful and lies ugly, are endowed with the spirit that once will break the tyrants' fortresses and the servants' yokes and inspire the poets:

> Now all men are free and equal
> In a pure and noble race.

Translated by David Schiffman and Renate Steinchen

APPENDIX

The Law against the Socialists
(Law against Social Democratic Endeavors which Threaten Public Peace)

§1. Associations aiming at the overthrow of the existing political system or social order by means of social democratic, socialist or communist objectives are to be prohibited. Socialist or communist endeavors aiming at the overthrow of the existing political system or the social order surface in ways threatening public peace, particularly to the unity among the different classes of the population.

Associations rank equally with organizations of any kind.

§2. In the case of registered mutual benefit societies, §55 of July 4, 1868, concerning the status of trade and economic mutual benefit societies under civil law (BGB1. p. 415) is applicable, instead of §1, subparagraph 2.

By the same token, §29 of the law pertaining to registered aid funds of April 7, 1876 (BGB1. p. 125), is applicable.

§3. Independent funds (not registered) aiming at the mutual support of their members according to their statutes shall not be prohibited immediately if §1, subparagraph 2, is applicable, but to be put under special government control.

If several independent associations of the above-mentioned kind are consolidated into a society and if the endeavors described in §1, subparagraph 2, surface in one of the associations, the exclusion of the association from the society and its supervision may be decreed.

If the described endeavors are displayed in one of the associated organizations, the supervision is to be limited to this one organization likewise.

§4. The government board that has been entrusted with the supervision is authorized as follows:

1. to attend all of the association's meetings and conventions;
2. to call and to preside over general assemblies;

3. to inspect the books, documents, and cash holdings and to request information on the association's conditions;
4. to prohibit the execution of resolutions, promoting the endeavors described in §1, subparagraph 2;
5. to entrust the care of the executive committee's functions or those of the association's other executive bodies to a person deemed suitable;
6. to impound and to administer the funds.

§5. Should the orders set up by the control authority within the framework of its competence be violated by the general assembly, the executive committee or any other executive body of the association, or should the endeavors described in §1, subparagraph 2, surface even after the introduction of the supervision, then the association may be prohibited.

§6. The regional police authorities are in charge of the prohibition and the ordering of the supervision. The prohibition of foreign associations is under the Reich's Chancellor's control.

In all cases the prohibition shall be announced in the *Reich's Gazette*. The prohibition decreed by the regional police authorities, in addition, shall be publicized in the paper designated by the authorities for public notices for a township or a district.

The prohibition is effective for the entire country and concerns all of the association's branches and every allegedly new association that factually represents the old one.

§7. On the basis of this prohibition the association's funds and all objects intended for the association's endeavors shall be confiscated by the authorities.

After the prohibition has become final the administrative board to be nominated by the regional police authorities shall entrust and supervise the winding up of the association (liquidation) to suitable persons and announce the names of the liquidators.

The laws or statutes provided by the general assembly's resolution shall be replaced by the administrative board's decision.

The liquidated association's funds shall be used according to the association's statutes, or according to the general provisions of the law, irrespective of legal claims by a third party or the association members.

(The date of the prohibition taking effect is to be considered the time of the liquidation or closure of the association and of the funds).

Against the administration's orders only an appeal to the supervising authorities is permissible.

§8. The prohibition decreed by the regional police authorities and the order for supervision shall be announced to the association's executive committee, if such exists in Germany, by a written substantiated administrative order. The association's executive committee has the right to appeal (§26).

The appeal shall be made within a week to the authority that issued the prohibition.

The appeal has no suspensive effect.

§9. Meetings at which social democratic, socialist, or communist endeavors aimed at the overthrow of the existing political system or social order are displayed, shall be dissolved.

Meetings that by objective facts give rise to the assumption that they are intended for the promotion of the endeavors described in the first subparagraph shall be prohibited.

Meetings rank equally with public celebrations and demonstrations.

§10. The police authorities are in charge of the prohibition and the dissolution.

Appeals can only be made to the control authorities.

§11. Publications in which social democratic, socialist, or communist endeavors aimed at the overthrow of the existing political system or social order are displayed in ways threatening public peace, particularly harmony among the social classes, shall be prohibited. In the case of periodicals, this prohibition may also be extended to future publication, when on the basis of this law the prohibition of one edition has occurred.

§12. The regional police authorities are in charge of the prohibition. In the case of periodicals issued in Germany, the district police authorities at the place of publication are in charge. The Reich's Chancellor is directly responsible for the prohibition of further dissemination of periodicals issued abroad.

The prohibition shall be announced in the way described in §6, subparagraph 2, and is effective for the entire federal territory.

§13. The prohibition of a publication ordered by the regional police authorities shall be announced to the publisher or editor; the prohibition of a publication not issued periodically shall also be announced to the author stated in the latter by a written, substantiated administrative order, provided that these persons reside in Germany.

The publisher or editor and the author have the right to appeal against the administrative order (§26).

The appeal shall be made within a week after the delivery of the administrative order to the authority that issued it.

The appeal has no suspensive effect.

§14. On the basis of the prohibition all publications affected by the law are to be confiscated where they are found for the purpose of dissemination. The confiscation may be extended to the blocks and plates used for printing; in the case of printed matter in a stricter sense the printing blocks may be distributed instead of being confiscated after an application has been made by the interested party. The confiscated blocks and plates shall be destroyed after the prohibition has become final.

An appeal can only be made to the supervising authority.

§15. The police authorities have the right to confiscate temporarily the publications of the kind described in §11 and the block and forms used for printing even before prohibition takes effect. The confiscated publication shall be submitted to the regional police authorities within twenty-four hours. The latter shall either give immediate orders to repeal the confiscation or shall issue a prohibition within a week. If a prohibition is not issued within this fixed period of time the confiscation becomes void and the individual objects, blocks and forms shall be released.

§16. Collecting contributions for the promotion of social democratic, socialist, or communist endeavors aimed at the overthrow of the existing political system or social order and the public call for contributing to such payments shall be prohibited by the police. The prohibition is to be announced publicly.

An appeal may only be made to the supervising authorities.

§17. Any person who joins such a prohibited association (§6) as a member or engages in activities in the interest of such an association shall be fined up to five hundred marks or be sentenced to prison for up to three months. The same penalty shall be imposed on a person participating in a prohibited meeting (§9) or who does not leave immediately after its breaking up by the police.

Those who participate in an association or a meeting as president, chairman, supervisor, agent, speaker, or cashier, or those who call up a meeting, shall be sentenced to prison for a period of between one month and one year.

§18. Any person who makes premises available to a prohibited association or to a prohibited meeting shall be sentenced to prison for a period of between one month and one year.

§19. Any person who disseminates, continues, or reprints a prohibited publication (§§11, 12) shall be fined up to one thousand marks or be sentenced to prison of up to six months.

§20. Any person who violates a prohibition according to §16 shall be fined up to five hundred marks or be sentenced to prison for up to three months. In addition, everything received or its respective value as a result of prohibited collections or appeals shall fall to the local poor-relief fund, where the collection was made.

§21. Any person who commits any of the prohibited acts of §§17, 18, 19 unknowingly, but after the prohibition has been announced in the *Reich's Gazette,* shall be fined up to one hundred and fifty marks or be sentenced to prison.

The same punishment shall be inflicted upon a person committing a prohibited act according to §16 after the public announcement was made. The final provision of §20 shall apply.

§22. Persons engaging in agitation for endeavors described in §1, subparagraph 2, shall—in case of a conviction for violating §§17 to 20—not only be sentenced to imprisonment, but the admissibility of restricting their right of abode shall also be under consideration.

On the basis of this sentence the convicted may be denied the right of abode in certain districts or townships by the regional police authorities, however, in his residence only, if he has not been residing there for six months. Aliens may be deported from the federal territory by the regional police authorities.

Violations shall be punished with imprisonment for between one month and one year.

§23. Under the provisions described in §22, subparagraph 1, innkeepers, saloonkeepers, persons engaging in the petty trade with brandy or spirits, book printers, book dealers, librarians of rental libraries, and owners of reading cabinets may, apart from being sentenced to prison, also be sentenced to closing their businesses.

§24. Persons who engage in promoting endeavors described in §1, subparagraph 2, or who on the basis of a regulation of this law have been sentenced to a nonappealable penalty, may be subject to the revocation of their license to disseminate, professionally or non-professionally, publications or engaging in the itinerary trade of discriminating publications by the regional police authorities.

An appeal may only be made to the supervising authorities.

§25. Any person who violates a pronounced sentence on the basis of §23 or an issued administrative order on the basis of §24 shall be fined up to one thousand marks or sentenced to incarceration or imprisonment for up to six months.

§26. For the arbitration of appeals made in the cases of §§8, 13, a committee shall be formed. The Federal Council elects four members from its midst and five from the number of members of the Reich's highest court or the individual federation states.

The election of these five members is valid for the duration of the law and for the duration of their tenure in their juridical office.

The Kaiser selects the chairman and his deputy from among the committee's members.

§27. Arbitration is issued by the committee's five members, three of whom at least have to be judicial members. Before the final decision on the appeal the participants shall have the opportunity to give an oral or written substantiation of their appeals. The committee is authorized to take evidence to the fullest extent, particularly by means of interrogation under oath of witnesses and experts, or to take evidence by means of request to an agency of the Reich or a federal state. Concerning the obligation to testify as a witness or an expert, and in view of the imposed penalties in the case of disobedience, the regulations in effect at the committee's seat or the rules of procedure of the appealed administration shall be applied. The decisions are made at the committee's discretion and are final.

As for the rest, the committee's agenda shall be structured by regulations that are to be drafted by the committee and subject to the Federal Council's confirmation.

§28. For districts and townships whose public peace is threatened by the endeavors characterized in §1, subparagraph 2, the central authorities of the federation states may decree the following orders. In case they are not yet in effect as the law of the state, they may take effect with the Federal Council's permission for a maximum duration of one year:

1. that meetings may only take place with the police authorities' prior permission; this restriction does not extend to meetings

with the purpose of an ordered election for the Reich's Parliament or the state's House of Representatives;

2. that the dissemination of publications on public paths, streets, squares or in other public places may not take place;
3. that persons who are suspected of posing a danger to public security or order may be prohibited from residing in the districts or townships;
4. that the possession, carrying, import, and sale of weapons is prohibited, restricted, or subject to certain provisions.

Every order issued on the basis of the existing regulations shall be reported to the Reich's Parliament immediately, or during its next convening, respectively.

The orders issued shall be announced in the *Reich's Gazette* and in ways provided by law for administrative orders made by the state police authorities.

Any person who violates these orders or the administrative orders issued on this basis knowingly or after public announcement has been made, shall be fined one thousand marks or be sentenced to detention or prison for up to six months.

§29. Whichever of each federal state's authorities are meant by the term *state police authorities* or *police authorities* shall be announced by the Federal Council's central authorities.

§30. This law takes effect on the day of its pronouncement and shall be valid until March 31, 1881.

Translated by Renate Steinchen

August Bebel

Model Statutes for German Trade Unions

Goals and Objectives

§1. The trade union of the German . . . workers was founded with the goal of maintaining and promoting the participants' dignity and material interests.

§2. In order to achieve this goal the trade union pledges itself to use and utilize all means and ways that are made available to the trade union by the institutions of state and society, the experience and findings of the sciences, and the class consciousness of the workers.

As the next step for achieving its goal the union pledges in particular to establish the following institutions or to maintain and carry them on, respectively:

a. The establishing of a fund (1) for the support of those members of the union who are out of work as a result of a reprimand by the employers or a strike; (2) for relief in times of hardship.
b. The founding of a general sick and funeral fund.
c. The founding of an invalids' and old-age pension fund.
d. The establishing of a general travel allowance fund.
e. The providing of the members' protection against pressure or unjustified demands made by employers and authorities, and if necessary, payment from the union's fund for all expenses resulting from legal action or nonlitigious complaints and conducting of litigations.

f. Statistical inquiries into the standard of wages, working hours, prices for food and the general situation on the labor market at large. Procurement of work.

g. Organizing and supervision of the training of apprentices.

h. The founding or, respectively, the support of a newspaper that represents the trade unions' interests.

i. The endeavor to establish an association of German trade unions or a consolidation with the same, if such should be in existence already.

Additional measures and organizations for the promotion of the union's goals may be decided by the general assembly's resolution.

Membership

§3. (Admission). Every . . . worker may become a member irrespective of age and gender and every small craftsperson, either male or female. The admission is handled by the local executive committee. Should doubts arise as to whether someone is a small craftsperson or not, the local trade union shall decide on that prior to admission. If, however, at least one-sixth of the local trade union members protest against the admission or rejection, a report shall be made to the central executive committee within eight days and the latter has the right to come up with a final decision. The central executive committee's decision shall also be delivered to the local trade union within eight days.

§4. Persons who are not employed at the . . . industrial plant or workshop cannot be admitted as members under any circumstances.

§5. On admission into the union every member shall pay a registration fee of . . . *silbergroschen* and shall receive the membership card, statutes, and receipt book in return. Besides every member is obliged to make a weekly payment of . . . *silbergroschen* to the trade union funds.

§6. The weekly payments of . . . *silbergroschen* shall only be used for the association's general goals (see §2a, e, f, g, h, i). The registration fees and contributions to the funds concerning sickness, funerals, journeys, old age, and invalids shall be determined and administered separately.

§7. Should a raise of dues be necessitated as a result of extraordinary claims on the union's funds, the central executive committee shall order such a measure, if two-thirds of its members advocate in favor of it at a meeting called in due order. The management is obliged, however, to seek approval of all the local unions within four weeks at the latest. If the majority of all the voting trade union members rejects the charging of dues, the charges shall be annulled immediately by the central executive committee.

Temporary Forfeiture of Membership Rights

§8. If a member is behind with his dues for longer than six weeks he shall lose his due rights according to §2 for two weeks.

Forfeiture of Membership

§9. Membership shall be declared as forfeited to those who

a. are behind with their dues for longer than eight weeks;
b. committed a dishonorable crime;
c. knowingly violated the union's interests and objectives and abused the funds in fraudulent ways;
d. withdraw by means of written notice.

§10. The local executive committee is obliged to announce the names of the new and the withdrawn members (in case of the latter by stating the reasons) to the members at least once a month. As in the case of admission of new members, the local union has the right of judgment also concerning the withdrawal or exclusion of members in controversial cases. The excluded member may, however, appeal with the central executive committee, and the latter may annul the decision.

§11. If members are drafted for military service they shall be suspended of their rights and obligations.

§12. Every member has seat and vote in the local union meetings and may be elected into all of the union's offices; except for those cases where the existing laws of a state stipulate for a certain age or make other provisions.

The Formation of Local Unions

§13. If at least ten workers of . . . an industrial plant join up in a town or a district within a radius of at most one mile, they may form a local union.

In larger cities and districts where the trade union comprises more than three hundred members the formation of several local unions is permissible.

§14. As soon as a local trade union has been constituted, the central executive committee of the trade union shall be informed of the new formation immediately, that is, five days after the constitution occurred at the latest, and the number, names, and offices of the members of the executive committee and the overall number of members shall be announced. Changes should likewise be reported to the central executive committee immediately as they occur.

Administration

§15. Each local union elects an executive committee for the administration and the handling of the current affairs for the duration of one year by secret ballot.

The executive committee may not comprise less than three and no more than seven members. The chairman, or his deputy, respectively shall be elected by separate ballot, the rest by joint ballot. Each executive committee shall at least have one chairman, one treasurer, and one secretary, as for the rest it may furnish offices according to its own discretion.

§16. The election is valid, only if those elected have obtained the absolute majority (one vote above half) of those present. Should the absolute majority for all or for one single candidate(s) not have been reached, a second or, respectively, third ballot shall take place. In the case of parity of votes a decision shall be made by lot. Each winner of the election will have to accept the election.

The resigning members of the executive committee may be reelected immediately.

§17. The executive committee shall hold a meeting regularly at least once every fourteen days during which all the necessary affairs shall be handled. As a rule the meetings of the executive committee are public and open to the trade union's members. A secret meeting shall only be held, if the chairman or the majority of the executive committee members present make a resolution to that effect. The executive committee only constitutes a quorum if the majority of its members is present.

The executive committee shall establish parliamentary regulations for the structuring of the debates, for the beginnings and endings of the meetings, and for penalties for latecomers or absentees.

§18. As a rule reimbursements or recompensations shall not be paid to the executive committee or to individual members by the union fund. It is at the local union's discretion to make exceptions; such expenses may not, however, affect the mandatory dues to the general trade union treasury.

§19. Special executive committee meetings may be called by the chairman or by request of one-third of the executive committee members.

§20. Should one or several executive committee members re-sign—a new election shall take place during the next scheduled assembly of the members.

§21. The rights and obligations of the executive committee include:

a. The chairman: He shall call and preside over the trade union executive committee meetings and assemblies, represent the union to the outside and shall countersign all dispatched letters and documents, and the minutes of the meetings. In case of his absence the deputy chairman shall take his place. If such a position should not exist, another member of the executive committee authorized by the chairman should do so.
b. The secretary shall register all incoming and outgoing mail, take the minutes of all meetings of the executive committee and local union meetings and sign them after prior approval. Furthermore he shall be entrusted with the handling of the entire correspondence.
c. The treasurer shall keep the membership records, collect the dues, and register them in due manner. The delivery of the funds to the central treasury or other forms of organization necessary for unitary accounts shall be regulated by guidelines for the distribution of funds that shall be issued by the central executive committee.

§22. Should the creation of new positions and offices prove necessary as a result of the provisions made in §2 of this statute, the scope of their activities shall be determined by the local union or its executive committee, respectively. Provisions shall be made in such a way that—on the one hand—the fund's cash holdings and the union's property shall be taken care of properly and, on the other hand, that the expediency and the promptness of the management shall not be impaired.

Board of Supervisors

§23. The board of supervisors is comprised of one to three members depending on the size of the local union. It shall be elected at the same meeting in the same way and for the same duration of time as the local executive committee. The resigning members may be reelected. Generally the same rules apply for the election of the members of the board of supervisors and for the executive committee members (§16). Should a member of the board of supervisors resign in the course of his year in office, a new election shall take place during the next regular or special assembly of members.

§24. The tasks of the board of supervisors include:

a. supervising the executive committee's entire administration;
b. supervising the execution of resolutions made by the assembly of members;
c. inspecting the monthly and annual financial statements, giving account thereof to the assembly of members, and submitting said financial statements for final approval by the assembly.

In addition, the board of directors has the right to inspect all documents, files, books, and records, to revise the fund's cash balances at any time and to take them into custody if necessary and to suggest the suspension or removal of individual or all members of the executive committee during an assembly of members that has been duly and lawfully scheduled.

Local Union Meetings

§25. As a rule there shall be local assemblies of members every fourteen days, on a day and at a place to be scheduled, where union matters shall be discussed and resolutions be passed. It is at each local union's own discretion to determine the ways of announcing the meeting and the number of members necessary to make a quorum. Absent members shall acquiesce to the resolutions made.

§26. The agenda of each regular or special meeting shall be announced on the union local's bulletin board at least three days before the meeting or shall be published by means of a circular or through the press, depending on the circumstances. Individual suggestions that are not included on the agenda can only be dealt with if at least two-thirds of the members present declare themselves in their favor. All resolutions shall be passed by absolute majority.

§27. Special meetings may be called by the central executive committee, the chairman of the local executive committee, the local executive committee, and the board of supervisors. In the case of a written request made by a certain number of members the executive committee shall call a special meeting. With local unions of up to twenty members this number of members shall comprise one-third, with unions of up to fifty members one-quarter, and of up to one hundred members one fifth; with local unions of over one hundred members, at least forty members shall participate.

If the chairman or the executive committee does not comply with the members' request within three days the proponents have the right to issue the invitation independently.

§28. Should the subject of the meeting's discussion concern complaints against the chairman or the entire executive committee the meeting shall be presided over by a member of the board of supervisors or by a member from the meeting's midst that shall be elected.

§29. The supervision of the meetings shall be handled according to bylaws that have yet to be issued.

§30. The scope of the local union meetings includes all matters that are not part of this statute or of other regulations that shall still be issued by the local or central executive committee or the general assembly.

Accordingly, in controversial cases, they shall decide on the admission or exclusion of members, make decisions concerning the election and removal of executive committee members, the board of supervisors, or other committees that might become necessary. They settle disputes between the executive committee and the board of supervisors, they decide requests and complaints made to the central executive committee and to the general assembly. Finally they alone have the right to appropriate all special expenses provided they are not restricted to the competence of the general assembly and the central executive committee and to seek approval for strikes from the central executive committee.

District Unions

§31. If several local unions of the German . . . trade union exist in a city, a province, or a state the trade union may consolidate into a district union for the better representation of their interests.

§32. At least once a year a general district meeting shall take place on which the matters concerning the current affairs of the district union shall be discussed. Only elected local union representatives have the right to vote and the delegate's number of votes depends on the number of members he represents.

§33. The district assembly elects an executive committee for the management of the district union that shall comprise at least three but no more than seven members. All executive committee members shall reside in the same town or in the same district within a radius of no more than two miles from each other. The chairman's residence shall be the district union's seat of the executive.

§34. It is at the district assembly's discretion to define the scope of the district union's executive committee. It goes without saying that these regulations may not be in any conflict with this statute.

Central Executive Committee and Seat of the Executive

§35. The local unions consolidate into a district union and elect a central executive committee for the duration of one year.

§36. The central executive committee comprises eleven members, namely one president and his deputy, one secretary, one main treasurer, one comptroller, and six members who shall handle the rest of the current affairs according to the central executive committee directives that have yet to be determined.

§37. The election of the central executive committee shall be handled in the following way: The general assembly elects a president and his deputy, each of them in a separate ballot. Both of them shall reside in the same town or within a radius of at most two miles from each other. The president's residence is also seat of the union. After the election, the president and his deputy shall schedule a meeting of all of the trade union's members at their place of residence and in its vicinity within a two-mile radius, and organize an election by ballot from the members' midst for the rest of the nine central executive committee members, by absolute majority.

The central executive committee has to establish itself within three days after the election and the establishment shall immediately be reported to all the trade unions duly and lawfully.

§38. In addition to the rights granted to the central executive committee in accordance with the preceding paragraphs of these statutes, the central executive committee shall have the following rights and duties:

a. Admission and exclusion of local unions. In case of nonadmission or exclusion the local unions have the right to appeal to the general assembly;

b. to determine the beginning or end of strikes by the trade union members or, respectively, to procure the necessary funds for distribution to the strikers;

c. administering the trade union's returns and expenses according to the regulations issued by the general assembly.

§39. The meetings of the central executive committee shall take place at least once a week and shall usually be open to the trade union members. A secret meeting, however, can be ordered at any time by the president or his deputy and by resolution of the majority of the members of the executive committee.

§40. Whenever seven members are present the meetings of the central executive committee make a quorum. All of the resolutions are made by absolute majority; only where the beginning or end of strikes is concerned is a majority of two-thirds of the present members necessary.

§41. The competence of individual members of the executive committee shall be defined by the central executive committee according to the bylaws that shall be drafted and announced to all trade union members in due manner.

§42. The salaries, compensations, and sureties for members of the executive committee are at the general assembly's discretion. The general assembly shall allot an annual lump sum for travel expenses necessary for propagandistic endeavors intended for the expansion of the trade union; the central executive committee shall administer the moneys allotted for this purpose.

§43. If vacancies in the central managing board occur in the course of an office term, a general assembly of members at the seat of the executive and from its two-mile vicinity shall be called for a by-election.

Central Board of Supervisors

§44. The central board of supervisors comprises three members who, like the central committee, shall reside at the seat of the executive or within a two-mile vicinity. The election takes place by ballot and absolute majority during the general assembly.

§45. The scope of the central board of supervisors includes:

a. supervision of the entire administration by the central executive committee;
b. supervising the execution of the resolutions made in the general assemblies;
c. inspecting the monthly and annual financial statements, giving report thereof at general assemblies, and submitting said financial statement for final approval.

In addition, in urgent cases, the central board of directors may suspend the central executive committee or some of its individual members. In the latter case it is obliged to give the necessary orders—with the approval of the union members' assembly that shall be called immediately at the seat of the executive and within a two-mile radius thereof—for the provisional handling of the current affairs, until the next regular general assembly.

General Assembly

§46. Every year a trade union general assembly shall take place in the month of . . . at the central executive committee's seat. The local unions, either separately or in conjunction with others, elect either one or several but no more than five deputies as their representatives for this purpose. The representatives' number of votes depends on the number of members they represent. The guideline for the number of votes is the statistics of the month prior to the election. Travel expenses and allowances for the deputies shall be paid by the central treasury, however, only in the following way: In case of individual or consolidated local unions consisting of 200 members only one, of 400 members two, of 800 three, of 1,200 four and of over 1,200 members five deputies shall receive reimbursement.

§47. The right to call and preside over a general assembly resides with the central executive committee. However, the general assembly may, by special resolution entrust the chairmanship to any other member at any time.

§48. Each general assembly, including the provisional agenda, shall be announced by the central executive committee to the local unions at least six weeks in advance. Within ten days after the announcement, suggestions for the general assembly shall be submitted to the central executive committee by the local unions, and these suggestions shall be announced together with the central executive committee's suggestions to local unions as the final agenda at least four weeks prior to the general assembly. Individual suggestions that are not announced on the agenda can only be dealt with if at least two-thirds of the members present declare themselves in their favor. Requests for changing the statutes and the trade union's dissolution are excluded from these regulations.

§49. The general assembly's scope includes:

a. electing the president of the executive committee and the three members of the central board of supervisors; removal of members of the executive committee and the central board of supervisors;
b. deciding in the last instance on the admission or expulsion of local unions;
c. approving the request made by the central board of supervisors for the annual financial statement;

d. appropriating all ordinary and extraordinary contributions to the trade union treasury;

e. interpreting and changing the statutes;

f. determining the salaries and sureties of the central executive committee;

g. deciding on a consolidation with the association of German trade unions or the withdrawal from it, determining ordinary and extraordinary expenses for the same;

h. deciding on the dissolution of the trade union.

§50. All elections and resolutions require an absolute majority, except for resolutions concerning a change of the statutes that require a majority of two-thirds of the vote, and the resolution concerning the dissolution of the trade union that requires a three-quarters majority of all votes.

Trade Union Newspaper

§51. In order to represent its interests expressly and to be able to inform the members promptly and conveniently about all resolutions and regulations the trade union shall either found a trade union paper of its own or nominate an already-existing paper as its organ working in the interest of the workers.

§52. At least one copy of each issue of the newly founded or nominated organ shall be subscribed to by the local unions, the central executive committee, and the central board of supervisors at the expense of the trade union fund. In addition, the trade union members shall be encouraged to subscribe to the paper regularly at their own expense.

Finances

§53. All of the local unions', district unions', and the central executive committee's funds are the common property of the trade union. Accordingly, all the statutory expenses made by them shall be considered as the entire trade union's account and risk.

If the existing funds of a local union are not sufficient for the statutory expenses, the executive committee in question may make a request to the central executive committee specifying the fund's circumstances and the subsidy needed, upon which the central executive committee shall procure the needed covering funds within eight days at the latest.

§54. After the end of the business year, which shall coincide with the calendar year, the financial statement and balancing of all local unions' funds shall be made by the central executive committee. This shall be done by means of calculating the entire trade union's cash holdings per capita and—after deducting a sum, to be determined by the central executive committee and the central board of supervisors, for the trade union's central treasury to keep—every local union shall receive a compensation in proportion with the number of its members. By mid-February of every year the balancing shall be completed.

§55. The central managing board shall take care that the fund's cash holdings do not exceed the amount of the security deposited by the main treasurer. All sums exceeding the deposit shall be invested in a safe, interest-yielding manner, however, in such ways as to render the procurement of money easy and prompt in case of need.

Unemployment

§56. In case of a dispute between workers (union members) and employer as a result of which the members are laid off from their work, the local executive committee shall immediately call a meeting inviting representatives of the strikers and look into the matter. Depending on the result of the inquiry the executive committee shall either request the workers to accept the conditions made or to prevail upon the employer to submit to the workers' demands, respectively to arrange the meeting of an arbitral tribunal. If the workers (members) refuse to comply with the executive committee's resolutions they shall forfeit all eligibility for assistance. They may, however, appeal with the local assembly or the central executive committee. If the employers refuse to accept an arbitration tribunal's settlement or ruling, the local executive committee has the right to grant the usual assistance of . . . *silbergroschen* per diem to the strikers, provided the assembly of members approves. The central executive committee shall be informed immediately of the agreed strike and of assistance benefits available, or be requested to take care of the timely provision of the means therefor. It is at the central executive committee's discretion to determine the duration of the assistance payments. The central committee's decision to suspend the assistance benefits shall be reported to the corresponding local unions within three days.

§57. The members have the right to go on strike and to apply for assistance only when their dignity has been insulted, they have been physically injured without a fault of their own, or have been cheated out of their due wages. In all other cases §56 shall apply.

§58. If more than half of a local union's members are not working as a result of a layoff or a strike, the central executive committee has the right to decide on the assistance benefits.

§59. If the trade union's funds are insufficient for an extended period of assistance payments, the central executive committee shall turn to the president of the umbrella organization of the trade union, if such should exist, in due time, and request the aid deemed necessary. If this aid is not offered, and should the rendering of further assistance either by the existing funds or by means of special contributions from the trade unions be impossible, the central executive commiteee shall order the strikers to resume work, which will automatically end the need to pay assistance benefits. It may, however, be decided by the general assembly or by general members' vote, to take up loans or to appeal to the workers or the general public for financial assistance or other means of support, in order to be able to continue the strike.

§60. If there is a sound prospect for a striking member to find work elsewhere during a layoff or a strike, an unmarried member shall be ordered by the central executive committee to go to the place in question within three days, a married member within fourteen days; every member traveling for this reason is eligible to have his travel expenses paid for by the union's funds. If work should be unavailable in the place to which the member has been sent, the respective local executive committee, with consent of the central executive committee, shall either order him to return or go to a third place where work is available. In both cases the travel expenses shall be procured. The union fund shall also pay the traveling expenses—the amount of which has yet to be determined—for the families of married members moving to the new place later on.

§61. If striking members resume work against the orders given by the local executive committee, the local assembly or the central executive committee, without the causes for the unemployment having been eliminated, the workers shall be excluded from the union and be declared to have forfeited all privileges and rights. The same applies to members (from out of town or residents) who accept jobs vacant as a result of the local union bodies' resolution or approval.

§62. In case of general unemployment resulting from slackening of business or a state of general distress the local or the central executive committee shall—apart from requesting assistance from union comrades and other unions—also enlist the services of the public or the community and the state in order to alleviate the general need in an appropriate way, either by means of assistance or by promoting mobility or emigration.

Travel Assistance

§63. If the trade union declares itself in favor of travel assistance the following regulations shall apply: Every member traveling in order to find work, and who has been a trade union member for at least three months, shall receive travel assistance of . . . *silbergroschen* per mile from the place where he last received assistance. This assistance shall be noted in his traveler's membership book and may be granted by the same local union only once within a period of six months.

Training of Apprentices

§64. In order to put an end to the abuses that have been caused by degradation and exploitation of apprentices, the local and central executive committees and all members shall pay special attention to this issue. Particularly, they shall see to it that apprentices not be engaged in any activities other than work-related, be treated humanely, and obtain sufficient instruction in all works pertaining to the trade. In the case of an impending or an already existing surplus of apprentices in an industry, they shall make use of all lawful possibilities such as: public warnings and lodging complaints with the parents, guardians, and employers, etc., against the acceptance of new apprentices. Care shall also be taken to give the apprentices moral and technical training by means of having them attend Sunday schools or other educational facilities available to them.

Protection against Pressure by Employers and Authorities

§65. If a member feels justified to raise complaints against unreasonable demands or pressure by an employer or an administrative body he shall report the matter to a member of the executive committee who in turn shall give account of it during the next meeting of the executive committee. The executive committee shall make up its mind on the issue by hearing the interested parties, if possible. If the problem cannot be settled amicably the executive committee has the right to make use of all legal means to settle the matter. In particular, it should be intent on publishing all cases of flagrant pressures in the trade union newspaper. If the dispute can only be resolved by taking legal action, the litigation shall be made at the expense of the trade union fund, provided the member's or the members' innocence has been ascertained. In all major cases, namely when litigation is impending, the central executive committee shall be informed and asked for approval.

Procurement of Work and Statistics

§66. Any member becoming jobless shall report this fact to the local executive committee. The latter is obliged to announce the name of the member seeking employment on the union premises or otherwise, and to publish the list of names in the trade union newspaper.

As a rule, the statistical inquiries take place quarterly and concern wages, working hours, volume of business, number of apprentices, sickness and death cases, etc. The local executive committee shall receive the forms of these inquiries from the central executive committee and shall return the completed questionnaires to the latter within a certain period of time. The central executive committee shall then compile and publish them in the union newspaper at the expense of the fund.

Sickness and Funeral Funds, Old-Age Pension and Invalid's Fund

§67. The statute drafts concerning these matters shall be furnished by the central executive committee and be brought to the members' attention in due manner and submitted to the general assembly for further deliberation and final decision.

Trade Union Dissolution

§68. A local union is dissolved whenever the number of its members drops below ten or if a majority of three-quarters of the members present in a statutory meeting makes a resolution to this effect. All existing funds, documents, books, and liquid and immobile assets fall to the trade union; the central executive committee of this union shall impound and administer the latter in the interest of the trade union.

§69. The trade union may only be dissolved as a result of insolvency or the general assembly's resolution during which at least a three-quarters majority of all votes shall advocate such action.

In the first instance the members are obliged to make themselves liable and to make good for liabilities incurred; in the second case the general assembly shall establish a liquidation commission. The general assembly shall decide on the use of the property remaining.

Translated by Renate Steinchen

The Authors

AUGUST BEBEL, born 1840 in Cologne, died 1913 in Switzerland. Active in the working class movement since early 1860s; one of the founders of the *Sozialdemokratische Arbeiterpartei* (Social Democratic Workers Party) in 1869; leader of the Social Democratic Party, member of Parliament. Main publication: "Woman and Socialism," translated into many languages, with many editions.

EDUARD BERNSTEIN, born 1850 in Berlin, died 1932 in Berlin. Editor of exile party paper *Der Sozialdemokrat* since 1881; main representative of revisionist faction; main publication "Evolutionary Socialism: A Criticism and Affirmation" *(Die Voraussetzungen des Sozialismus und die Aufgaben der Sozialdemokratie).*

JOSEPH DIETZGEN, born 1828 in Siegburg/Bonn, died 1888 in Chicago. A tanner and autodidactic philosopher of the materialist school. Interpreted Marx to workers; spent last 10 years of his life in the US advocating democratic Socialism as editor of German-language revolutionary press.

FRIEDRICH ENGELS, born 1820 in Barmen, died 1895 in London. One of the main revolutionaries and socialist writers in Europe; met Karl Marx initially in 1841 in Berlin.

KARL KAUTSKY, born 1854 in Prague, died 1938 in Amsterdam. Leading contemporary theoretician of the German Social Democratic Party; editor of the party periodical *Die Neue Zeit* since 1883. Wrote, among many books, a popularized version of Karl Marx's *Das Kapital,* several books on the history of socialism.

FERDINAND LASSALLE, born 1825 in Breslau (now Poland), died 1864 in Geneva. Founder and first chairman of the Allgemeiner Deutscher Arbeiterverein; activist in the revolution of 1848/49; major organizer and writer for the working class until his death.

EMIL LEDERER, born 1882 in Pilsen/Bohemia (now CSR), died 1939 in New York. Professor of political economy, successor to Max Weber in Heidelberg. Many publications, *Die Privatangestellten in der modernen Wirtschaftsentwicklung* (1912), *The State of the Masses* (1940).

KARL LIEBKNECHT, born 1871 in Leipzig. Son of Wilhelm L., godson of Karl Marx; lawyer; since 1900 member of the SPD, radical member of the Spartacist League in the revolution of November 1918; founding member of the German Communist Party; murdered in January 1919, together with Rosa Luxemburg, by right-wing extremists, in Berlin.

WILHELM LIEBKNECHT, born 1826 in Giessen, died 1900 in Berlin. Father of Karl L. Revolutionary of 1848 in Southern Germany. Exiled in Switzerland and England; close collaborator with A. Bebel; editor of SPD periodicals; member of Parliament since 1874. Biographer of Karl Marx.

ROSA LUXEMBURG, born 1871 in Zamość (Poland) now Russia. Early activity in Polish labor movement. Since 1898 in Germany; professor at SPD academy; antirevisionist; murdered in January 1919, together with Karl Liebknecht, by right-wing extremists in Berlin. Major works: *The Accumulation of Capital* (1913), *The Crisis of the German Social-Democracy* ("Junius" pamphlet).

KARL MARX, born 1818 in Trier, died 1883 in London. Leading theoretician and activist of the international working class movement since 1840s; lived most of his life in exile. Major work: *Das Kapital* (1867 ff.).

FRANZ MEHRING, born 1846 in Schlawe, Pomerania (now Poland), died 1919 in Berlin. Journalist; member of the SPD since 1891; editorial writer for *Die Neue Zeit;* historian of the SPD, biographer of Karl Marx.

CLARA ZETKIN, born 1857 in Wiederau (now GDR), died 1933 in exile in the Soviet Union. Editor of the SPD women's journal *Die Gleichheit* (Equality) 1891–1917; founding member of the German Communist Party.

Bibliographical Notes

Karl Marx/Friedrich Engels, *Manifesto of the Communist Party* (New York: New York Labor News Company, 1888). Translation by Samuel Moore. First chapter: "Bourgeois and Proletarians." Original title: *Das Kommunistische Manifest* (London: Bildungs-Gesellschaft für Arbeiter, 1848).

Karl Marx, *A Contribution to the Critique of Political Economy* (Chicago: Charles H. Kerr and Company, 1904) translated from the second German edition by N. I. Stone. Original title: *Ein Beitrag zur Kritik der Politischen Ökonomie*, 1859.

Friedrich Engels, Speech at the Graveside of Karl Marx (1883). Original title: Grabrede für Karl Marx, *MEW*, vol. 19, pp. 333–34.

August Bebel, *On Workers' Clubs and Labor Associations in the 1860s*. From: *Bebel's Reminiscences*. (New York: The Socialist Literature Company, 1911), pp. 56–61. Translated by E. Untermann.

Friedrich Engels, *Socialism in Germany*. Translated by Irene Schmied. From: Friedrich Engels, "Sozialismus in Deutschland," in *Die Neue Zeit*, vol. 10 (1891/92), pp. 580–89.

Wilhelm Liebknecht, *On May Day*. Translated by Renate Steinchen. From: *Protokoll über die Verhandlungen des Parteitages der Sozialdemokratischen Partei Deutschlands* (Cologne: 1893), pp. 164–71.

Ferdinand Lassalle, *What is Capital?* (New York: New York Labor News Company, 1899). Freely translated by F. Keddell. Translation

of chapter 4 of *Herr Bastiat-Schulze von Delitzsch, der ökono-
mische Julian, oder Capital und Arbeit* (Berlin: R. Schlingmann,
1864).

Emil Lederer, "The Problem of the Modern Salaried Employee, Its
Theoretical and Statistical Basis," chapters 2 and 3 of *Die Privatangestellten in der modernen Wirtschaftsentwicklung* (Tü-
bingen: Mohr, 1912). Translation by E. E. Warburg. Published by
the State Department of Social Welfare and the Department of Social
Science, Columbia University, as a report on project no. 165-
6999-6027 conducted under the auspices of the Work Progress
Administration (New York: 1937).

Karl Marx, "Social Classes in America." Letter to Joseph Weydemeyer, London, March 5, 1852.

Friedrich Engels, "The Labor Movement in the United States."
Preface to the American edition of *The Condition of the Working
Class in England in 1844* (New York: Louis Weiss, 1887).

Friedrich Engels, "Why There Is No Large Socialist Party in America." Letter to Friedrich A. Sorge, London, December 2, 1893.

Ferdinand Lassalle, *Open Letter to the National Labor Association
of Germany* (New York: International Publishing Co., 1901). Translation by John Ehrmann and Fred Bader. Translation from: Ferdinand Lassalle, *Offenes Antwortschreiben an das Central-Comité
zur Berufung eines Allgemeinen deutschen Arbeitercongresses zu
Leipzig* (Zürich: Meyer & Zeller, 1863).

Franz Mehring, "The Law against the Socialists." Translation by
Irene Schmied, from: Franz Mehring, *Geschichte der Deutschen
Sozialdemokratie* (Stuttgart: J. H. W. Dietz), vol. 4, pp. 155–69,
325–28.

Eduard Bernstein, "The Most Pressing Problems of Social Democ-
racy." Excerpts from: Eduard Bernstein, *Evolutionary Socialism: A
Criticism and Affirmation*. Translation by Edith C. Harvey (New
York: B. W. Huebsch, 1909). Original title: Eduard Bernstein, *Die*

Voraussetzungen des Sozialismus und die Aufgaben der Sozial-demokratie (Stuttgart: J. H. W. Dietz, 1899).

Rosa Luxemburg, "Reform or Revolution" (New York: Three Arrow Press, 1937). Translation by Integer. Original title: *Sozialreform oder Revolution* (Leipzig: Leipziger Buchdruckerei, 1899).

Karl Kautsky, "The Revisionist Controversy." From: Karl Kautsky, *Selected Political Writings* (London: Macmillan Press, 1985), edited and translated by Patrick Goode. Excerpts from original title: Karl Kautsky, *Bernstein und das sozialdemokratische Programm* (Stuttgart: J. H. W. Dietz, 1899).

"Report of the Executive Committee of the German Social Democratic Party on the Activities of the Party." Original title: "Report of the Executive Committee of the German Social-Democratic Party to the International Socialist Congress at Copenhagen on the Party's Activity Since the Stuttgart Congress" (Berlin: 1910).

August Bebel, *Woman and Socialism* (New York: Socialist Literature Co., 1910). Translation by Meta L. Stern. 50th ed., pp. 226–33, 285–306. Original title: *Die Frau und der Sozialismus* (Stuttgart: J. H. W. Dietz, 1895).

Clara Zetkin, "What the Women Owe to Karl Marx." From: Clara Zetkin, *Selected Writings* (New York: International Publishers, 1984), pp. 93–97. Original article in *Die Gleichheit*, Stuttgart, March 25, 1903.

Karl Liebknecht, "Military Pedagogy." From: Karl Liebknecht, "Militarism" (New York: B. W. Huebsch, 1917), pp. 59–79. Revised lecture from 1906. Translation by Sidney Zimand.

Rosa Luxemburg, "Working Class and Militarism." Translation by Renate Steinchen. Original title: Rosa Luxemburg, *Arbeiterklasse und Militarismus* (1899).

Friedrich Engels, "On Anti-Semitism." Translation by Renate Steinchen. Original title: *Über den Antisemitismus (Ein Brief nach Wien)*. In: *Die Arbeiterzeitung*, no. 19, May 9, 1890.

August Bebel, "Anti-Semitism and Social-Democracy." Translation by Renate Steinchen. Original title: *Antisemitismus und Sozialdemokratie*. In: *Protokoll über die Verhandlungen des Parteitages der Sozialdemokratischen Partei Deutschlands* (Cologne: 1893), pp. 223–37.

Joseph Dietzgen, "Scientific Socialism." From: Joseph Dietzgen, *Some of the Philosophical Essays on Socialism and Science, Religion, Ethics, Critique-of-Reason, and the World-at-large* (Chicago: Charles H. Kerr & Co., 1906), pp. 79–89. Translated by M. Beer and T. Rothstein. Originally published in *Volksstaat*, 1873.

Franz Mehring, "On the Philosophy of Capitalism." Translation by Renate Steinchen. Original title: *Zur Philosophie und Poesie des Kapitalismus*. Chapter 9 of Franz Mehring, *Kapital und Presse* (Berlin: K. Brachvogel, 1891).

Franz Mehring, "Christianity and Social Democracy." Translation by Renate Steinchen. Original title: *Christentum und Sozialdemokratie*. In: *Die Neue Zeit*, vol. 19, 1900–1901, pp. 257ff.

Franz Mehring, "Proletariat and Religion." Translation by David Schiffman and Renate Steinchen. Original title: *Proletariat und Religion*, in *Leipziger Volkszeitung*, May 17, 1902.

The Law against the Socialists (Law against Social Democratic Endeavors which Threaten Public Peace). Translation by Renate Steinchen. Original title: *Gesetz gegen die gemeingefährlichen Bestrebungen der Sozialdemokratie*, in Ignaz Auer, *Nach zehn Jahren. Materialien und Glossen zur Geschichte des Sozialistengesetzes* (Nürnberg: Fränkische Verlagsanstalt & Buchdruckerei GmbH, 1913), pp. 86–92.

August Bebel, "Model Statutes for German Trade Unions." Original title: *Musterstatuten für deutsche Gewerksgenossenschaften, ausgearbeitet von August Bebel, Vorsitzender des "Vororts des Verbands deutscher Arbeitervereine,"* in *Demokratisches Wochenblatt* (Leipzig) suppl. for no. 48, November 28, 1868.

Bibliography

In the bibliography, we concentrate primarily on those historical studies that have a direct bearing on some of the aspects of the development of German socialism and the Social Democratic Party, *and* that are available in English—with one exception: the collection of "Programmatic Documents of German Social Democracy" (which is, as yet, not available in English.)

The list of literary texts is a suggestion only for scholars and students outside the Humanities who are proficient in German. It includes works of the high-culture canon as well as from popular and "trivial" literature with a social content.

Historical Studies

Angress, Werner T. *Stillborn Revolution*. Princeton, 1963.

Braunthal, Gerard. *The West German Social Democrats, 1969–1982: Profile of a Party in Power*. Boulder, 1983.

Braunthal, Julius. *History of the International*. London, 1967.

Craig, Gordon. *Germany, 1866–1945*. New York, 1978.

———. *The Germans*. New York, 1982.

Dowe, Klotzbach, eds. *Programmatische Dokumente der deutschen Sozialdemokratie*. Berlin and Bonn, 1984.

Fletcher, Roger, ed. *Bernstein to Brandt—A Short History of German Social Democracy*. London, 1987.

Gay, Peter. *The Dilemma of Democratic Socialism—Eduard Bernstein's Challenge to Marx*. New York, 1952.

Grebing, Helga. *History of the German Labor Movement*. London and New York, 1969.

Guttmann, W. L. *The German Social Democratic Party, 1875–1933: From Ghetto to Government.* London, 1981.

Joll, James. *The Second International.* London, 1975.

Kremp, Werner. " 'Variations on America'—Some Remarks about the Role of America in the Political Thought of the SPD from the 1860ies to the 1930ies" in *German Social Democracy and the United States: Past, Present, and Future Attitudes.* Occasional Papers of the Friedrich Ebert Foundation. Washington, DC, 1988.

Landes, David S. *The Unbound Prometheus: Technological Changes and Industrial Development in Western Europe from 1750 to the Present.* Cambridge, UK, 1969.

Lidtke, Vernon. *The Outlawed Party.* Princeton, 1975.

———. "Songs of the German Labor Movement, 1864–1914" in *Geschichte und Gesellschaft 5,* No. 1, 1979, pp. 54–82.

Moore, Barrington. *Injustice—The Social Bases of Obedience and Revolt.* New York, 1978.

Morgan, David W. *The Socialist Left and the German Revolution: A History of the Independent Social Democratic Party (USPD), 1917–22.* Ithaca, 1975.

Morgan, R. *The German Social Democrats* and the *First International, 1864–72.* Cambridge, UK, 1965.

Moses, John A. *Trade Unionism in Germany from Bismarck to Hitler, 1869–1933.* London, 1982.

Nettl, Peter. "The German Social Democratic Party 1890–1914 as a Political Model" in, *Past and Present,* No. 30, 1965, pp. 29–65.

Rivinius, Karl Josef. *The Social Movement in 19th Century Germany.* München, 1979.

Roth, Günther. *The Social Democrats in Imperial Germany: A Study in Working Class Isolation and National Integration.* Totowa, 1963.

Schoenbaum, David. "Early Perceptions of Social Democracy (in America)" in, *German Social Democracy and the United States: Past, Present, and Future Attitudes.* Occasional Papers of the Friedrich Ebert Foundation. Washington, DC, 1988.

Schorske, Carl E. *German Social Democracy 1905–1917: The Development of the Great Schism.* New York, 1972.

Thonessen, W. *The Emancipation of Woman: The Rise and Decline of the Women's Movement in German Social Democracy, 1863–1933.* London, 1973.

Literary Texts

Büchner, Georg. *Der hessische Landbote; Woyzeck; Dantons Tod.*
Fontane, Theodor. *Effi Briest.*
Hauptmann, Gerhart. *Die Weber; Rose Bernd.*
Heine, Heinrich. *Deutschland ein Wintermärchen; Lutetia;* "Die Schlesischen Weber"; *Zur Geschichte der Religion und Philosophie in Deutschland; Die romantische Schule.*
Lassalle, Ferdinand. *Franz von Sickingen.*
Mann, Heinrich. *Der Untertan; Professor Unrat.*
May, Karl. *Schacht und Hütte.*
Viebig, Clara. *Das Weiberdorf.*

Acknowledgments

Every reasonable effort has been made to locate the owners of rights to previously published works and the translations printed here. We gratefully acknowledge permission to reprint the following material:

"The Revisionist Controversy" by Karl Kautsky from *Karl Kautsky: Selected Political Writings,* edited and translated by Patrick Goode. © Patrick Goode 1983; Chapter 2 © J. H. W. Dietz 1899, and reprinted by permission of St. Martin's Press Inc. and Macmillan, London and Basingstoke.

"What the Women Owe to Karl Marx" by Clara Zetkin, translated by Kai Schoenhals, © International Publishers Co., New York, 1984.